SOUTH-EAST

Other Chambers Scottish Guides

South-West Scotland
Stuart Bathgate

Highlands and Islands
Roger Smith

Chambers Scottish Guides

SOUTH-EAST SCOTLAND

Kristina Woolnough

Series editor
Kristina Woolnough

Chambers

Published 1992 by W & R Chambers Ltd
43–45 Annandale Street, Edinburgh EH7 4AZ

British Library Cataloguing in Publication Data

A catalogue record for this book is available from the British
Library

ISBN 0–550–22100–X

Acknowledgements
National and Regional Fact Files compiled by Donald Grieg
Maps and town plans by Baynefield Carto-Graphics Ltd

Cover design by Creative Link, Edinburgh
Typeset by Hewer Text Composition Services, Edinburgh
Printed in England by Clays Ltd, St Ives, plc

CONTENTS

Preface   vi

How to use this book   viii

Introduction to the South-East   xi

National Fact File   1

Regional Fact File   29

Gazetteer   57

Maps and town plans

Scotland   2

Regional map of South-East Scotland   30

Town plan of Dundee   92

Town plan of Edinburgh   100

Edinburgh and environs   107

Town plan of Perth   159

Town plan of St Andrews   166

Chambers Scottish Guides

Scotland has traditionally been celebrated for two outstanding features: its history and its scenery. Romantic, compelling figures such as Robert the Bruce, Mary Queen of Scots and Bonnie Prince Charlie move across an historical landscape which is spiced with power-broking, love, political and religious intrigue, lust, murder and treachery.

Their names are known all over the world and the enduring appeal of their stories is given additional impetus by the tangible, remaining historical sites. Scattered throughout Scotland, from the Borders northwards, are battlefields where lands and crowns were won and lost and where uprisings succeeded and failed. There are caves, churches and castles where secular and religious courts were held and where refuge was sought. And there are palaces where kings and queens were born and died. As well as the buildings and ruins that document the fortunes of nobles and Scottish royalty, humbler stone monuments, settlements, houses and cottages can also be seen. These, from the prehistoric stone circles and standing stones to the 'black houses' of the Western Isles, represent largely unknown, unrecorded people who were either too ancient or too ordinary to capture the world's imagination.

Scotland's historical heritage is complemented by the country's natural heritage. The stock images of Scotland are invariably the photogenic Highland ones: jagged mountains, clear-eyed lochs and shaggy heath. Often overlooked are the more subtle charms of the Borders hills, or the hidden south-western corner of Scotland which lies around the Solway Firth. Mistakenly by-passed too is the sometimes dramatic, often picturesque east coast of the country, which stretches with indents of sandy crescents and fishing harbours from the Borders to Duncansby Head.

History, natural setting and human achievement marry in Scotland's towns and cities. Each place's architectural diversity, whether it involves loved and cherished buildings from the 17th, 18th and 19th centuries or the frequently controversial and sometimes hated efforts of the 20th century, fuses the past and the present.

For Scotland is not a museum, nor is it a national park, nor just a monument to past human endeavour. The fact of contemporary Scotland is a vital, intriguing one. New industries are slowly replacing old ones. A thriving contemporary urban culture – theatre, fiction, popular music – is successfully blending with the traditional, predominantly Highland, culture of dancing, tartan, bagpipes, accordion bands and Gaelic ceilidhs. This blending exists at the large cultural annual fixtures like the Edinburgh Festival and Glasgow's Mayfest and it exists across Scotland at the plethora of smaller-scale, local celebrations which include music festivals, family fun-days and Highland shows.

The historical and the scenic, the traditional and the contemporary – *Chambers Scottish Guides* confirm all that is known and celebrated about Scotland and they also uncover the unknown, the less familiar and the forgotten corners. The guides will be an invaluable source of reference for visitors and for residents alike. Both can take advantage of the comprehensive Gazetteer of places and attractions, both can make use of the listings of theatres, cinemas, festivals, local media, nightlife, transport and galleries. Whether employed for suggestions for family outings, Sunday jaunts or for all-season holidays, *Chambers Scottish Guides* will inform, inspire and enlighten.

As well as providing the invaluable Gazetteer and listings, *Chambers Scottish Guides* offer a broad, sometime idiosyncratic, view of Scotland in the subject panels which are interspersed throughout the Gazetteer. These panels look at aspects of Scottish history, Scottish culture and contemporary Scottish life from football to conservation. From these panels, an impression emerges of a diverse, challenging, fascinating country, one that is inspired by its past and is also tripped up by it, and one that is struggling consciously and successfully for its future. If you think you know Scotland well, there is yet more to discover. If you are travelling in Scotland for the first time, these books will guide your journey.

How to use this book

Each *Chambers Scottish Guide* consists of three sections:

The **National Fact File**, which includes information on national Scottish organizations, sports associations, airports, mainline train stations, media, Scottish currency and accommodation.

The **Regional Fact File**, which contains listings of cinemas, theatres, media, festivals, public transport facilities, tourist information offices, airports, galleries and museums specifically for the area covered by each book.

The **Gazetteer**, which provides comprehensive A–Z information about cities, towns, villages, historical sites and visitor attractions within the regions covered by each book.

The **National Fact File** is arranged alphabetically by subject and then alphabetically by entry.

The **Regional Fact File** is ordered alphabetically by subject, then by town, city or village and then alphabetically by entry.

The **Gazetteer** is alphabetical and contains entries on cities, towns and villages, and visitor attractions within each guide's area. The Gazetteer also contains several special-feature panels, which look more closely at subjects, phenomena, people and historical events associated with the area. In addition, there are a number of maps and town plans. Gazetteer entries begin with the entry heading and then give an indication of location. Mileages given are for guidance only and are not strict road mileages. Addresses, opening hours, telephone numbers and an indication of disabled access follow where appropriate. 'Free' denotes no admission charge; an entrance fee should otherwise be assumed. The letters HS or NTS before the telephone number show that the property or land is owned or managed by Historic Scotland or the National Trust for Scotland. We have adopted the Scottish Tourist Board's definitions of disabled access, and it should be noted that in many cases the visitor attractions have defined their own accessibility. It is advisable for disabled visitors to check in advance. The symbols used are:

D – unassisted disabled access
D (P) – partial access
D (A) – access with assistance

Where no letter is given, it should be assumed that access has not been assessed in the STB's scheme or that access is difficult or impossible.

Comprehensive cross-references to other Gazetteer entries and to panels have been included for ease of use. For example: **Burke and Hare**, see panel p74. Other cross references from within one gazetteer or panel entry to another are highlighted by the use of **bold type**.

In the case of the major cities and towns – Aberdeen, Dundee, Edinburgh, Glasgow, Inverness, Perth and St Andrews, visitor attractions have been alphabetically entered as sub-headings under the main city or town heading. This procedure has also been adopted for islands and island groups.

It should be noted that three-figure telephone numbers are in the process of being phased out in Scotland. At the time of going to press, number changes had not all been implemented.

INTRODUCTION TO THE SOUTH-EAST

The Borders, Lothian, Fife and Tayside are the subject of this book. Whatever the sometimes arbitrary nature of the imposed political boundaries, each region has its unifying, identifiable features – landscape, local architecture, customs, dialect, industry – and each region has its contrary-minded rebel towns and terrains which buck the generalization.

For centuries the Borders, the south-eastern gateway for Scotland, has been the venue for England–Scotland warfare. Intermittent cross-Border cattle raids were preceded and succeeded by all-out armed conflict. In the firing line were the Borders towns of Melrose, Selkirk, Hawick, Galashiels, Kelso and Jedburgh whose inhabitants followed the cycle of defending and raiding that was the Borders way of life for hundreds of years. Today, the ruins of the great Borders abbeys and crumbling Borders castles are reminders of this violent past.

War and conflict left the Borders with another legacy: a strong sense of identity and tradition. Today, most Borders towns hold festivals, or Common Ridings, which recall various aspects of their precarious past in rigorously traditional ceremonies. The Common Ridings, because they usually involve a procession of horse-riders, introduce another Borders theme: horses. Pony clubs and gymkhanas, hunts and hunt balls are very much a part of the region's social calendar.

The green rolling hills of the area feed a mainstay of the Borders' economy, the wool industry. As well as grazing land for sheep, the hills are the source of several of the River Tweed's tributaries. On the banks of these tributaries woollen mills were developed, which now double up as manufacturing bases and visitor attractions. The magnificent Tweed brings other economic advantages: its inherent visual appeal, so celebrated by the great champion of the Borders and of Scotland, Sir Walter Scott, boosts tourism; its waters are world-famous and much sought after by salmon fishermen; and it nurtures the rich agricultural land, the Merse, in the east of the region.

The coastal strip of the Borders, bullied by the grey North Sea, is the region's contrary face. Here, small fishing villages, built in warm red sandstone, and unfrequented sandy beaches merge atmospherically and visually into the coast of another region, Lothian. In turn, the picturesque red sandstone and orange pantile-roofed villages of East Lothian – Dirleton, Tyninghame, East Linton – seem worlds apart from industrial West Lothian. At the heart of Lothian, with its sprinkling of listed ancient sites, and its more recently protected shale bings, lies Scotland's capital city, Edinburgh.

Edinburgh is the city which hardly needs to promote itself. Edinburgh Castle, sitting on its rocky outcrop, the narrow medieval Old Town and the elegant Georgian New Town give the city its striking visual appeal. Year-round festivals, the magnetic August Edinburgh Festival and a full complement of theatres, cinemas, galleries, parks and attractions complete the visitor's itinerary.

Just to the north of the city is the Firth of Forth, the watery expanse separating Lothian and Fife which is spanned by the mighty red cantilever Forth Bridge and the slimline suspension Forth Road Bridge. Once across the Forth, the city is left behind. Fife lies on a broad peninsula of land, with the Firth of Forth in the south and the Firth of Tay in the north. The region is a mishmash: heavily industrial and densely populated from Dunfermline to beyond Kirkcaldy, with the occasional interruptions of seaside resorts and small fishing harbours becoming more frequent. The east of the region, towards St Andrews, has a rich agricultural interior and a necklace of pretty fishing villages along its coast. St Andrews, the home of golf, of Scotland's oldest university and the country's one-time religious centre, is the visitor magnet of Fife.

North of St Andrews is Newport-on-Tay. From here, the Tay Bridge stretches over the Firth of Tay towards the city of Dundee and into Tayside. The river which gives the region its name runs in a dog-leg through the hilly splendour of the southern Highlands. In the process, it threads together several of Tayside's most important settlements, including Dunkeld and its ruined cathedral, the city of Perth and, of course, Dundee. At Dundee, the Tay estuary has been central to the city's past fortunes as a fishing and whaling harbour and as a bustling port. Today, Dundee is redeveloping its maritime heritage, this time for the leisure and tourist industries.

The River Tay, like the Tweed, is legendary in the eyes of salmon fishers. Rarely do you see salmon fishing in a city centre as you can in Perth in season, when fly rods whip over the wide river. This unusual urban pastime is one of the factors that has contributed, in recent years, to Perth's reputation as a city which offers considerable quality of life. Perth has prospered: its situation just south of the Highlands, its range of shops and its handsome buildings have obvious appeal for residents and visitors.

North of Perth, Dundee and the Firth of Tay, the urban and the man-made attractions give way to the agricultural, the rural and to the lure of the outdoors. The Highlands slice diagonally across the region up to Stonehaven. South of the Highland wall (of mountains), around the well-heeled town of Blairgowrie, is a particularly fertile area, the Carse of Gowrie, where much of Scotland's soft fruit is grown. On the coast, fishing around Arbroath continues to make an economic and a culinary contribution to north Tayside.

The greatest scenic and recreational asset of Tayside is the southern Highlands. The mountains of the Highlands and the lochs which loop around their bases provide a beautiful and challenging arena for traditional Highland activities – fishing, stalking, grouse-shooting, hill-walking – and for newer developments – watersports, skiing and photo-stalking.

National Fact File

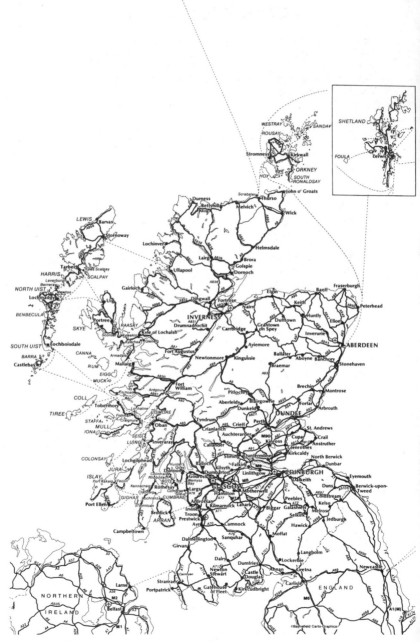

Scotland

ACCOMMODATION

The Scottish Tourist Board (STB: see under **Information – Associations and Organizations**) publishes a number of annual guides containing details of accommodation and grading systems throughout the country. A comprehensive booking service is offered by **Hi-Line**, run as part of the **Highland Direct Reservation System**.

CARAVANS AND CAMPING

A voluntary classification and grading scheme exists, run by the National Federation of Site Operators and the National Caravan Council, with the support of the Scottish Tourist Board (STB). Range of facilities is indicated on a descending scale from A to D, and quality of facilities by the number of ticks, varying 4–1. Other symbols are used to denote facilities, size and location of park, nature of park (static or touring), and standard of static caravans available for hire (also graded A–D). All parks in the scheme comply with the basic requirements of their site licence and, in general, with STB standards, and all have water and fire points and, where necessary, toilet blocks etc. In addition, a Thistle Commendation Scheme also indicates Holiday Static Caravan Parks, which let first-class caravans, combined with good facilities and an attractive environment. All commended parks which meet the requirements will display a Thistle plaque. Full details of sites involved in the scheme are available in STB's *Scotland: Camping and Caravan Parks*.

HOTELS, GUEST HOUSES AND SELF-CATERING

A voluntary classification and grading scheme is run by the STB, which sends inspectors to all hotels, guest houses, self-catering and bed and breakfast establishments wishing to be included. Gradings are awarded for quality, and classification indicates the range of services and facilities. Gradings are categorized as Approved (acceptable quality); Commended (good); Highly Commended (high), and Deluxe (excellent). Classification is signified by the number of crowns, varying 1–5 (minimum–comprehensive). Highly Commended Two Crown therefore indicates higher quality than Commended Four Crown, but offering fewer services and facilities. Full details of listed establishments are available in STB's *Scotland: Hotels and Guest Houses, Scotland: Bed and Breakfast* and *Scotland: Self-Catering Accommodation*.

YOUTH HOSTELS

There are 80 youth hostels in Scotland, categorized A–C in descending order, indicating facilities available. All offer dormitory accommodation and self-catering facilities. Full details are available from the Scottish Youth Hostels Association (see **Information – Associations and Organizations**), which publishes a handbook for youth hostellers in Scotland.

HIGHLAND DIRECT RESERVATION SYSTEM (HI-LINE)

Run by Highlands and Islands Enterprise, Highland Direct is an accommodation reservation service specifically for the Highlands and Islands. A brochure of all participating establishments is available by calling 0349 63434, while reservations (as well as travel information) can be made on 0349 65000 (see Highland Direct under **Information – Associations and Organizations**).

ACTIVITIES AND PASTIMES

The organizations listed here cover a range of sports and pastimes which may be of interest to the visitor. Anyone wishing to become involved with a certain activity during their stay in Scotland should contact the relevant organization. A complete list is available from the Scottish Sports Council (see **Information – Associations and Organizations**).

ARCHERY

Scottish Archery Association: Coaching Organizer, 4 Glowrorum Drive, Denny (0324 814380). Central body for archery in Scotland. Visitors may be invited to shoot with local clubs, 'as long as they hold FITA membership' (the international body for archery).

Scottish Field Archery Association: Don S. Smith, Secretary, 83 Woodend Road, Rutherglen, Glasgow (041–634 3108). Outdoor archery on a permanent woodland course of 28 targets.

ATHLETICS

Scottish Amateur Athletic Association/Scottish Women's Amateur Athletic Association: Secretary, Caledonia House, South Gyle, Edinburgh (031–317 7320/1).

BADMINTON

Scottish Badminton Union: Secretary, Cockburn Centre, 40 Bogmoor Place, Glasgow (041–445 1218).

BASKETBALL

Scottish Basketball Association: Secretary, Caledonia House, South Gyle, Edinburgh (031–317 7260).

BOWLING

Scottish Bowling Association: Secretary, 50 Wellington Street, Glasgow (041–221 8999).

Scottish Indoor Bowling Association: Secretary, 41 Montfode Court, Ardrossan, Ayrshire (0294 68372).

Scottish Women's Bowling Association: Secretary, 55A Esplanade, Greenock (0475 24140).

Scottish Women's Indoor Bowling Association: Secretary, 1 Underwood Road, Rutherglen, Glasgow (041–647 5810).

CAMPING

The Camping and Caravanning Club (Scottish Region): Ally Park, 56 Polwarth Avenue, Brightons, Falkirk (0324 715264). Scottish branch of the international affiliated organization for campers and caravanners.

CANOEING

Scottish Canoe Association: Secretary, Caledonia House, South Canoeing *cont* Gyle, Edinburgh (031–317 7314). Produces a number of videos and supplies, as well as a booklet listing names and addresses of clubs and coaching organizations throughout Scotland. Also produces a guide to

Scottish rivers, available from the above address.

CAVING

Grampian Speleological Group: 8 Scone Gardens, Edinburgh (031–661 1123).

CRICKET

Scottish Cricket Union: Secretary, Caledonia House, South Gyle, Edinburgh (031–317 7247. Produces a *Guide to Scottish Cricket* giving details of fixtures and results and including a Scottish directory of clubs, associations, universities and schools.

CURLING

Royal Caledonian Curling Club: Secretary, 2 Coates Crescent, Edinburgh (031–225 7083). A popular game among the Scots, curling is played on ice and involves sliding heavy stones with handles (curling stones) down a rink towards a target (tee).

CYCLING

CTC Scottish Cycling Council: Secretary, 11 Torridon Place, Kirkcaldy, Fife (0592 262944).

DANCE

Royal Scottish Country Dance Society: Secretary, 12 Coates Crescent, Edinburgh (031–225 3854). Worldwide society promoting Scottish Country Dance, organizing dances and events and offering instruction from beginner level to teaching standard.

Scottish Official Board of Highland Dancing: Secretary, Heritage House, 32 Grange Loan, Edinburgh (031–668 3965 a.m. only). World governing body for Highland Dancing offering information to visiting Highland dancers about championships, competitions and Highland Games they may wish to attend, and procedure for entering events.

DISABLED

Scottish Sports Association for the Disabled: Administrator, Fife Sports Institute, Viewfield Road, Glenrothes (0592 771700).

FISHING

Scottish Anglers National Association: Secretary, 5 Cramond Glebe Road, Edinburgh (031–312 7618). Governing body for the sport of game fishing in Scotland. The association does not provide an advice service to visitors, but does produce an annual report, available for a fee, which includes a useful 'Guide to SANA Club Waters', detailing clubs, waters, species, seasons and permit addresses.

Scottish Salmon Angling Federation: Secretary, 18 Abercromby Place, Edinburgh (031–556 4466).

FOOTBALL

Scottish Amateur Football Association: Secretary, Beechwood, Gateside Road, Barrhead, Glasgow (041–881 4025).

Scottish Football Association: 6 Park Gardens, Glasgow (041–332 6372). The sport's main governing body.

Scottish Football League: Secretary, 188 West Regent Street, Glasgow

(041–248 3844). Publishes the *Scottish Football League Review* giving details of all clubs, and contact names and addresses.

Scottish Women's Football Association: Administrator, Kelvin Hall, Argyle Street, Glasgow (041–337 1455).

GAMES
(HIGHLAND AND BORDER)

Scottish Games Association: Secretary, 24 Florence Place, Perth (0738 27782). Central organization for Highland and Border Games throughout Scotland.

GENEALOGY

Scottish Genealogy Society: 15 Victoria Terrace, Edinburgh (031–220 3677). Nominal membership fee. Does not carry out professional record searching, but can supply members with a list of professional researchers.

GLIDING

Scottish Gliding Association: Secretary, Glenfinart Park, Ardentinny, near Dunoon, Argyll (0369 81256).

GOLF

Scottish Golf Union: Secretary, The Cottage, 181A Whitehouse Road, Edinburgh (031–339 7546).

Scottish Ladies Golfing Association: Secretary, Chacewood, 49 Fullarton Drive, Troon (0292 313047).

HANG GLIDING

Scottish Hang Gliding Federation: Peter Shields, Secretary, 1 Lochbrae

Drive, High Burnside, Glasgow (041–634 6688). Scotland has only one hang gliding school, Cairnwell Hang Gliding School, Cairnwell Mountain, by Braemar, Aberdeenshire (03397 41331). Visitors already qualified should contact the above address in Glasgow for information on the nearest club.

HOCKEY

Scottish Hockey Union: Executive Administrator, Caledonia House, South Gyle, Edinburgh (031–317 7254). Contact point for non-national clubs and associations interested in participating in Scotland.

ICE HOCKEY

Scottish Ice Hockey Association: President, 16 Glencairn Road, Ayr (0292 266203).

LACROSSE

Scottish Lacrosse Association: Secretary, Geddes House, Parleyhill, Culross, Dunfermline (0383 880602).

LAWN TENNIS

Scottish Lawn Tennis Association: Secretary/National Coach, 12 Melville Crescent, Edinburgh (031–225 1284).

LITERATURE

Association for Scottish Literary Studies: c/o Department of English Literature, University of Glasgow, Glasgow (041–339 8855 ext 5549). National association promoting the study, teaching and writing of

Scottish literature and the study and teaching of Scottish languages.

Poetry Association of Scotland: Secretary, 38 Dovecot Road, Edinburgh (031–334 5241). Originally established in 1924, the association is today a registered charity promoting poetry through readings and related activities.

MOUNTAINEERING

The Mountaineering Council of Scotland: Kevin Howett, National Officer, Flat 1R, 71 King Street, Crieff (0764 4962). Representative body for Scottish hill-walkers, rock and ice climbers, ski mountaineers and cross-country skiers of all standards. It directly funds winter and summer training courses for members at Glenmore Lodge in the Cairngorms (the national Scottish Outdoor Centre).

ORIENTEERING

Scottish Orienteering Association (SOA): Secretary, 7 Lawson Avenue, Banchory (033 02 3145). Formed in 1961, the association is now a subsidiary branch of the British Orienteering Federation (BOF), the governing body of the sport in the UK, which is affiliated to the International Orienteering Federation.

PARACHUTING

Scottish Sport Parachute Association: Secretary, 47 Great Southern Road, Aberdeen (0224 586510).

PARAGLIDING

Cloudbusters Paragliding School: Peter Shields, Chief Inspector,

9 Lynedoch Place, Glasgow (041–634 6688). Courses available for novices to advanced pilots. Information about nearest clubs available from the above address.

PÉTANQUE

Scottish Pétanque Association: Bob Boyle, National Secretary, 1 Arbroath Crescent, Stirling (0786 70619). The National Secretary of the association defined pétanque (peytonk) as being the 'proper name for the French game of boules'. With the exception of a few events which are only open to licensed players, all games are open to the public. Lists of affiliated clubs and contacts and a fixtures list are available from the above address.

RAMBLING AND RIGHTS OF WAY

The Ramblers' Association (Scotland): Scottish Officer, Kelinbank, Church Place, Freuchie, Fife (0337 58065).

Scottish Rights of Way Society: Secretary, Mrs Judith Lewis, John Cotton Business Centre, 10/2 Sunnyside, Edinburgh (031–652 2937).

RIDING

Scottish Trekking and Riding Association: Secretary, Tomnagairn Farm, Trochry, by Dunkeld (035 03 220).

ROWING

Scottish Amateur Rowing Association: Secretary,

11 Spottiswoode Street, Edinburgh (031–229 2366).

RUGBY

Scottish Rugby Union: Secretary, Murrayfield, Roseburn Street, Edinburgh (031–337 9551).

SHINTY

The Camanachd Association: Secretary, Algarve, Badabrie, Banavie, Fort William (0397 772461). A game like hockey, shinty is played mainly in the Highlands and Islands with a curved stick called a caman.

SHOOTING

British Association for Shooting and Conservation: Director of Development – Scotland, Scottish Centre, Trochry, by Dunkeld (035 03 226).

Scottish Clay Target Association: Secretary, 10 Balgibbon Drive, Callander (0877 31323).

SKIING

Scottish National Ski Council: Administrator, Caledonia House, South Gyle, Edinburgh (031–317 7280). Governing body representing and regulating skiing in Scotland. Produces a number of leaflets about its activities and skiing in Scotland.

SUB AQUA

Scottish Sub Aqua Club: Secretary, Cockburn Centre, 40 Bogmoor Place, Glasgow (041–425 1021). Central organization for sub aqua and diving clubs throughout Scotland.

SURFING

Scottish Surfing Federation: Secretary, South Pitblae House, Fraserburgh (0346 23600).

TUG-OF-WAR

Scottish Tug-of-War Association: Fiona Watson, Secretary, Laurelbank, 3 Riverside Villas, Catrine, Mauchline (0290 51502).

WATER SKIING

Scottish Water Ski Association: Secretary, Caledonia House, South Gyle, Edinburgh (031–317 7217).

WINDSURFING

Scottish Windsurfing Association: Secretary, c/o RYA Scotland, Caledonia House, South Gyle, Edinburgh (031–317 7217). The association publishes a guide to recognized windsurfing centres throughout the UK and abroad.

YACHTING

Royal Yachting Association Scotland: Secretary, Caledonia House, South Gyle, Edinburgh (031–317 7388). Videos, handbooks and log books for all RYA training and examination schemes are available from the above address. The *RYA Yearbook and Race Programme* is a useful guide to sailing in Scotland, giving comprehensive details of affiliated clubs and organizations, events and topics of general interest to all in the sailing community.

FESTIVALS (NATIONAL) AND PUBLIC HOLIDAYS

FESTIVALS

Burns Night: 25 January.
Celebrations marking the birthday of Scotland's national poet Robert Burns in 1759 have no effect on public facilities and services. Burns Night Suppers are held either on the evening of the 25th or on nearby dates at hotels, local halls, and in private houses.

St Andrew's Day: 30 November.
Celebrations for Scotland's patron saint do not constitute a statutory public holiday, and few amenities are affected. In the evening, St Andrew's Night dances and ceilidhs are held in hotels and local halls.

PUBLIC HOLIDAYS

English public holidays do not apply in Scotland, although some English-associated companies do recognize them. Bank holidays affect banks only. The following list gives the main bank holidays each year: 1 January*, 2 January, Friday before Easter, first and last Monday in May, first Monday in August, 30 November, 25 December*, 26 December. Spring and autumn holidays are taken instead of public holidays. Dates vary from year to year, but are usually on a Monday. Local holidays marking particular dates or occasions relevant to specific areas vary considerably between towns and regions. Full details of public holidays are available in *Public Holidays in Scotland*, published and updated annually by the Glasgow Chamber of Commerce (30 George Square, Glasgow (041–204 2121). The booklet costs £1.00. The STB publishes a free booklet, *Events in Scotland*, which lists events and festivals for the year throughout the country.

* New Year's Day and Christmas Day are taken by shops, offices, factories etc, although many hotels may remain open.

FOOD AND DRINK

DRINKING

Licensed hotels can serve drinks to residents at any time. Although licensing laws allow bars to open for 12 hours a day, public houses are usually open 1100–1430, and 1700–2300, Monday–Sunday, although not all choose to open on Sunday, and many, especially in cities, stay open later (some until 0130–0200). The same restrictions apply to licensed restaurants.

The legal age for drinking in Scotland is 18. Some landlords and publicans reserve the right to refuse admittance to minors, so it is always advisable to ask permission to bring children in.

Off-licences (liquor stores) selling beers, wines and spirits for private consumption are generally open 1100–2200 (Monday–Saturday, closed Sunday). It is illegal for anyone under the age of 18 to attempt to buy alcohol from an off-licence.

Scottish beer comes in a variety of forms. The standard request is for a pint of 'heavy' or 'special' but what exactly this means depends on what part of the country you're in. Generally, heavy is the equivalent of the Englishman's 'bitter', but is sweeter and fuller bodied. If you ask for a pint of heavy in Edinburgh, you're likely to be served '80 shilling' or, if you specifically request it, '70 shilling'. A few pubs also serve '90 shilling'. All three are cask-conditioned beers which have carbon dioxide pumped through them, making them creamy rather than fizzy. Their names – 70, 80 and 90 shilling – refer to the original

price of a keg of beer in days gone by. Ninety shilling has the greatest proof (alcoholic content) and 70 the least. Elsewhere, the same request for a pint of heavy is likely to secure a pint of Special. These are pressurized beers which are fizzy rather than creamy. Lager is another option, originally imported from Germany and Denmark, but now produced in Scotland. A pressurized beer, it is roughly equal in strength to 70 shilling, although some stronger lagers are available.

Chasers are a small measure of spirit (usually whisky), drunk simultaneously with a pint of beer. Whisky remains one of Scotland's favourite drinks and best-known exports. A nip and a dram are both equal to roughly one measure. Visitors should note, however, that measures in Scotland tend to be larger than those in England.

PUBLIC HOUSES

The Scottish pub is something of an institution. Although in larger towns restaurants are now widely available, in more rural areas they can be few and far between, in which case it is the pub which provides a focal point for eating. Pubs provide an excellent alternative for a cheap and filling lunch or dinner. Some pubs offer a 'Family Room', usually to one side of the main bar, where minors can eat either on their own or with their parents.

RESTAURANTS

A voluntary listing scheme for restaurants was introduced by the STB in 1973. Called 'The Taste of Scotland', it is now independently run, and covers restaurants, inns and coffee shops throughout Scotland which have applied for membership and paid the required fee. All applicants are visited by inspectors and, if up to standard, subsequently included in *The Taste of Scotland Guide*. Participants display the Taste of Scotland logo, a soup tureen encircled by the words 'The Taste of Scotland'. A list of all participating establishments is available from the Taste of Scotland office (see **Information – Associations and Organizations**). Restaurant guides, such as *Michelin* and the *Good Food Guide*, generally contain a Scottish section, albeit somewhat limited, and there are one or two specifically Scottish food guides.

LANGUAGE

ENGLISH

Spoken throughout Scotland, although variations in accent can often be difficult to understand.

SCOTS

Dialects vary from region to region. Visitors are most likely to hear 'broad' Scots around Glasgow and the Central Region. Geographically, in the Borders and from Dundee northwards, dialects change frequently.

GAELIC

Gaelic is still a living language in the Outer Hebrides (road signs on the Isle of Lewis are exclusively in Gaelic and bilingual in the rest of the region) and in pockets elsewhere, such as the Isle of Skye. Roughly 87 000 people in Scotland (about 2 per cent of the population) either speak, read or write Gaelic. The language is undergoing something of a renaissance at present, and it is estimated that over 3000 Scots are now learning Gaelic. Forecasts are that by 1993 broadcasting time for Gaelic television programmes will have trebled to 300 hours (see **Sabhal Mor Ostaig**, and **An Comunn Gaidhealach** under **Information – Associations and Organizations**).

MEDIA

The magazines and newspapers listed below are published in Scotland for a specifically Scottish market. British national papers often have Scottish sections or correspondents. Freesheets are free local newspapers distributed to each home in a particular area, often aimed at a certain district of a city or rural community. Some, along with regional newspapers, are listed in the Regional Fact File.

MAGAZINES

The List: 14 High Street, Edinburgh (031–558 1191). Contemporary magazine covering art, books, clubs, film, music, sport, television, theatre and travel, particularly in the Central Belt, covering Glasgow and Edinburgh. Published fortnightly (Thursday) and available from bookshops and newsagents.

Scots Magazine: Bank Street, Dundee (0382 23131). Scotland's oldest magazine was first published in 1739 in Edinburgh. In addition to articles of general Scottish interest, it has regular features on areas of Scotland and aspects of Scottish culture, and a classified section covering holidays, accommodation, books, shooting, fishing, livestock, and public notices. On sale on the last Friday of every month, it is available either by subscription or from newsagents and some bookshops.

Scottish Field: The Plaza Tower, The Plaza, East Kilbride (03552 46444). Up-market, glossy magazine offering the best of Scottish contemporary life. Articles cover people, lifestyles, fashion, culture, landscape, natural history and attractions, as well as history and heritage. Published monthly and available from newsagents.

Scottish Historical Review: Company of Scottish History Ltd, Aberdeen University Press, Farmers Hall, Aberdeen (0224 630724). Intellectual/academic magazine of essays on Scottish history, book reviews and lists of articles written about Scotland. Available by subscription only from the above address.

Scottish Home and Country: 42 Heriot Row, Edinburgh (031–225 1934). 'The Magazine of the Scottish Women's Rural Institutes' was founded in 1924. Published monthly, it offers features on crafts, fashion, gardening, books and cookery, all with a strong Scottish emphasis. Available on subscription in Scotland and abroad.

Scottish World: PO Box 1, Oban, Argyll (0631 62079). Covers all aspects of life in Scotland, such as clans, history and art; published quarterly and available on subscription or from newsagents.

What's On: 9a St Bernard's Crescent, Edinburgh (031–332 0471). Describing itself as 'the magazine for the Scottish leisure and tourism industry', *What's On* rivals *The List* as Scotland's equivalent of *Time Out*, providing details of events around Scotland. Covers exhibitions, theatre, film, music, food and drink; published monthly and available from newsagents.

DAILY NEWSPAPERS

Daily Record: Anderston Quay, Glasgow (041–248 7000).

Dundee Courier and Advertiser: 7 Bank St, Dundee (0382 23131).

The Herald: 195 Albion Street, Glasgow (041–552 6255). Formerly called the *Glasgow Herald*.

Press and Journal: PO Box 43, Lang Stracht, Mastrick, Aberdeen (0224 690222).

The Scotsman: 20 North Bridge, Edinburgh (031–225 2468).

SUNDAY NEWSPAPERS

Scotland on Sunday: 20 North Bridge, Edinburgh (031–225 2468).

Scottish Sunday Express: Park House, Park Circus Place, Glasgow (041–332 9600).

Sunday Mail: Anderston Quay, Glasgow (041–242 3403).

Sunday Post: Courier Place, Dundee (0382 22214); 144 Port Dundas Road, Glasgow (041–332 9933).

NATIONAL RADIO

(Regional channels listed under Regional Fact File)

BBC Radio Scotland: Broadcasting House, Queen Margaret Drive, Glasgow (041–330 2345); Broadcasting House, Queen Street, Edinburgh (031–225 3131). MW: 810 kHz/370m, VHF: 92.95 MHz.

BBC1–5: can be received throughout the country on the following frequencies, although quality of reception varies:
Radio 1 – MW: 1053 kHz/285m, 1089 kHz/275m
VHF: 97.7–99.6 MHz.

Radio 2 – VHF: 88–90.2 MHz.
Radio 3 – MW: 1215 kHz/247m.
VHF: 90–92.5 MHz.
Radio 4 – LW: 198 kHz/1515m.
VHF: 95.8, 94.9 MHz.
Radio 5 – MW: 693 kHz, 909 kHz.
In addition, BBC Radio Scotland is broadcast on MW: 810 kHz/370m, VHF: 92.95 MHz.

There is no national independent radio channel (in 1992); some independent regional channels (listed separately) are available.

TELEVISION

BBC Scotland: Broadcasting House, Queen Margaret Drive, Glasgow (041–330 2345); Broadcasting House, Queen Street, Edinburgh (031–225 3131). BBC1 and BBC2 are both received throughout the country, with some programme variations from England, including Scottish news bulletins.

British Sky Broadcasting: 6 Centaurs Business Park, Grant Way, Isleworth, Middx (071–782 3000). Broadcasts five channels to special receivers.

Channel 4 Television Company Ltd: 60 Charlotte Street, London (071-631 4444). Programmes received nationally throughout Britain.

Independent Television Association: Knighton House, 56 Mortimer Street, London (071–636 6866). Central organization for independent television stations. ITV programmes vary between regions: Scottish Television (STV), Borders Television and Grampian Television are listed in Regional Fact Files.

MONEY AND BANKS

BANKING

Scotland has four national banks.

Bank of Scotland plc: Head Office, The Mound, Edinburgh (031–442 7777). Fully independent.

The Royal Bank of Scotland plc: Head Office, 42 St Andrew Square, Edinburgh (031–556 8555). Fully independent.

Clydesdale Bank plc: Head Office, 30 St Vincent Place, Glasgow (041–223 2000). Part of National Australia Bank group.

TSB Scotland plc: Head Office, 120 George Street, Edinburgh (031–225 4555). Part of the TSB Group (head office in London).

All four banks have branches in the major Scottish cities, while both the Royal Bank of Scotland and the Bank of Scotland provide a comprehensive network of branches and autotellers throughout the country, which can be used by cardholders from other banks. Signs showing which cards can be used are displayed at autotellers.

CURRENCY

Scottish currency is the same value as English currency, although there are variations in the design of banknotes depending on the bank of issue. One pound notes are still legal tender in Scotland, along with the new one pound coins.

TRAVEL AND TRANSPORT

AIRPORTS

Scotland's main airports are at Glasgow and Edinburgh. Regional airports are located at Aberdeen and Prestwick, and there are a number of smaller airfields throughout the country (Dundee, Inverness and around the Highlands and Islands). Regional airports are listed in Regional Fact Files. Central address: **Scottish Airports Ltd**: St Andrews Drive, Glasgow Airport, Paisley, Renfrewshire (041–887 1111).

BUSES/COACHES

Scottish Citylink: St Andrew Square Bus Station, Edinburgh (031–557 5717); Victoria Coach Station, 164 Buckingham Palace Road, London (071–730 0202).

Caledonian Express/Stagecoach: Walnut Grove, Kinfauns, Perth (0738 33481).
Both run services from London and cities throughout England to Aberdeen, Dumfries, Dundee, Edinburgh, Fort William, Glasgow, Inverness, Lochalsh, Oban, Perth and Stirling. Stagecoach also run to Thurso.
Details of coach times and routes are available from the **Travel Centre**, Buchanan Street Bus Station, Glasgow (041–332 7133).

Scottish Postal Board: Royal Mail Public Relations Unit, West Port House, 102 West Port, Edinburgh EH3 9HS. Post enquiries only. Produces an annual *Scottish Postbus Guide*, giving full details of postbus services throughout Scotland.

DRIVING

Driving in Scotland is on the left-hand side. The road network throughout the country is generally good, with either motorway or dual carriageway links between Glasgow, Edinburgh and the north, including Stirling, Perth and Dundee.
Visitors should take extra care when driving on small country roads – many of which are single-track – particularly in the north of the country. In addition, during wintertime it is advisable to check on relief maps whether routes go over high roads, as snow can soon block them.

FERRIES

Comprehensive ferry services are run, particularly around the north of the country and to outlying islands.

Caledonian MacBrayne Ltd (popularly known as Cal Mac): The Ferry Terminal, Gourock (0475 33755).

Orkney Islands Shipping Company Ltd: 4 Ayre Road, Kirkwall, Orkney (0856 2044).

P&O European Ferries: Enterprise House, Channel View Road, Dover (0304 203388).

P&O Ferries Orkney and Shetland Services: P&O Ferries Terminal, Jamieson's Quay, Aberdeen (0224 589111).

Sealink British Ferries: Sea Terminal, Stranraer (0776 2262).

Shetland Islands Council: Grantfield, Lerwick, Shetland (0595 2024).

Western Ferries (Argyll) Ltd/Western

Ferries Clyde Ltd: 16 Woodside Crescent, Glasgow (041–332 9766).

TRAINS

InterCity trains connect Scotland with the rest of the UK. If taking a bicycle on trains, check in advance about availability of space, as reservations are compulsory on some services. Full details are available in the leaflet *ScotRail Welcomes Cyclists*.

Edinburgh Waverley Station: Waverley Bridge (031–556 2451).

Glasgow Central Station: Gordon Street (041–204 2844).

Glasgow Queen Street Station: (041–204 2844).

TRAVEL TICKETS

Reduced Price Tickets: Issued by British Rail, these can save money on most routes around the country. Ask for details of Standard, Cheap Day and Saver tickets, as well as Weekly, Monthly and 3-Monthly season tickets if your stay in Scotland is longer.

Travelpass: Issued by Highlands and Islands Enterprise, Travelpass allows 8 or 13 days' unlimited travel around the Highlands and Islands, including the Outer Hebrides, by bus, train and ferry. Passes also cover travel by train or bus (Scottish Citylink) from Glasgow, Edinburgh or Aberdeen to the Highlands and back again. Further details, and passes, are available from British Rail in Edinburgh, Glasgow, Paisley, Aberdeen, Stirling and Inverness; from St Andrew Bus Station (Edinburgh), Buchanan Street Bus Station (Glasgow); and from Caledonian MacBrayne (address under Ferries above).

Festival Cities Rover: Issued by British Rail, this allows unlimited travel for any three or seven consecutive days between Edinburgh, Kirkcaldy, North Berwick, Stirling, Glasgow and intermediate stations.

Freedom of Scotland Rover Ticket: Issued by British Rail, this allows unlimited train travel (also covering Caledonian MacBrayne ferries and Firth of Clyde steamers) from Wick and Thurso in the north to Carlisle and Berwick in the south, for 4, 7, 10 or 15 days.

Highland Rover Airpass: British Airways offers a 'Highland Rover Airpass', which allows travel on up to eight Highlands and Islands flights over a minimum of eight days.

WEATHER

Misconceptions about Scottish weather are common: that the whole of Scotland is covered by snow in winter for example, and that it rains a lot in summer.

In fact the eastern part of Scotland is rather dry; the annual average rainfall for Edinburgh is similar to that for London. The higher areas are wet, but even there the rainfall is seasonal. In the west of Scotland the driest months are April, May and June and the wettest are September to January.

As for sunshine, the chart shows the extreme east of Scotland (Dunbar) to have an excellent sunshine record (although the absolute record for hours of sunshine in a day is held by Tiree with 329 hours in a month in May 1946 and May 1975).

Full details of Scotland's climate are available in *The Climate of Scotland – Some Facts and Figures*, on sale at HMSO Bookshops or from the Meteorological Office, Saughton House, Broomhouse Drive, Edinburgh (031–244 8362/3).

Average number of days with snow on ground at 9am (1951–80)

Location	Jan	Feb	Mar	Apr	May	Jun	Jul	Aug	Sep	Oct	Nov	Dec	Year
Shetland													
Lerwick	7.5	7.8	3.8	1.4	0.1	0.0	0.0	0.0	0.0	0.2	2.4	4.9	23.1
Western Isles													
Stornoway	3.5	2.8	1.4	0.2	0.0	0.0	0.0	0.0	0.0	0.0	1.0	1.5	10.4
Highland													
Wick	5.4	5.6	2.2	0.5	0.0	0.0	0.0	0.0	0.0	0.0	1.5	3.0	18.2
Nairn	5.5	5.6	1.7	0.2	0.0	0.0	0.0	0.0	0.0	0.0	0.8	2.7	16.5
Grampian													
Braemar	15.6	15.9	9.7	2.4	0.1	0.0	0.0	0.0	0.0	0.3	4.6	10.4	59.0
Craibstone (nr Aberdeen)	9.6	9.6	4.9	0.9	0.1	0.0	0.0	0.0	0.0	0.2	2.6	4.7	32.6
Tayside													
Perth	5.7	5.2	1.2	0.1	0.0	0.0	0.0	0.0	0.0	0.0	0.5	2.4	15.1
Lothian													
Edinburgh													
Royal Botanic Gdn.	5.0	5.3	1.1	0.2	0.0	0.0	0.0	0.0	0.0	0.0	0.5	1.9	14.0
Royal Observatory	5.5	6.1	1.8	0.3	0.0	0.0	0.0	0.0	0.0	0.0	1.0	2.0	16.7
Penicuik	9.6	9.3	3.8	0.9	0.1	0.0	0.0	0.0	0.0	0.0*	1.9	4.7	30.3
Dunbar	1.7	2.6	0.4	0.1	0.0	0.0	0.0	0.0	0.0	0.0	0.2	0.6	5.6
Strathclyde													
Tiree	1.4	1.2	0.4	0.1	0.0	0.0	0.0	0.0	0.0	0.0	0.1	0.4	3.6
Glasgow Airport	3.5	1.8	0.7	0.1	0.0	0.0	0.0	0.0	0.0	0.0	0.6	1.3	8.0
Auchincruive (nr Ayr)	2.3	1.7	0.7	0.1	0.0	0.0	0.0	0.0	0.0	0.0	0.5	0.6	5.9
Dumfries & Galloway													
Eskdalemuir	10.1	9.6	4.7	0.7	0.0*	0.0	0.0	0.0	0.0	0.0*	1.9	5.0	32.0

Note: 0.0* in the 30-year period indicates there was only one day with snow lying at 0900 hours in this month.

Average rainfall in mm (1951–80)

Location	Jan	Feb	Mar	Apr	May	Jun	Jul	Aug	Sep	Oct	Nov	Dec	Year
Shetland													
Lerwick	127	93	93	72	64	64	67	78	113	119	140	147	1177
Orkney													
Kirkwall	105	71	72	54	53	57	55	77	88	110	120	121	983
Western Isles													
Benbecula	129	86	89	62	65	76	83	83	119	139	140	132	1203
Stornoway	115	77	80	66	62	67	72	74	103	126	129	125	1096
Highland													
Ullapool	119	84	93	76	73	83	80	92	115	155	159	161	1290
Achmore (nr Plockton)	104	68	70	56	56	63	78	82	107	112	124	112	1032
Portree (Skye)	182	116	129	93	91	104	113	118	170	204	203	210	1732
Onich (nr Fort William)	200	132	152	111	103	124	137	150	199	215	220	238	1981
Wick	81	58	55	45	47	49	61	74	68	73	90	82	783
Fort Augustus	112	72	83	58	72	61	65	82	103	124	126	140	1098
Nairn	48	34	33	36	43	46	62	75	50	54	60	52	593
Glenmore Lodge	96	64	71	68	76	73	87	107	80	96	100	106	1024
Grampian													
Gordon Castle	55	44	42	42	51	55	77	89	57	66	75	67	720
Braemar	93	59	59	51	65	55	58	76	73	87	87	96	859
Craibstone (nr Aberdeen)	77	57	54	51	62	54	79	83	68	78	80	80	821
Tayside													
Pitlochry	94	59	52	47	64	62	65	72	70	76	69	94	824
Arbroath	50	40	40	38	48	44	62	67	50	52	54	54	599
Perth	70	52	47	43	57	51	67	72	63	65	69	82	738
Fife													
St. Andrews	62	48	44	39	50	44	61	68	55	55	63	64	653
Lothian													
Edinburgh (Royal Botanic Garden)	47	39	39	38	49	45	69	73	57	56	58	56	626
Dunbar	46	33	33	33	47	41	55	68	47	48	55	49	555
Borders													
Floors Castle (Kelso)	55	43	38	40	55	51	63	75	57	59	63	57	656
Central													
Callander	164	113	115	81	97	86	97	113	141	147	175	193	1522
Strathclyde													
Tiree	120	71	77	60	56	66	79	83	123	125	123	123	1106
Inveraray Castle	210	132	150	115	106	124	137	148	209	225	228	252	2036
Eallabus (Islay)	139	85	92	70	67	74	93	93	128	139	149	149	1278
Glasgow Airport	96	63	65	50	62	58	68	83	95	98	105	108	951
Auchincruive (nr Ayr)	82	50	53	47	51	58	80	91	100	97	99	93	901
Aros (Mull)	210	116	142	97	96	109	120	133	199	208	203	220	1853
Dumfries & Galloway													
West Freugh (nr Stranraer)	100	65	67	53	55	57	70	82	98	100	105	103	955
Loch Dee	236	154	168	130	121	122	142	184	214	222	241	263	2197
Dumfries	103	72	68	55	71	63	77	93	104	106	109	104	1023
Eskdalemuir	150	99	108	86	94	95	107	122	142	140	153	160	1456

1″ = 25.4mm

Average bright sunshine in hours (1951–80)

Location	Jan	Feb	Mar	Apr	May	Jun	Jul	Aug	Sep	Oct	Nov	Dec	Annual	Annual total
Shetland														
Lerwick	0.7	1.9	2.7	4.5	4.9	5.3	4.0	3.8	3.2	2.0	1.1	0.5	2.9	1056
Orkney														
Kirkwall	1.0	2.3	3.1	4.9	5.2	5.4	4.3	4.1	3.4	2.4	1.3	0.7	3.2	1160
Western Isles														
Stornoway	1.2	2.5	3.6	5.2	6.0	5.9	4.2	4.4	3.6	2.5	1.5	0.8	3.4	1256
Benbecula	1.3	2.5	3.7	5.8	6.5	6.5	4.6	4.9	3.8	2.5	1.6	0.9	3.7	1361
Highland														
Prabost (Skye)	1.3	2.7	3.5	5.2	6.0	5.8	4.1	4.3	3.3	2.3	1.5	1.0	3.4	1243
Onich (nr Fort William)	0.9	2.2	2.9	4.4	5.3	5.0	3.7	3.8	2.9	2.1	1.1	0.6	2.9	1059
Wick	1.3	2.6	3.4	5.0	5.2	5.4	4.4	4.3	3.7	2.8	1.6	1.0	3.4	1240
Nairn	1.4	2.8	3.6	4.9	5.3	5.6	4.7	4.3	3.9	2.9	1.8	1.2	3.5	1290
Fort Augustus	0.8	2.1	2.9	4.2	5.0	5.0	3.8	3.8	2.9	2.0	1.0	0.6	2.9	1044
Glenmore Lodge (nr Aviemore)	0.8	2.4	3.4	4.4	5.1	5.2	4.2	4.1	3.5	2.6	1.1	0.5	3.1	1137
Grampian														
Braemar	0.8	2.0	2.9	4.5	5.2	5.5	4.9	4.2	3.4	2.1	1.1	0.6	3.1	1137
Craibstone (nr Aberdeen)	1.7	2.7	3.4	5.0	5.6	6.0	5.2	4.7	3.9	3.1	2.1	1.5	3.7	1367
Tayside														
Perth	1.4	2.3	3.2	5.1	5.7	6.0	5.5	4.5	3.7	2.7	1.8	1.1	3.6	1309
Arbroath	1.8	2.9	3.6	5.6	6.1	6.4	5.9	5.2	4.4	3.2	2.4	1.6	4.1	1499
Fife														
St. Andrews	1.8	2.6	3.4	5.1	5.8	6.2	5.6	4.9	4.2	3.1	2.2	1.5	3.9	1415
Lothian														
Edinburgh														
(Royal Botanic Garden)	1.5	2.4	3.2	4.9	5.7	6.1	5.5	4.8	4.0	3.0	2.0	1.3	3.7	1400
Dunbar	1.8	2.8	3.7	5.4	6.1	6.7	6.1	5.4	4.4	3.4	2.4	1.7	4.2	1523
Strathclyde														
Tiree	1.4	2.4	3.7	5.8	6.9	6.6	5.1	5.2	3.9	2.5	1.5	0.9	3.8	1400
Glasgow Airport	1.3	2.2	3.1	5.1	6.0	6.2	5.3	4.7	3.7	2.6	1.6	1.0	3.6	1303
Prestwick Airport	1.6	2.8	3.5	5.6	6.8	6.7	5.7	5.2	4.0	2.9	1.9	1.3	4.0	1465
Dumfries & Galloway														
Dumfries	1.5	2.5	3.2	4.9	5.8	6.1	5.1	4.9	3.7	2.9	2.0	1.3	3.7	1338
Eskdalemuir	1.3	2.2	2.9	4.5	5.3	5.4	4.6	4.3	3.3	2.5	1.8	1.2	3.3	1198

MISCELLANEOUS

EMERGENCY PHONE NUMBERS

Directory Enquiries: 192. Free from phone-boxes; 42 pence per call otherwise.

Operator: 100. Free.

Police/Fire/Ambulance/Mountain Rescue/Coastguard: 999. Free.

LAW

The Scottish legal system differs from that in England. Unlike most legal systems, it is based neither solely on Roman Law (as in France and Germany), nor is it derived completely from English law (as in America). Instead, it is a mixture of composite sources, having evolved its principles over the centuries on the basis of past cases.

The most senior lawyer in Scotland is the Lord Advocate, who is responsible for all criminal prosecutions, discharging his functions through the Crown Office. He is also a member of the government, although his role as a lawyer takes precedence over that as a politician.

The legal profession in Scotland has two branches: advocates and solicitors. Further information is available from the **Law Society of Scotland** (see under **Information – Associations and Organizations**).

LOCAL GOVERNMENT

Scottish local government as it is recognized today came into existence on 16 May 1975. It is on a two-tier basis, with nine regional councils (such as Strathclyde, Tayside and the Borders) and 53 district councils (such as Glasgow City, Angus and Berwickshire). In addition there are three island councils for Orkney, Shetland and the Western Isles which perform the tasks of both regional and district councils. In general, regional councils provide large-scale services such as transport and education within their area, while district councils are responsible for local planning, housing, environmental affairs, tourism and amenity services.

POPULATION

Britain: 55 780 000 (1981).

Scotland: 5 130 735 (1981).

At the time of going to press, preliminary figures of the 1991 census put Scotland's population at 4 957 289. Also apparent is the first evidence of the 'urban clearances' which have pushed up house prices in many rural areas of the country, with increasing numbers of people leaving their homes in the city for a peaceful retreat in the country. It is estimated that over the past two years (1989–91), almost 14 000 people have migrated to Scotland, many from England. Islands such as Skye, Mull and Arran now have sizeable English populations.

RELIGION*

Of Scotland's various Christian denominations, the largest is the Church of Scotland, with an official membership of 822 985 (1988), although it is likely that considerably more people identify themselves as belonging to the Church of Scotland without formally being members of it. Its structure is presbyterian, with regions split into parishes, and its doctrine evangelical. It is governed by the General Assembly of the Church of Scotland, which meets once a year in Edinburgh in May to review policies and discuss reports. The Roman Catholic Church is Scotland's second largest, with 793 620 members (1988), while Scottish Episcopal Church membership stands at 59 940 (1987).

Also functioning along the lines of the presbyterian tradition is a conservative presbyterian group, with a membership of around 12 250 (1988). This includes the Reformed Presbyterian Church, found mostly in the Lowlands, and the Free Church of Scotland and Free Presbyterian Church, which are found mostly in the western Highlands and Islands.

Other religious groups present in Scotland include the Religious Society of Friends (Quakers), whose membership is around 550 (1988), and a number of Christian organizations, including Independent Evangelical Churches, various house Churches and the Christian Brethren, which have a combined total membership of over 17 800 (1984). Judaism is represented, with Hebrew congregations in each of Scotland's four major cities accounting for 4200 people, while the Muslim population, mostly Asian, is estimated to be between 15 000 and 20 000 (1988). Hindus and Sikhs are also present (although no figures are available), and for several years now there has been a Buddhist community at Langholm in the Borders.

TELEPHONES

British Telecom pay-phones can be found throughout the country. Although the Mercury·network is increasing, Mercury telephones are still found mostly in larger cities. British Telecom telephones accept either coins (all except one penny and the new five pence coins) or phone-cards; the latter are available from post offices and some newsagents. British Telecom has replaced the traditional red call-box (telephone booth) with modern glass booths, although a handful of old ones have been allowed to remain in locations where they have been thought more appropriate. New booths marked with a green stripe or sign accept phone-cards and those with a pink stripe or sign, coins. International Direct Dialling is possible to most countries.

TOURISM IN SCOTLAND

Tourism in Scotland has traditionally consisted of a three-month summer influx of visitors from June to August, followed by increased activity (both domestic and international) at the end and beginning of the year for the skiing season. Attributes constantly

* Statistics throughout are based on the Fact Sheet *Religion in Scotland*, issued by the Scottish Office (see Information – Associations and Organizations), in conjunction with HMSO. At the time of going to press a new Fact Sheet is being prepared, updated to provide comprehensive information on religion in Scotland, and available from the Scottish Office.

highlighted have been beautiful scenery, wild open spaces, the Edinburgh Festival in August, and the opportunity to indulge in some healthy country living.

This situation is changing, however, and the emphasis is no longer on making the most of a few months of the year, but on how to sustain tourism in Scotland right through from January to December, and in a way that brings maximum benefits to visitors and locals alike. As in so many countries around the world, Scotland is now trying to make the most of her resources without allowing them to become worn, run-down and over-exploited. To this end, moves are afoot throughout the country to implement new policies aimed at opening up less visited areas, raising standards of accommodation, and, generally, spreading the load more evenly in terms of both geographical location of attractions and seasonal accessibility. In addition, conservation bodies are continually working with all aspects of Scottish wildlife, fauna and flora (see **Information – Associations and Organizations** for a number of the main ones). For the visitor this will ensure a better quality of stay at any time of the year, while for the Scots it means the continued preservation of their land, and the ensuing economic benefits.

INFORMATION – ASSOCIATIONS AND ORGANIZATIONS

An Comunn Gaidhealach: 109 Church Street, Inverness (0463 231226). One of several Gaelic organizations based at the Church Street office, dealing with the Gaelic language and culture past and present.

Forestry Commission: 231 Corstorphine Road, Edinburgh (031–334 0303). A government department, the Forestry Commission manages over one million hectares of forest (60 per cent in Scotland), provides a source of employment and revenue in more rural areas, is responsible for training and research, and provides many recreational facilities.

Friends of the Earth Scotland: Bonnington Mill, 70–2 Newhaven Road, Edinburgh (031–554 9977). Scottish headquarters of environmental group.

Highlands and Islands Enterprise: Bridge House, 20 Bridge Street, Inverness (0463 234171). Development agency for the Highlands and Islands, investing roughly 25 per cent of its budget in tourism.

Highland Direct: Hi-Line House, Station Road, Dingwall, Ross-shire (0349 65000). A comprehensive holiday booking service run by Highlands and Islands Enterprise.

Historic Scotland: 20 Brandon Street, Edinburgh (opening times and admission charges, 031–244 3101; Friends of Historic Scotland, 031–244 3099; all other enquiries, 031–244 3144). Government body working to protect Scotland's built heritage, caring for over 330 properties throughout Scotland, including Edinburgh and Stirling Castles, Dryburgh Abbey, the Meigle Sculptured Stones, Dallas Dhu Distillery and St Andrews Cathedral. Membership of 'Friends of Historic Scotland' is open to anyone and benefits include 'unlimited free entry (and directory) to all properties; concessions at English and Welsh monuments, and a quarterly newsletter'. For non-members Scottish Explorer Tickets are available for 7 or 14 days (family tickets also), offering reduced entrance fees to over 70 sites.

Law Society of Scotland: 26 Drumsheugh Gardens, Edinburgh (031–226 7411). The governing body of the solicitor branch of the Scottish legal profession.

National Trust for Scotland: 5 Charlotte Square, Edinburgh (031–226 5922). There are over 100 historic castles, houses, gardens and areas of open countryside in the Trust's care in Scotland. A registered charity, the National Trust for Scotland was formed in 1931 and now welcomes in excess of one and a half million people per year to properties in its care. Members are admitted free to all properties, while non-members are charged an entrance fee at most sites.

Royal Highland and Agricultural Society of Scotland: Edinburgh Exhibition and Trade Centre, Ingliston, Edinburgh (031–333 2444).

Royal Society for the Protection of Birds (Scotland): Scottish

Headquarters, 17 Regent Terrace, Edinburgh (031–557 3136). Scottish branch of the national organization, working to protect birds throughout Scotland. Produces a series of useful leaflets, as well as an excellent map, *Where to Watch Birds in Scotland*, matching areas of the country with species of birds.

Sabhal Mor Ostaig Gaelic School: An Teanga, Isle of Skye (04714 373). Started in 1973 as a summer school, Sabhal Mor Ostaig (The Big Barn) has grown to become a popular centre for innovative further education, as well as one of the world's leading authorities on Gaelic language and culture. Courses and information are offered on every aspect of Gaelic culture, from song and clarsach to language and writing skills.

Saltire Society: 9 Fountain Close, 22 High St, Edinburgh (031–556 1836). Promotes culture and heritage of Scotland through lectures, publications etc.

Scotland's Gardens Scheme: 31 Castle Terrace, Edinburgh (031–229 1870). Works with and publishes details of several hundred private gardens around Scotland which are periodically opened to the public. Directory available from the above address, or from outlets such as National Trust shops and Tourist Information Offices.

Scottish Arts Council: 12 Manor Place, Edinburgh (031–226 6051). Part of the Arts Council of Great Britain, promoting the arts in Scotland. Information on theatres throughout the country.

Scottish Conservation Projects: Balallan House, 24 Allan Park, Stirling (0786 79697). Conservation charity founded in 1984, inviting people of all ages to become involved in preserving the Scottish countryside. Working 'holidays' learning skills such as dry-stone dyking and wildlife management.

Scottish Enterprise: 120 Bothwell Street, Glasgow (041–248 2700). A Government-funded body which oversees and monitors development throughout the country. Grants aid towards development and administers the Enterprise Trust scheme.

Scottish Field Studies Association: Kindrogan Field Centre, Enochdhu, Blairgowrie, Perthshire (0250 81286). Offers courses at its Perthshire field centre aimed at increasing understanding of the Scottish countryside.

Scottish Natural Heritage: Battleby, Redgorton, Perth (0738 27921) and 12 Hope Terrace, Edinburgh (031–447 4784). In existence from 1 April 1992, created by the merger of the Countryside Commission for Scotland and the Nature Conservancy Council in Scotland. Functions include giving planning advice to authorities, providing financial assistance for tree-planting, landscape enhancement and recreation provisions establishing nature reserves, researching species and sites and granting aid to conservation bodies.

Scottish Office: Information Department, New St Andrew's House, Edinburgh (031–244 5199). The publicity office of Scotland's administrative headquarters produces a number of useful fact sheets about issues relevant to Scottish life today. These cover a wide range of topics, including religion, education and social work and are available by post or phone-call from the above address. No personal callers.

Scottish Sports Council: Caledonia House, South Gyle, Edinburgh (031–317 7200). Umbrella organization for sports in Scotland, information on main sporting bodies throughout the country.

Scottish Tartans Society: Scottish Tartan Museum, Drummond Street, Comrie, Perthshire (0764 70779). International headquarters maintaining the Register of all Publicly Known Tartans. Research department will answer questions 'on the origin of Scottish names, their connections with clans and families, and their associated tartans'. Fees are charged for time spent searching records and compiling reports. The society does not deal with enquiries concerning heraldry or genealogy. Individual and associate membership available.

Scottish Tourist Board: 23 Ravelston Terrace, Edinburgh (031–332 2433); 19 Cockspur Street, London (071–930 8661).

Scottish Wildlife Trust: 25 Johnston Terrace, Edinburgh (031–226 4602). Voluntary body conserving Scottish wildlife, with over 60 reserves throughout the country.

Scottish Youth Hostels Association: 7 Glebe Crescent, Stirling (0786 51191). Central office and information point for Scotland's 81 youth hostels.

Taste of Scotland: 33 Melville Street, Edinburgh (031–220 1900). (See listings under **Food and drink – Restaurants**.)

Regional Fact File

Regional map of South-East Scotland

CINEMAS

Dundee

Cannon: Seagate (0382 25247).

Dunfermline

Orient Express Cinema: East Port
(0383 721934).

Edinburgh

Cameo: 38 Home Street, Tollcross
(031–228 4141).

Cannon: 119 Lothian Road
(031–229 3030 (information);
031–228 1638 (box office)).

Dominion: Newbattle Terrace,
Morningside (031–447 2660).

Filmhouse: 88 Lothian Road
(031–228 2688).

Odeon: 7 Clerk Street
(031–667 7331/2).

UCI (United Cinemas International):
Newcraighall Park, Newcraighall
(031–669 0777) (box office);
031–669 0711 (information).
Twelve-cinema complex.

Galashiels

Kingsway: Channel Street
(0896 2767).

Glenrothes

Kingsway: Glenrothes Leisure Centre,
Church Street (0592 750980).

Kelso

Roxy Cinema: Horse Market
(0573 24609).

Kirkcaldy

Cannon: High Street (0592 260143).

Perth

Playhouse: Muir Street (0738 23126)

St Andrews

New Picture House: North Street
(0334 73509).

FESTIVALS/EVENTS

The festivals listed below are those which are likely to be of most interest to visitors. Dates are based on those of 1991 and should be checked with Tourist Information Offices.

Aberfeldy
Mid June: Provincial Gaelic Mod.
June, third week: Kenmore to Aberfeldy Raft Race.

Anstruther
July: Holiday Fair Week.

Birnam
August, fourth Saturday: Highland Games.

Blair Atholl
End May (Saturday before the Games): Atholl Highlanders' Parade at Blair Castle.
End May (usually last Sunday): Highland Games.

Burntisland
Mid July: Burntisland Highland Games, reputed to be the second oldest in the world.

Ceres
End June: Highland Games, the oldest in Scotland (1314).

Comrie
July/August: Comrie Fortnight.
31 December: Flambeaux Torchlight Procession.

Crail
July: Festival Week.

Crieff
August, third Saturday: Highland Gathering.

Cupar
June/July: Gala Week.

July: Highland Games.

Dundee
June and July: Dundee City Festival.
July: Highland Games.
July/August: Jazz Festival.
July/August: Folk Festival.
July/August: Children's Festival.
August, first two weeks: Water Festival.

Dunfermline
June: Civic Week.

Dunkeld
June, third week: Dunkeld and Birnam Arts Festival.

Edinburgh
March/April: International Folk Festival.
Mid April: Opening of Royal Scottish Academy Annual Exhibition.
June, third week: Royal Highland Show.
Mid August: International Film Festival, for two weeks.
Mid August: International Festival of Music, Drama and the Arts, for three weeks.
Mid August: Festival Fringe.
Mid August: Military Tattoo, for three weeks.
Mid August: Book Festival (biennial, next 1993).
August, third week: International Jazz Festival.
November, third week: Antiques Fair.

Elie
July: Elie Fair, Arts and Crafts Festival.

Falkland
June, last week: Falkland Festival.
End July: Craft Fair.

Galashiels
End June: Braw Lads' Gathering/
Common Riding event.

Gleneagles
July, first or second week: Bells
Scottish Open Golf.

Haddington
May/June: Festival Week.

Hawick
June, second week: Common Riding.

Jedburgh
July, first week: Jetharts Callants
Festival. Traditional celebrations.
July: Jedburgh Border Games.

Kelso
February/March: Berwickshire Hunt
point-to-point.
March, third week: Kelso Races.
May: Great Tweed Raft Race.
July: Kelso Games; Civic Week/
Common Riding event; Border
Union Agricultural Show.

Kenmore
June, third week: Kenmore to
Aberfeldy Raft Race.
June/July: Highland Games.

Kirkcaldy
April: The Links Market, Britain's
oldest and largest fair.

Langholm
End July: Common Riding.

Lauder
July/August: Common Riding.

Leuchars
Mid September: Military and Civil
Air Show.

Leven
Mid May: Fife Agricultural Show.

Melrose
June: Summer Festival.

Newburgh
Mid June: Highland Games and
Haggis Market.
August: Newburgh Festival.

Peebles
June, around 21: Beltane Festival.

Perth
Early February: Aberdeen Angus
Cattle Show and Sales.
Mid May: Perth Festival of the Arts.
August, second week: Highland
Games.
October, third week: Aberdeen
Angus Cattle Show and Sales.

Pitlochry
April/May: Golf Week.
May–October: Pitlochry Festival
Theatre Season.
September, second Saturday:
Highland Games.

St Andrews
February: St Andrews Festival
(biennial, next 1993).
March: International Festival of Food
and Wine.
April: St Andrews and NE Fife
Golf Week.
April: Kate Kennedy Procession.
End May: Craigtoun Country Fair.
June, third week: East Neuk of Fife's
'Spice of Fife' fish festival.
End July: Highland Games.
August, first week: Lammas
Medieval Market Fair.
September/October: Dunhill Cup
Golf Week.

Scone
End June: Coronation Pageant, Scone
Palace.

Selkirk
June, second week: Common Riding.

GALLERIES

Galleries listed below are intended as a quick reference guide only and cover those of most interest in each area. Galleries which are included as part of a museum are listed under Museums, unless they merit particular mention, in which case there is an entry for both the gallery and the museum.

Ancrum

Ancrum Gallery: Cross Keys Inn (083 53 340). Monthly exhibitions by leading Scottish artists.

Anstruther

Halcyon Gallery: 32 Rodger Street (0333 311954). Local scenes in oils, watercolours and prints.

Arbroath

Arbroath Art Gallery: Public Library, Hill Terrace (0674 73232). Local work, including watercolours by J.W. Herald and oils by Pieter Brueghel.

Auchterarder

Shinafoot Gallery: High Street (0764 63843). Original Scottish works and limited editions.

Broughton

Broughton Place: off A701 north of Broughton village (08994 234). Collection of works by contemporary artists and craftsmen housed in an imposing modern castle designed by Sir Basil Spence in 1938.

Dalkeith

Dalkeith Arts Centre: White Hart Street (031–663 6986). Changing exhibitions, mostly local.

Dundee

Dundee Printmaker's Workshop and Seagate Gallery: 38–40 Seagate (0382 26331). Changing exhibitions promoting contemporary arts.

Francis Cooper and Matthew Galleries: Duncan of Jordonstone College of Art, Perth Road (0382 23261 ext 291). National and international exhibitions of fine art, design, photography and architecture.

McManus Galleries: Albert Square (0382 23141). Dundee's principal museum and gallery. Works by Flemish, Dutch, French, British and Scottish artists. Regular modern exhibitions.

Windsor Gallery: Perth Road (0382 202863). Pictures for sale.

Edinburgh

City Art Centre: Market Street (031–225 2424 ext 6650). Edinburgh City's Art Gallery, including many Scottish works. Holds exhibitions from throughout the world.

Edinburgh College of Art Sculpture Court and Andrew Grant Gallery: Lauriston Place (031–229 9311). Open during term times, exhibitions of contemporary art, diploma shows.

French Institute: 13 Randolph Crescent (031–225 5366). Yearly programme, mostly contemporary French and Scottish artists.

Fruitmarket Gallery: 29 Market Street (031–225 2383). Contemporary Scottish and international works.

National Gallery of Scotland: The Mound (031–556 8921). Neoclassical building housing works by Scottish and European artists, including William McTaggart, Allan Ramsay, David Wilkie, as well as Raphael,

El Greco, Turner, Rembrandt and Van Gogh. Old Masters and Impressionists included.

Netherbow Arts Centre: 43 High Street (031–556 9579/2647). New works in regular exhibitions.

Rias Gallery: 15 Rutland Square (031–229 7545). Architectural exhibitions in a house gifted to the Royal Incorporation of Architects.

Royal Scottish Academy: The Mound (031–225 6671). Annual exhibition (summer) and Festival exhibition of painting, sculpture and architecture.

Scottish National Gallery of Modern Art: Belford Road (031–556 8921). Twentieth-century paintings, sculptures and graphic art, including works by Derain, Matisse, Moore, Picasso, Hockney and Caulfield.

Scottish National Portrait Gallery: Queen Street (031–556 8921). Scotland's famous faces through the ages.

Stills Gallery: 105 High Street (031–557 1140). National and international photography.

Talbot Rice Gallery: University of Edinburgh, Old College, South Bridge (031–667 1011 ext 4308). New works in regular exhibitions.

369 Gallery: 233 Cowgate (031–225 3013). Contemporary Scottish exhibitions.

Galashiels

Old Gala House and Christopher Boyd Gallery: off A7 at Galashiels (0750 20096). Temporary art galleries housed in the former home of the Lairds of Gala, built in 1583.

Haddington

Peter Potter Gallery Trust: 10 The Sands (062 082 2080). Original work by local artists.

Kelso

Stichill Smithy Gallery: The Smithy House, Ednam Road, Stichill (05737 346), three miles north of Kelso on B6364). Exhibitions of artists and craftsmen housed in the former 'shoeing-end' of an old smithy.

Kirkcaldy

Kirkcaldy Museum and Art Gallery: War Memorial Gardens (0592 260732). Major collection of 19th- and 20th-century Scottish paintings, Wemyss Ware pottery, natural history and archaeological exhibition.

Kirriemuir

Kirriemuir Art Gallery (0575 74409). Temporary exhibitions by local artists.

Montrose

Montrose Art Gallery: Panmure Place (0674 73232). Local works, including William Lamb sculptures and paintings by George Paul Chalmers.

William Lamb Memorial Studio: Market Street (0674 73232). Sculpture and etchings by William Lamb, including heads of HRH Queen Elizabeth and HRH Princess Margaret as girls.

North Berwick

Westgate Gallery: 39–41 Westgate (0620 4976). Photographs and paintings covering a wide range of styles and subjects.

Peebles

Clockmhor Gallery: 7 Bridgegate (0721 20254/29733). Scottish fine art prints and originals.

Galleries (cont.)

Perth

Fair Maid's House: North Port
(0738 25976). Contemporary Scottish
crafts and studio workshop.

Perth Art Gallery and Museum:
George Street (0738 32488). Local
history exhibitions, including fine
and applied art.

St Andrews

Crawford Arts Centre: University
of St Andrews, 93 North Street
(0334 74610). Regular Scottish and
international art exhibitions.

GOLF CLUBS/ASSOCIATIONS

Visitors are welcome at the courses listed below, but are advised to telephone ahead to check times. Note that many clubs require written applications, particularly for groups, and often with at least 21 days' notice. Full details of golf clubs are usually available from Tourist Information Offices in the relevant areas.

Aberfeldy

Aberfeldy: (0887 20535). 9 hole.

Crail

Crail Golfing Society: Balcomie (0333 50960 professional, 50278 clubhouse). 18 hole.

Crieff

Crieff Golf Club: Perth Road (0764 2909). 18 hole.

Dunkeld

Dunkeld and Birnam Golf Club: Fungarth, Dunkeld (03502 524). 9 hole.

Edinburgh

Braid Hills Golf Course: Braid Hills Road (031–447 6666). 18 hole.

Falkland

Falkland Golf Club: The Myre (0337 57404). 9 hole.

Gullane

Gullane Golf Club (0620 84255). 18 hole.

Muirfield Golf Club: Muirfield (0620 842123). 18 hole.

Haddington

Haddington Golf Club: Amisfield Park (062 082 3627). 18 hole.

Hawick

Minto Golf Club: Denholm (0450 72180). 18 hole.

Kenmore

Kenmore Golf Club: Taymouth Castle (08873 228). 18 hole.

Ladybank

Ladybank Golf Club: Annsmuir (0337 30814). 18 hole.

Longniddry

Longniddry Golf Club: Links Road (0875 52141); 18 hole.

Pitlochry

Pitlochry Golf Club: (0796 2792). 18 hole.

St Andrews

St Andrews Links (0334 75757). Four 18 hole and one 9 hole, including the Old, New, Eden and Jubilee Courses.

HALF-DAY CLOSING

Tuesday
Dalkeith, Glenrothes, Hawick,
Innerleithen.

Wednesday
Arbroath, Bathgate, Burntisland,
Dunbar, Dundee, Dunfermline,
Duns, Edinburgh (in some areas),
Eyemouth, Galashiels, Kelso,
Kirkcaldy, Linlithgow, Montrose,
Peebles, Perth.

Thursday
Coldstream, Haddington, Jedburgh,
Lauder, Leven, Melrose, North
Berwick, St Andrews, Selkirk.

LEISURE/SPORTS CENTRES

These include swimming pools, ski slopes, bowling alleys, ice rinks, general athletic grounds and gymnasia.

Aberfeldy

Recreation Centre: Crieff Road (0887 20922). Swimming pool, multi-gym, squash, rifle range and snooker.

Arbroath

Arbroath Sports Centre: Keptie Road (0241 72999). Squash, racquet ball, table tennis, multi-gym and swimming pool.

Bathgate

Sports Centre: Balbardie Park of Peace (0506 634561).

Blairgowrie

Recreation Centre: Beeches Road (0250 3724). Swimming pool, games hall, gym and fitness room.

Cupar

Sports Centre: Elmwood Carslogie Road (0334 54793). Swimming pool, fitness room, gym, games hall, squash, sunbed, steam bath.

Eden Park Leisure Centre: Eden Park East Road (0334 54968). Squash, swimming pool, sauna and sunbed.

Dunbar

Castle Park Leisure Pool: The Harbour (East Lothian Tourist Board for details, 031–665 3711). New swimming pool, to be opened May or June 1992. Flumes, steam room, sunbed, fitness centre and aerobics.

Edinburgh

Ainslie Park Leisure Centre: 92 Pilton Drive (031–551 2400). Scotland's only eight-lane, 25-metre swimming pool.

Edinburgh Mega Bowl: Newcraighall Park, Newcraighall. Ten-pin bowling. (031–657 3731).

Hillend Ski Centre: Biggar Road (031–445 4433). Dry ski slope.

Meadowbank Sports Stadium: 139 London Road (031–661 5351). Wide range of indoor and outdoor sports.

Murrayfield Ice Rink: 13 Riversdale Crescent (031–337 6933). Ice rink and curling.

Royal Commonwealth Pool, Dalkeith Road (031–667 7211). 50-metre pool, diving pool, flumes, sunbed, sauna and weights.

For other sports centres and pools, see under Edinburgh District Council in the Edinburgh and Lothians telephone directory.

Glenrothes

Fife Institute of Physical and Recreational Education: Viewfield Road (0592 771700). Swimming pool, games hall, squash, artificial grass tennis courts, sauna, sunbed.

Glenshee

Glenshee Chairlift: off A93, 25 miles north of Blairgowrie (033 97 41320).

Hawick

Teviotdale Leisure Centre: Mansfield Road (0450 74440/75644). Swimming pool, squash and sunbed.

Kenmore

Croft-na-Caber Watersports and Activities Centre (08873 235). Mainly

Leisure/Sports Centres (cont.)

outdoor watersports centre on Loch Tay.

Loch Tay Boating Centre: Pier Road (08873 291). Boats for hire.

Montrose

Montrose Sports Centre: (0674 76211). Games hall, squash court, multi-gym.

Swimming Pool: The Hall (0674 72026). Indoor pool.

Musselburgh

Musselburgh Sports Centre: Newbigging (031–653 6367). Badminton, squash, table tennis, fitness room.

North Berwick

Sports Centre: Grange Road (0620 3454). Games hall, squash, trampoline, fitness room, table tennis, indoor bowling.

Perth

Dewar's Rinks: Glover Street (0738 24188). Ice rink, indoor bowling.

Gannochy Trust Sports Complex: Hay Street (0738 22301). Games hall, squash, badminton.

Perth Leisure Pool: Glasgow Road (0738 30535). Swimming pool, flumes, sauna and sunbed.

Pitlochry

Atholl Leisure Centre: West Moulin Road (0796 3866). Wide range of indoor sports.

St Andrews

East Sands Leisure Centre: at East Sands beach (0334 76506). Swimming pool (indoor), sauna and sunbeds.

Tranent

Loch Centre: Well Wynd (0875 611081). Swimming pool, fitness room, games hall, squash.

LIBRARIES

Aberfeldy

Aberfeldy Library: Bank Street
(0887 20475).

Arbroath

Arbroath Library: Hill Terrace
(0241 72248).

Bathgate

Bathgate Library: Hopetoun Street
(0506 53416).

Buckhaven

Buckhaven Library: College Street
(0592 712192).

Burntisland

Burntisland Library: 102 High Street
(0592 872781).

Crieff

Crieff Library: Comrie Street
(0764 3418).

Cupar

Cupar Library: Crossgate
(0334 53001).

Dalkeith

Dalkeith Library: White Hart Street
(031–663 2083).

Dunbar

Dunbar Library: Castellau, off Delisle
Street (0368 63521).

Dundee

Central Library: Wellgate Centre,
Victoria Road (0382 23141; 26115
after 5 p.m. and at weekends).

Dunfermline

Central Library: Abbot Street
(0383 723661).

Edinburgh (city centre)

Central Library: George IV Bridge
(031–225 5584).

National Library of Scotland:
George IV Bridge
(031–226 4531).

Scottish Poetry Library: Tweeddale
Court, 14 High Street
(031–557 2876).

Galashiels

Galashiels Library: Lawyers Brae
(0896 2512).

Glenrothes

Cadham Centre: Huntsman Road
(0592 741784).

Glenwood Centre: Shopping Centre
(0592 755866).

Glenrothes Library: 50 Woodside Way
(0592 751187).

Haddington

Haddington Library: Newton Port
(062 082 2531).

Hawick

Hawick Library: North Bridge Street
(0450 72637).

Innerpeffray

Innerpeffray Library: by Crieff
(0764 2819). Oldest surviving

Libraries (cont.)

lending library in the country
(1690).

Jedburgh

Jedburgh Library: Castlegate
(0835 63592).

Kelso

Kelso Library: Bowmont Street
(0573 23171).

Kinghorn

Kinghorn Library: Balliol Street
(0592 891036).

Kirkcaldy

Central Library: War Memorial
Gardens (0592 260707).

Leven

Greig Institute: Forth Street
(0333 26766).

Linlithgow

Linlithgow Library: The Vennel
(0506 842869).

Livingston

Carmondean Library: Carmondean
Centre, Deans (0506 34266).

Melrose

Melrose Library: 18 Market Square
(089 682 3052).

Methil

Methil Library: Wellesley Road
(0333 27229).

Montrose

Montrose Library: High Street
(0674 73256).

North Berwick

North Berwick Library: School Road
(0620 3470).

Peebles

Peebles Library: Chambers Institute,
High Street (0721 20123).

Perth

Sanderean Library: Kinnoull Street
(0738 23329).

Pitlochry

Pitlochry Library: Atholl Road
(0796 2323).

St Andrews

St Andrews Library: Church Square
(0334 73381).

University of St Andrews Library:
North Street (0334 76161).

Selkirk

Selkirk Library: Ettrick Terrace
(0750 20267).

LOCAL MEDIA

NEWSPAPERS

Angus

Angus County Press Ltd: Craig o' Loch Road, Forfar (0307 64901). Publishes the **Forfar Dispatch**.

Arbroath Herald Ltd: Brothock Bridge, Arbroath (0241 72274). Publishes the **Guide and Gazette** and the **Arbroath Herald**.

D.H. Edwards: 20 Swan Street, Brechin (03562 2767). Publishes the **Brechin Advertiser**.

Montrose Review: Old St John's Church, John Street, Montrose (0674 72605).

Borders

Border Telegraph: 113 High Street, Galashiels (0896 58395).

Borders Gazette: 54 Bondgate Within, Alnwick, Northumberland (0665 602234).

Hawick News: 24 High Street, Hawick (0450 72204).

Peeblesshire News: 40 Northgate, Peebles (0721 20884).

Selkirk Weekender: 5 Scotts Place, Selkirk (0750 21969).

Tweeddale Press Group: The Hermitage, High Street, Selkirk (0750 21581). Publishes the **Southern Reporter, Berwickshire News, Berwickshire Advertiser, Morpeth Herald** and **Alnwick Advertiser**.

Fife

Dundee Courier: Bank Street, Dundee (0382 23131).

Strachan and Livingston Ltd: 23 Kirk Wynd, Kirkcaldy (0592 261451).

Publishes the **Fife Free Press, East Fife Mail, Fife Herald, St Andrews Citizen, Glenrothes Gazette**, and the freesheets, the **Advertiser** and the **Fife Leader**.

Forth Valley

Johnston Falkirk Ltd: 1 Newmarket Centre, Newmarket Street, Falkirk (0324 24959). Publishes the **Falkirk Herald, Falkirk and Grangemouth Advertiser, Cumbernauld News, Cumbernauld Advertiser, Linlithgow Gazette, Carluke and Lanark Gazette** and the freesheet, the **Linlithgow Advertiser**.

Linlithgowshire Journal and Gazette: 114 High Street, Linlithgow (0506 844592).

Lothian

East Lothian Herald: 90 Marygate, Berwick-upon-Tweed (0289 306677).

Edinburgh Evening News: 20 North Bridge, Edinburgh (031–225 2468).

Lothian Courier: 20/22 King Street, Bathgate (0506 633544).

Scottish County Press: Sherwood Industrial Estate, Bonnyrigg (031–663 2404). Publishes **East Lothian News, Musselburgh News, Midlothian Advertiser** and the freesheets, the **Lothian Times** and the **Peebles Times**. Also publishes **Month by Month in the Lothians** during the summer (see magazines below).

Tayside

Dundee Evening Telegraph and Post, Dundee Courier: Bank Street, Dundee (0382 23131).

Perthshire Advertiser: 38 Tay Street, Perth (0738 36031). Also publishes a weekly freesheet, the **Perthshire Shopper**.

Local Media (cont.)

MAGAZINES

Lothian

The List: 14 High Street, Edinburgh (031–558 1191). Central Scotland events guide covering music, sport, theatre, art, books, television, travel and food.

Month by Month in the Lothians: Scottish County Press, Sherwood Industrial Estate, Bonnyrigg (0506 633544). Published throughout the summer months with features on locations in the Lothians, and information on hotels, restaurants and facilities in the area. Free from hotels and Tourist Information outlets, and included on the last Friday of the month with paid-for newspapers published by the Scottish County Press.

RADIO

Borders

Radio Borders: Tweedside Park, Tweedbank, Melrose (0896 59444). 96.8 FM (Selkirk), 103.1 FM (Peebles), 103.4 FM (Eyemouth).

Radio Tweed: Municipal Buildings, High Street, Selkirk (0750 21884). 93.5 FM.

Fife and Tayside

Radio Forth: Forth House, Forth Street, Edinburgh (031–556 9255). Broadcasting two stations: Radio Forth RFM – VHF: 97.3MHz; Radio Forth MAX AM – MW: 1548 kHz/194m.

Radio Tay: North Isla Street, Dundee (0382 200800). MW Dundee: 1161kHz/258m, VHF: 102.8 MHz, MW Perth: 1584 kHz/189m, VHF: 96.4 MHz.

Lothian

Radio Forth: Forth House, Forth Street, Edinburgh (031–556 9255). Broadcasting two stations: Radio Forth RFM – VHF: 97.3MHz; Radio Forth MAX AM – MW: 1548 kHz/194m.

TELEVISION

Borders

Border Television: Television Centre, Carlisle (0228 25101).

Fife and Tayside

Grampian Television: Queens Cross, Aberdeen (0224 646464).

Lothian

Scottish Television (STV): Cowcaddens, Glasgow (041-332 9999). STV also received in some areas of Borders and Fife.

MUSEUMS

The list of museums below represents a cross-section of those found throughout the area and is intended as a quick reference guide only. Full details of museums in specific locations are obtainable from the relevant Tourist Information Office. Museums of special interest are included in the Gazetteer.

Aberlady

Myreton Motor Museum: six miles SW of North Berwick off A198 (087 57 288). Cars, motorcycles, bicycles and military vehicles from 1896 onwards.

Alyth

Alyth Folk Museum: Commercial Street (0738 32488). Local, folk and farming history.

Anstruther

North Carr Lightship. Floating museum showing conditions aboard a lightship.

Bathgate

Bennie Museum: 9–11 Mansefield Street (0506 634944). Local history, including inventors of chloroform and paraffin, and early photographs.

Blair Atholl

Atholl Country Collection: Old School (079 681 232). Extensive display of local life, folklore and trades, including Smiddy, Post Office and Crofter's Stable.

Clan Donnachaidh Museum: Bruar Falls, three miles north of Blair Atholl on A9 (079 683 264). Exhibitions relating to a number of clans, and the Jacobite risings of 1715 and 1745.

Brechin

Brechin Museum: St Ninian's Square (0674 73232). Local history and some artwork.

Burntisland

Burntisland Museum: High Street (0592 260732). 'Burntisland Edwardian Fair' display.

Coldstream

Coldstream Museum: Market Square (0890 2630). Coldstream Guards exhibition, and history of Coldstream.

Crail

Museum and Heritage Centre: 62 Marketgate (0333 50869). History and fishing, heritage of Crail, run by Crail Preservation Trust.

Crieff

Highland Tryst Museum: Burrell Street (0764 5202). History of Crieff, and hand-loom tartan weaving and leatherwork demonstrations.

Muthill Museum: by Crieff (Historic Scotland, 031–244 3101). Local history and heritage.

Dundee

Barrack Street Museum: Barrack Street (0382 23141). Wildlife and geology in Dundee and Scotland, including the skeleton of the great whale which beached near Dundee in the late 19th century.

Broughty Castle Museum: St Vincent Street, Broughty Ferry (0382 23141). Local history, including maritime, whaling, fishing, arms and armour.

Dunfermline

Andrew Carnegie Museum: Moodie Street (0383 724302). Birthplace of

Museums (cont.)

rags-to-riches weaver's son Andrew Carnegie, who made his fortune in the USA.

Dunkeld

Museum of the Scottish Horse Regiment: The Cross (035 02 296). History of this Yeomanry Regiment.

Dysart

McDougall Stuart Museum: Rectory Lane (0592 260732). Birthplace of the first explorer to cross Australia, now a small award-winning museum recalling his journeys.

Edinburgh

Brass Rubbing Centre: Trinity Apse, Chalmers Close, High Street (031–556 4364). Medieval brasses, Scottish stone carvings and rubbing facilities.

Living Craft Centre: 12 High Street (031–557 9350). Working craft exhibitions, including kilt-making, bagpipe-making, pottery, hand weaving, silversmith and Arran and cashmere hand-knitters.

Royal Museum of Scotland: Chambers Street (031–225 7534). Comprehensive science, art, natural history and history exhibition.

Royal Museum of Scotland (Museum of Antiquities): Queen Street (031–225 7534). Artefacts from prehistoric times to present day.

Royal Observatory Visitor Centre: Blackford Hill (031–668 8405). Astronomy exhibition.

Russell Collection of Early Keyboard Instruments: St Cecilia's Hall, Niddry Street, Cowgate (031–667 1011 ext 4415). Collection includes clavichords, chamber organs and early pianos, housed in a concert hall built in 1762 for the Edinburgh Musical Society.

Scottish Record Office: General Register House, Princes Street (031–556 6585). Population records, exhibition of historic documents, and research rooms.

Scottish Agricultural Museum: Ingliston, near Edinburgh Airport (031–333 2674). Social and economic history of Scottish agriculture.

Stock Exchange Information Office: 91 George Street (031–220 1684). International stock exchange information point, group visits welcomed.

The People's Story: Canongate Tolbooth, Canongate (031–225 2424 ext 6638). The story of the Scottish people from late 18th century to today.

University Collection of Historic Musical Instruments: Reid Concert Hall, Bristo Square (031–667 1011 ext 2573). Over 1000 instruments, including woodwind, brass, strings, percussion, bagpipes, ethnic, and acoustic.

West Register House: Charlotte Square (031–556 6585). More modern documents of the Scottish Record Office (see above), exhibition of Scottish history, including the Declaration of Arbroath (1320).

Errol

Errol Station Railway Heritage Centre: Errol Station (05754 222). History of Tayside rural railways in an 1847 station, now restored to 1920s period.

Eyemouth

Eyemouth Museum: Manse Road (08907 50678). History of Eyemouth and surroundings.

Galashiels

Galashiels Museum: Nether Mill, Huddersfield Street (0896 2091). History of Galashiels and textile industry.

Glamis

Angus Folk Museum: Kirkwynd Cottages (030 784 288). Local and farming history, photographs and archives.

Haddington

Jane Welsh Carlyle Museum: Lodge Street (062 082 3738). Restored house dating from the 18th century.

Hawick

Hawick Museum: Wilton Lodge Park (0450 73457). History of Hawick set in beautiful parkland. Also here, the **Scott Gallery**, temporary exhibitions.

Museum of Border Arms and Armour: Teviothead, by Hawick (045 085 237). Exhibition relating to the Border reiver. Also here, **Johnny Armstrong Gallery** of crafts, Celtic jewellery and old maps.

Inverkeithing

Inverkeithing Museum: The Friary (0383 413 344). Local history, including Rosyth dockyard and Admiral Greig, reputed founder of the Russian navy.

Kelso

Kelso Museum: Turret House, Abbey Court (0573 25470). History of Kelso and surroundings.

Kinross

Kinross Museum: High Street (0783 32488). Local history, including Loch Leven.

Kirkcaldy

Kirkcaldy Museum and Art Gallery: War Memorial Gardens (0592 260732). Art, craft and local history exhibition in an award-winning museum.

Meigle

Meigle Museum: eight miles east of Blairgowrie (08284 307). Collection of 25 Celtic Christian sculptured monuments.

Montrose

Montrose Museum: Panmure Place (0674 73232). Local history, including silver, pottery and maritime displays.

Newburgh

Laing Museum: High Street (0334 53722 ext 141 – NE Fife District Council). Exhibition relating to life in Victorian Scotland.

North Berwick

Museum of Flight: East Fortune, by North Berwick (062 088 308). Aircraft, rockets and engines in the hangars of a wartime RAF station.

North Berwick Museum: School Road (062 082 4161). Local history.

Peebles

Cornice Museum of Ornamental Plasterwork: 31 High Street (0721 20212). Cornice plasterwork display and methods of casting.

Tweeddale Museum: Chambers Institute, High Street (0721 20123). Local history (including environment and industry). **Picture Gallery** also here, changing exhibition of arts and crafts.

Museums (cont.)

St Andrews

Preservation Trust Museum:
12 North Street (0334 72152). History
of the working town, including
19th-century grocer's and chemist's
shops, furniture, photographs and
paintings.

**St Andrews Cathedral Museum and St
Rule's Tower** (031–244 3101). Relics
from the town and cathedral, and St
Rule's Tower, built around 1127.

Selkirk

Town Hall: Market Place
(0750 20096). Exhibition relating to
Sir Walter Scott, Mungo Park, James
Hogg, Robert Burns and Andrew
Lang, and paintings by Tom Scott.

South Queensferry

South Queensferry Museum: Council
Chambers, High Street (031–225 2424
ext 6689, Huntly House Museum).
Local history, including the Forth
Bridges.

Walkerburn

Scottish Museum of Woollen Textiles:
The Mill Shop, Tweedvale Mills
(089 687 281/3). History of the
woollen industry.

NIGHTLIFE

The venues listed below are those which are known 'night-time spots'. Away from larger towns and cities it becomes more difficult to pin down regular venues but, as a guideline for entertainment-seekers, if you're in a more rural area, try the local hotels to see if they are either hosting events in their public bars or if they have a local information board. Tourist Information Centres may also have details.

Crieff

Scorpios Disco/Nite Spot: 35 James Square (0764 4772). Also in Crieff, the Drummond Arms Hotel (James Square, 0764 2151) and Crieff Hydro (0764 2401) all host dinner-dances. In addition, the latter two, along with a number of inns in the area, function as live music venues.

Dundee

Coconut Grove: 150 Marketgait (0382 27266). Nightclub and disco. Over 25s on Wednesdays, over 18 at all other times.

De Stihls: South Ward Road (0382 200066). Nightclub, over 18 Thursday and Sunday, over 21 Friday and Saturday. Occasional entertainment evenings, with local and touring acts such as hypnotists, comedians etc.

Fat Sam's Night Club, Disco/Diner: 31 South Ward Road (0382 26836). Popular with a young local crowd, events such as 'Fat Sam's Cocktail Night' on some evenings.

Edinburgh

Buster Brown's: 25/27 Market Street (031–226 4224). Disco Friday–Sunday.

Calton Studios: 24 Calton Road (031–556 7066). Nightclub/disco.

Dandies Night Club/Diner: King's Stables Road (031–228 6669). Cabaret every night. Over 23s only.

Madison's Nightclub and Liberty's: 18/22 Greenside Place (031–557 3807). Popular disco, over 21s only. **Club Sandino** takes place here on the first Saturday of every month to support the Nicaraguan Solidarity Campaign.

Maxie's Bistro: 32 West Nicholson Street (031–667 0845). Jazz and swing Monday–Thursday, classical folk music on Sunday.

Navaar House: 12 Mayfield Gardens, Newington (031–667 2828). Louisiana Ragtime Band on Tuesdays.

Network Discotheque: 3 West Tollcross (031–228 3252). Lively disco Thursday–Sunday.

Red Hot Pepper Club: 3 Semple Street (031–229 7733). One of Edinburgh's newest discos.

Shore Bar: 3 Leith Street (031–553 5080). Live music – jazz, folk and rock – Monday–Saturday.

The Mission: Cowgate (031–225 6569). Reggae, rock, 60s and 70s music depending on the night of the week. 'Shag' disco held here on Thursdays.

The Venue: 17/23 Carlton Road (031–557 3073). Live bands.

Walpole Hall: Chester Street, Haymarket (031–339 5374). Ceilidhs, international folk dance and local events.

Glenrothes

Follies Night Club: Kingdom Centre (0592 750988). Disco and nightclub.

Nightlife (cont.)

Kenmore

Croft-na-Caber Hotel: (08873 236). Hosts local and touring bands and evening events.

Kirkcaldy

Bentley's Night Scene: Victoria Road (0592 200417). Disco.

Jackie 'O': The Esplanade (0592 264496). Disco.

Leven

Manhattens: Burnmill Road (0333 21422). Disco.

Methil

'Ricks': 583–85 Wellesley Road (0592 715248). Disco.

Perth

Bianco's: 14–18 Princes Street (0738 23035). Bar/nightclub, occasional live bands.

Electric Whispers: 40–48 Canal Street (0738 30503). Nightclub and disco, occasional live bands.

Roxanne's: 32/34 Kinnoull Street (0738 33169). Nightclub and disco.

Yorky's: 15 York Place (0738 26467). Bar and disco.

Pitlochry

Town Hall: Local variety show each Thursday from June to September.

ORGANIZATIONS

The organizations included here have been chosen to cover those areas, places and subjects which are likely to be of most interest to the visitor. Scotland has many hundreds of local organizations which, as well as providing interesting information about their area, are also a good way of meeting local people. Tourist Information Offices usually carry some details of organizations, as do local libraries (listed above).

Auchterarder

Auchterarder Local History Group: Mr K.G. Young, Mansefield (0764 62671). Meets regularly, information on local history.

Aberfeldy

Locus Project: Town Hall, Aberfeldy (0887 20276). This is a new innovative project which has been set up in one of Scotland's most attractive areas. Visitors are requested to follow set trails and paths, so that the problems of erosion, over-use and visitor pressure are confined to a manageable area.

Dalkeith

Dalkeith Local History Society Museum and Workshop: 6 Buccleuch Street (031–663 2083, Dalkeith Library and Tourist Office).

Dunkeld

Dunkeld Historical Society: c/o Mrs Cox, Blackhill, Snaigow, by Dunkeld.

Edinburgh

An Comunn Gaidhealach: Rosemary Thomson, Top Flat, 24 Roseburn Terrace (031–337 0208). Monthly newsletter, regular ceilidhs and other social events as well as classes for Gaelic beginners.

Duddingston Village Preservation Society: Dr Windsor, 16 Old Church Lane EH15 3PX.

Edinburgh Folk Club: Frank or Jean Bechhoffer, 51 Barnton Park View (031–339 4083).

Edinburgh New Town Conservation Committee: The New Town Conservation Centre, 13a Dundas Street (031–557 5222). Guided walks available around the area; evening walks may include wine in a private house.

Strathearn

Strathearn Archaeological Society: contact Mrs E. Buchan, Lynemore, Madderty, by Crieff (0764 83 255).

THEATRES/CONCERT HALLS

Buckhaven

Buckhaven Theatre: Lawrence Street (0592 715577). New professional theatre in a converted listed church.

Dundee

Caird Hall: City Square (0382 23141). Concert hall and conference venue.

Dundee Repertory Theatre: Tay Square (0382 27684). Mainstream productions, often staging Scottish works.

Edinburgh

Assembly Rooms: George Street (031–220 4348). Mainstream and alternative work, primarily during the Festival period.

Bedlam Theatre: 2 Forrest Road (031–225 9873). Small theatre staging new, innovative and traditional works.

King's Theatre: Leven Street, (031–229 1201). Mainstream, occasionally hosting companies from the south such as London's National Theatre.

Leith Theatre: 28 Ferry Road (031–554 1408). Medium-sized theatre hosting local and touring companies. At present proposals are under discussion to convert the theatre into a multi-arts centre.

Netherbow Arts Centre: 43 High Street (031–556 9579). Small theatre, staging works by local and touring groups.

Playhouse Theatre: Greenside Place (031–557 2590). Musicals, ballet, concerts (pop), stand-up comedians, opera, solo artists and bands.

Queen's Hall: Clerk Street (031–668 2019). Classical music, choral work and chamber orchestras and ensembles.

Royal Lyceum Theatre: Grindlay Street, (031–229 9697). Repertory theatre, staging the occasional new play.

Theatre Workshop: Hamilton Place (031–226 5425). Small theatre staging in-house productions and hosting touring companies.

Traverse Theatre: Cambridge Street (031–226 2633). Recently reopened at its new address; innovative theatre, often performing new work and breaking new ground.

Usher Hall: Lothian Road (031–228 1155). Classical music, recitals, youth, chamber and national symphony orchestras.

Kirkcaldy

Adam Smith Theatre: Bennochy Road (0592 260498). Pantomimes, summer shows, plays and musicals.

Musselburgh

Brunton Theatre: High Street, Musselburgh (031–665 9900). Mainstream/family productions, classical and modern, traditional and new works.

Perth

Perth Theatre: High Street (0738 38123). Repertory theatre with a good reputation for its mixture of mainstream and innovative productions.

Pitlochry

Pitlochry Festival Theatre: Port-na-Craig (0796 3054). Repertory theatre, usually with three or four productions on at once.

St Andrews

Byre Theatre: Abbey Street
(0334 76288). Small theatre hosting
local and touring companies.

TOURIST INFORMATION

Area Tourist Boards

Angus Tourist Board: Market Place, Arbroath (0241 72609).

Dundee Tourist Board: 4 City Square, Dundee (0382 23141).

East Lothian Tourist Board: Brunton Hall, Musselburgh (031–665 3711).

Edinburgh Marketing: Waverley Market, 3 Princes Street, Edinburgh (031–557 1700).

Forth Valley Tourist Board: Burgh Halls, The Cross, Linlithgow, West Lothian (0506 844600).

Kirkaldy District Council: Information Centre, South Street, Leven, Fife (0333 29464).

Midlothian District Council: 7 Station Road, Roslin (031–440 2210).

Perthshire Tourist Board: 45 High Street, Perth (0738 38353).

St Andrews and North-East Fife Tourist Board: Tourist Information Centre, South Street, St Andrews, Fife (0334 72021).

Scottish Borders Tourist Board: Municipal Buildings, High Street, Selkirk (0750 20555).

Local Information Centres

Tourist Information Centres in main towns are usually open all year. Those in small towns, such as Dunfermline and Galashiels, and subsidiary offices, such as that at the Brunton Hall (Musselburgh) in Edinburgh are mostly open from April to October, although a small handful are just from May to August/September. As a general guideline, offices located in town car parks, libraries or museums are open for the summer season only.

Aberfeldy: The Square (0887 20276).

Anstruther: Scottish Fisheries Museum (0333 311073).

Arbroath: Market Place (0241 72609).

Auchterarder: 90 High Street (0764 63450).

Blairgowrie: 26 Wellmeadow (0250 2960).

Bonnyrigg: Bonnyrigg Libary, Polton Street (031–663 6762).

Brechin: St Ninian's Place (03562 3050).

Burntisland: 4 Kirkgate (0592 872667).

Coldstream: Henderson Park (0890 2607).

Crail: Crail Museum and Heritage Centre (0333 50869).

Crieff: Town Hall, High Street (0764 2578).

Cupar: Fluthers Car Park (0334 52874).

Dalkeith: Dalkeith Library, White Hart Street (031–663 2083).

Dunbar: Town House (0368 63353).

Dundee: 4 City Square (0382 27723).

Dunfermline: Abbot House, Marygate (0383 720999).

Dunkeld: The Cross (03502 688).

Edinburgh: Tourist Centre, Waverley Market, 3 Princes Street (031–557 1700); Edinburgh Airport, Tourist Information Desk (031–333 2167).

Eyemouth: Auld Kirk (08907 50678).

Forfar: The Library, West High Street (0307 67876).

Galashiels: Bank Street (0896 55551).

Glenrothes: Glenrothes House, North Street (0592 756684).

Haddington: Council Buildings (062 082 4161).

Hawick: Common Haugh (0450 72547).

Jedburgh: Murray's Green (0835 63435).

Kelso: Turret House (0573 23464).

Killin: Main Street (05672 254).

Kirkcaldy: Esplanade (0592 267775).

Kirriemuir: Bank Street (0575 74097).

Leven: South Street (0333 29464).

Melrose: Priorwood Gardens (089682 2555).

Montrose: The Library, High Street (0674 720000).

Musselburgh: Brunton Hall (031–665 6597).

North Berwick: Quality Street (0620 2197).

Peebles: Chambers Institute (0721 20138).

Penicuik: Penicuik Library, 3 Bellman's Road (0968 72340).

Perth: 45 High Street (0738 38353).

Pitlochry: 22 Atholl Road (0796 2215).

St Andrews: 78 South Street (0334 72021).

Selkirk: Halliwell's House (0750 20054).

TRANSPORT

Air

Dundee Airport: Riverside Drive
(0382 643242).

Edinburgh Airport: Ingliston
(031–333 1000).

Bus

Busline: 12 St Giles Street, Edinburgh
(031–225 3858). All questions
answered about any Edinburgh
public transport services: timetables,
destinations, concessionary travel
and services for disabled.

Eastern Scottish Omnibuses:
St Andrew Square Bus Station,
Edinburgh (031–556 8464).

Fife Scottish Omnibuses: Head Office,
Esplanade, Kirkcaldy (0592 261043).

Lothian Regional Transport: 14 Queen
Street (tours and bus information
for Edinburgh and the surrounding
area: 031–554 4494).

Lowland Scottish: (Borders)
Galashiels Bus Station (0896 58484).

MacEwan's Coach Services: (Edinburgh
to Dumfries and Galloway)
(0387 710357).

Midland Scottish: (Midlothian and
environs) Linlithgow (0506 842167).

Moffat and Williamson: (Fife) Main
Road, Gauldry, Newport-on-Tay
(0382 22155).

Tayside/Greyhound Coach Company:
East Dock Street, Dundee
(0382 201121).

Rail

Dundee (0382 28046).

Edinburgh (031–556 2451).

Perth (0738 37117).

Stirling (0786 64754).

Gazetteer

ABBEY ST BATHANS
Borders

Off A6112 5m N of Duns.

Situated on the Whiteadder Water, this small village was once the site of a 13th-century priory dedicated to St Bathan, a follower of St Columba. Abbey St Bathan's special appeal rests on its beautiful location beside the river in the **Lammermuir Hills**. A trout farm doubles up as an interpretive centre, illustrating life in the valley from prehistoric to modern times. There is also a gallery, a ceramics workshop, a tearoom and, on the slopes of Cockburn Law, a Pictish broch, or tower, known as **Edinshall**.

ABBOTSFORD HOUSE
near Galashiels, Borders

On A7 2½m SE of Galashiels.
Late Mar–end Oct, Mon–Sat 1000–1700,
Sun 1400–1700. D (P) (0896 2043).

Built between 1817 and 1822 for the author and largely designed by him, Abbotsford House was the last and most famous home of **Sir Walter Scott**. When building costs threatened Scott with bankruptcy, his creditors presented the house to him on behalf of the Scottish people, and he lived there until his death in 1832. A jamboree of turrets and crow-stepped gables, Abbotsford is as much visited today because of its architectural eccentricity as for its contents. Scott enthusiasts will be intrigued by the collection of historical oddities amassed by Scott – Rob Roy's purse and Robert Burns's drinking cup among others – as well as impressed by his study and his armoury. The house

is still owned by his descendants. Abbotsford is at the heart of what is known as 'Scott Country' which incorporates other places such as **Scott's View** and **Dryburgh Abbey**, where Scott is buried.

ABERCORN CHURCH
near South Queensferry, Lothian

On unclassified road 2m N of A904,
by Hopetoun. All year. D. Free
(031–331 1869).

The present building dates from the 12th century, with reconstructions taking place in 1579 and 1893 although it rests on the site of a seventh-century monastery. There is a display of eighth-century Anglican crosses.

ABERDOUR
Fife

On A921 5m E of Forth Bridge.

A summer resort with a sandy beach on the northern shore of the **Firth of Forth**, Aberdour also boasts a cluster of medieval buildings – **Aberdour Castle**, St Fillan's Church and a dovecot. The church, part Norman and part 16th century, has as a curiosity a leper squint, or window, in its west wall. Passenger ferries depart from Aberdour to **Inchcolm Island** which lies just out from Braefoot Point.

ABERDOUR CASTLE
Aberdour, Fife

On A921 5m E of Forth Bridge. All
year. Apr–Sept, Mon–Sat 0930–1900,

*Sun 1400–1900; Oct–Mar, Mon–Wed
0930–1600, Sun 1400–1600, closed
Thurs pm and Fri. D (P). HS (031
244 3101).*

In the 16th and 17th centuries, a
terraced garden and a bowling
green were added to the original
14th-century tower of Aberdour
Castle. There is also a fine circular
dovecot. Despite interior fire
damage, a 17th-century painted
ceiling survived and can be seen
today. The castle overlooks the
harbour at **Aberdour**.

ABERFELDY
Tayside

At junction of A826 and A827.

A well-heeled small town,
Aberfeldy lays claim to the title
of 'The Heart of Scotland'. Vying
with **Pitlochry**, it argues that it lies
at the very centre of Scotland. A
stone-built, largely Victorian town,
Aberfeldy sits beside the **River Tay**.
The river is spanned by Wade's
Bridge, begun at **General George
Wade**'s instigation to a William
Adam design in 1733. A steep
hump-back with four arches, it
is recognized as one of the finest
remaining Wade bridges. It is
also the finishing line for the June
Kenmore to Aberfeldy raft race.
Aberfeldy's restored and operational
water mill, a leisure centre and
Aberfeldy Distillery are the town's
main indoor attractions, while the
Birks (birch trees) of Aberfeldy
provide a scenic magnet. The Birks,
subject of a Robert Burns poem
of the same name, are reached
from the town centre. A loop path
takes walkers past the Birks, up
one side of the Urlar Burn to the

Falls of Moness and down the
other side.

ABERFELDY DISTILLERY
Aberfeldy, Tayside

*On A827 just E of Aberfeldy. Easter–Oct,
Mon–Fri 1000–1600. D (A/P). Free
(0887 20330).*

A small malt whisky distillery and
maturation warehouse built by the
Dewar family in 1898. Handsome
stone buildings and their less
attractive modern appendages,
visible from the road, are filled with
standard whisky-making equipment:
pot-bellied vats, wooden casks and
pressurized distillation chambers.
Guided tours uncover the secrets of
whisky production, and a shop sells
the finished result as do local pubs
and hotels.

ABERLADY
Lothian

On A198 8m W of North Berwick.

A pretty village of red sandstone
buildings with orange pantile
roofs, Aberlady's genteel ambience
is enhanced by its bowling green
and its church. A quiet seaside
resort on the southern shore of the
Firth of Forth, Aberlady was once
the thriving port of **Haddington**.
The one-time mooring place for
many ships, Aberlady Bay is now a
silted-up bird sanctuary frequented
by binocular-bearing enthusiasts.
Nearby are a golf course, **Luffness
Castle** (it can be visited by
appointment only), a castle with a
13th-century keep, and the Myreton
Motor Museum, which houses a
collection of vintage vehicles.

ABERLEMNO
Tayside

On B9134 6m NE of Forfar.

Aberlemno is famed for the Pictish standing stones decorated with Pictish symbols which lie in the churchyard and beside the road in the village. The churchyard stone dates from the eighth century and is engraved with a battle scene on one side and a Celtic cross on the other. One of the roadside slabs is carved with two angels and a hunting scene.

ABERNETHY
Tayside

On A913 9m SE of Perth.

With the Ochil Hills to the south and the Firth of Tay just to the north, the village of Abernethy was once an important Pictish capital and was also one of the ninth-century hubs of Christianity in Scotland. Its historical centrepiece is the **Abernethy Round Tower**.

ABERNETHY ROUND TOWER
Abernethy, Tayside

In Abernethy. Apply to key-keeper. Free. HS (031–244 3101).

The lower part of the 74-foot-high tower, one of only two of its type in Scotland (the other is at **Brechin**), is thought to date from the ninth century while its upper half is ascribed to the 11th or 12th centuries. Its role is believed to have been that of bell-tower and refuge for monks from the nearby monastery.

ROBERT ADAM, see panel p62.

ALMONDELL AND CALDERWOOD COUNTRY PARK
near East Calder, Lothian

On B7015 12m SW of Edinburgh. Visitor centre: Apr–Sep, Mon–Wed 0900–1700, Thurs 0900–1600, Sun 1030–1800; Oct–Mar, Mon–Thurs 0900–1700, Sun 1000–1630, closed for lunch 1200–1300. D (A/P). Free (0506 882254).

A former estate, Almondell and Calderwood Country Park is now a recreational area with riverside and woodland walks, picnic facilities and a visitor centre which includes freshwater aquaria and displays on natural and local history.

ALYTH
Tayside

Off B954 7m E of Blairgowrie.

At the southern end of Glen Isla, the small market town of Alyth sits on the **Highland Line**. A popular striking-out base for the Braes of Angus, Alyth's own visitor interest is its folk museum and the remains of its 13th-century church, St Moluag.

AMULREE
Tayside

On A822 10m S of Aberfeldy, 12m N of Crieff.

Not amounting to much more than a tiny cluster of buildings (including

Robert Adam and the Adam architects

There is one name that recurs repeatedly when you are discovering the world of 18th-century Scottish architecture: Adam. The Adam architectural dynasty began with William Adam, who introduced his sons, John, Robert and James, to the profession. When William Adam died in 1748, his eldest son John replaced him as Master Mason to the Board of Ordnance in North Britain. From 1750 onwards, he worked on the construction and fortification of Fort George on the Moray Firth. In the summers of 1750 and 1754, Robert Adam (1728–92) went to work with him. He was joined by his brother James, and the close partnership evolved that was to become the renowned Adam Brothers design team.

Before his death, William Adam had begun a series of drawings for **Hopetoun House** on the outskirts of **Edinburgh**. The brothers were commissioned to complete the interiors of the state rooms, among them the yellow and red drawing rooms that can be seen, virtually unaltered, today.

In 1754, Robert Adam departed on a 'Grand Tour' of Europe, something that was extremely fashionable at the time. Travelling with Charles Hope, the then Lord Hopetoun's brother, Adam made many useful and influential connections, among them French and Italian architects, and absorbed the designs of classical monuments and buildings which would so inform his own architecture.

(continued)

Robert Adam *(continued)*

Upon his return to Britain, he settled in London, opening up the Adam Brothers with John, James and the youngest brother, William. Robert Adam's work until the 1760s was largely related to restoring old English country houses. In 1761 he was appointed architect of the King's Works. Throughout the 1760s, the Adam Brothers, under the name of William Adam and Co, were expanding their business interests, into timber, brickworks, granite quarries, stone and paving. In 1768, they turned to property speculation, buying land and designing the Adelphi, an elegant street of houses, which nearly bankrupted them. Only a lottery of the properties saved them.

By the 1770s, commissions in Scotland were increasing dramatically, and an office was opened in Edinburgh. Meanwhile, Robert Adam's popularity in England was being overtaken by changing fashions and younger architects. Adam was given several prestigious castle commissions for Scottish ancestral seats, among them the dramatic Culzean Castle on the Ayrshire coast, Maudslie Castle in Lanarkshire and Auchencruive Tower in Ayrshire. Adam's principal Scottish urban designs were Register House in Edinburgh (1772–92), the north side of Edinburgh's Charlotte Square and Edinburgh University's Old College (1789). His death in 1792 occurred before the buildings were complete, and the Old College design was subsequently altered. John Adam died the same year, and James died two years later. Robert Adam is buried in Westminster Abbey.

a hotel), Amulree still serves in its historical role as a staging-post. Once frequented by cattle drovers, the hamlet is now a watering hole for car-borne tourists en route from the north to **Crieff**. Between Amulree and Crieff come the scenic delights of the **Sma' Glen**.

ANCRUM
Borders

On B6400 4m N of Jedburgh.

Ancrum is situated on the Ale Water, a tributary of the Teviot. The shaft of a 12th- or 13th-century mercat cross can be seen on the village green. There are a number of outlying points of interest. To the east is the **Woodland Visitor Centre** which has displays on the care and preservation of woodland. To the north-east on Peniel Heugh Hill, is the **Waterloo Monument**, erected in 1815 to mark the end of the Napoleonic Wars. To the north, Ancrum Moor, or, more precisely, Lilliard's Edge, was the scene of one of the last major Border conflicts in 1545.

PETER ANDERSON WOOLLEN MILL
Galashiels, Borders

Nether Mill, Galashiels. All year. Mon–Sat 0900–1700; also Jun–Sept, Sun 1200–1700. Conducted tours: Apr–Sept, Mon–Fri 1030, 1130, 1330, 1430. D (P) (0896 2091).

The Peter Anderson Woollen Mill combines a museum illustrating the general history and growth of **Galashiels** with tours of the manufacturing section of the mill,

where tweeds and tartans are produced. There is also a mill shop.

ANSTRUTHER
Fife

On A917 13m S of St Andrews.

More properly titled the United Burgh of Kilrenny, Cellardyke, Anstruther Easter and Anstruther Wester, Anstruther shrinks to 'Ainster' in local parlance. Until the wilful departure of the fish in the 1940s, Anstruther was a large herring port. Its links with its fishing heritage are maintained both by the **Scottish Fisheries Museum** and by the handful of local boats that ply the waters for shellfish. In the High Street, Buckie House, a restored 17th- and 18th-century merchant's house, doubles as an art gallery. Anstruther's Old Kirk was founded by Queen Margaret of Scotland in the 12th century. There is a manse at Anstruther Easter which dates from the late 16th century. Boat excursions run to the Isle of May, a birdwatcher's paradise, from Anstruther during the summer months.

ARBROATH
Tayside

On A92 18m E of Dundee.

Arbroath is an east coast fishing town, where the income from that traditional industry is supplemented by tourism. Beaches and an intriguing stretch of coast to the north-east, peppered with caves, have ensured that Arbroath has a loyal summertime following of holidaymakers. Literary connections include the town's appearance as 'Fairport' in **Sir Walter Scott**'s novel *The Antiquary*, while there are strong historical associations between Arbroath and various movements for Scottish independence. In 1320, the Declaration of Arbroath, asserting Scotland's independence from the English crown, was signed in **Arbroath Abbey**. The Stone of Destiny, stolen from Westminster Abbey in 1951, was eventually found on the high altar of the abbey. Arbroath has also made its way on to the culinary map of Scotland via the Arbroath smokie, dry-salted haddock which is smoked in oak chips. The **Arbroath Signal Tower** is also of interest. A seasonal attraction is **Kerr's Miniature Railway**.

ARBROATH ABBEY

In Arbroath town centre. Apr–Sept, Mon–Sat 0930–1900, Sun 1400–1900; Oct–Mar, Mon–Sat 0930–1600, Sun 1400–1600. D (P). HS (031–244 3101).

The impressive Gothic red sandstone ruins of Arbroath Abbey lie at the heart of the town. Founded in 1178 by William the Lion (who is reputedly buried here), and dedicated to the memory of the murdered Thomas à Becket, the abbey was the scene of the signing of the Declaration of Arbroath in 1320. The Declaration, which was sent to Pope John XXII, asserted that Robert the Bruce was king of Scotland. This was not recognized by Rome until 1324. Of the ruins, the circular window (known as the 'Round O of Arbroath' and once used when lit as a beacon for navigators) in the south transept and the Abbot's House are the most notable parts.

ARBROATH SIGNAL TOWER MUSEUM

Ladyloan, Arbroath. Apr–Oct, Mon–Sat 1030–1300 and 1400–1700 (Jul–Aug, Sun 1400–1700 in addition); Nov–Mar, Mon–Fri 1400–1700, Sat 1030–1300 and 1400–1700. D (P). Free (0241 75598 or 0674 73232).

Built as the shore base for the Bell Rock or Inchcape Lighthouse (itself considered the outstanding achievement of engineer Robert Stevenson, grandfather of Robert Louis Stevenson), the Signal Tower now houses Arbroath's history museum. The motley display of items tells the histories of the fishing and flax industries, locally made Shanks lawnmowers and of the lighthouse itself.

ARDESTIE AND CARLUNGIE EARTH-HOUSES
near Dundee, Tayside

Off A92. Ardestie: 6m E of Dundee at junction with B962. Carlungie: 1m N on unclassified road to Carlungie. All times. Free. HS (031–244 3101).

Both earth-houses are roofless, allowing easy viewing of these strange excavations. Ardestie has a curved underground gallery which is 80 feet in length, dating from the Iron Age, and originally attached to a surface dwelling. Carlungie earth-house comprises a long 150-foot twisting passage, with shorter tributary passages.

ARNISTON HOUSE
Gorebridge, Lothian

Off A7 11m S of Edinburgh. June–mid Sept Tues pm. Guided tours leave on the

½ hour. Otherwise by appointment for groups (0875 30238).

This **William Adam**-designed Palladian mansion lies on the site of what was the seat of the so-called 'uncrowned king of Scotland', the power-broking Henry Dundas, 1st Viscount Melville. The current house contains portraiture, fine stucco work and period furniture.

ATHELSTANEFORD
Lothian

On B1343 5m S of North Berwick.

Athelstaneford is known primarily as the place where the Scottish flag has its origins. A pictorial plaque by Athelstaneford Church tells the story of the St Andrew's Cross (the Saltire) and a floodlit flag is always on display here. Tradition has it that the Picts and Scots, about to enter battle against Northumbria's King Athelstan, saw a white St Andrew's cross of cloud in the blue sky. They vowed, if victorious, to make St Andrew their patron saint. They subsequently made a banner imitating the design they had seen and so it became Scotland's flag.

AUCHMITHIE
Tayside

On unclassified road off A92 2m N of Arbroath.

Perched precariously on a clifftop, the cluster of white-washed cottages that comprises Auchmithie has long been connected with the fishing industry. Down below is the village's harbour, which was built in the late 19th century. This coastline

here was notorious for smugglers, who made use of the caves which pepper the red sandstone cliffs.

AUCHTERARDER
Tayside

Off A9 12m SW of Perth.

An old market town, Auchterarder was spitefully burned down in 1715 by the Jacobite Earl of Mar after his withdrawal from the Battle of Sheriffmuir and the defeat of the 1715 Jacobite uprising. It was also the scene in the mid 19th century of a dispute which led to the division of the Church of Scotland, when the Free Church of Scotland was formed. There are several visitor attractions in and around Auchterarder, among them the Strathallan Aircraft Museum, the **Great Scots Visitor Centre** and **Tulliebardine Chapel**.

AYTON CASTLE
near Eyemouth, Borders

On A1 8m N of Berwick-upon-Tweed. At Ayton. Sun 1400–1700 or by appointment. D (P) (08907 81212).

This red sandstone Scottish baronial-style castle was built in 1846. Visible from the A1, the castle is now lived in as a family home.

SIR DOUGLAS BADER GARDEN FOR THE DISABLED
Cupar, Fife

Duffus Park, Cupar. All year. Daily during daylight hours. D (0334 53722 ext 437).

This garden, designed especially with disabled gardeners and disabled garden enthusiasts in mind, features raised beds, an aviary, paths, rock gardens and new products and plants.

BALERNO, see CURRIE.

BALGONIE CASTLE
by Markinch, Fife

On B921 2m E of Glenrothes. All year. Daily 1400–1700. D (0592 750119).

Balgonie Castle was built in the 14th century and additions were made to it until 1702. In the 17th century it was the home of Field Marshall Sir Alexander Leslie, who was made the Lord General of the Scottish Covenanting Army and who commanded the Scots at Marston Moor. He was also the 1st Earl of Leven. In 1716 the castle was garrisoned by Rob Roy MacGregor and 200 clansmen. Today Balgonie, with its restored chapel, a two-acre wildlife garden, a leather carver's workshop and a tapestry weaver's studio, leads a somewhat quieter life as an unusual family home.

BALHOUSIE CASTLE (BLACK WATCH MUSEUM), see PERTH.

BALMERINO ABBEY
near Newport-on-Tay, Fife

On S shore of River Tay on unclassified road 5m SW of Newport-on-Tay. All year. Viewing from outside only during restoration. Free. NTS (031– 336 2157).

Set amidst gardens in a picturesque site beside the **River Tay**, the ruined Cistercian abbey was founded in 1229 by Queen Ermingade and was built by monks from **Melrose**. It was largely destroyed in 1547, and the Reformation ensured that any attempts to rebuild it were thwarted.

BARRIE'S BIRTHPLACE
Kirriemuir, Tayside

9 Brechin Road, Kirriemuir. Easter weekend, end Apr–end Sept, Mon–Sat 1100–1730, Sun 1400–1730. D (P). NTS (0575 72646 or 0575 72538).

The playwright and inventor of Peter Pan, J.M. Barrie (1860–1937), was born in **Kirriemuir** in this white-washed two-storeyed house. The upper floor is furnished as it may have been when Barrie lived there. The adjacent house is now home to a museum containing literary, personal and theatrical memorabilia. A Peter Pan display is on show in the former wash-house, said to have been Barrie's first theatre.

BASS ROCK
by North Berwick, Lothian

In the North Sea, just off North Berwick. Boat excursions circumnavigate the rock (0620 2197).

One of the few protrusions on the generally flat East Lothian landscape, the piebald Bass Rock is a 350-foot-high volcanic plug which lies just over a mile off the coast at **North Berwick**. A lighthouse is wedged into the rock's shore-facing side. Otherwise, the Bass Rock's inhabitants are primarily sea-birds, including the residents of the third largest gannetry in the world. From 1671, the sea-girdled plug was used as a prison for Covenanters and then for Jacobite prisoners who seized the fort in 1691. The Jacobites held it until 1694 when they were granted an amnesty. The rock is designated a Site of Special Scientific Interest and is therefore protected by law.

BATHGATE
Lothian

Off M8 15m W of Edinburgh.

Bathgate's history is largely an industrial one: weaving in the 17th century, then coal mining and more recently, iron and steel foundries and the **shale oil** industry. The town was the birthplace in 1811 of James Simpson, pioneer of chloroform as an anaesthetic. At nearby Whiteside, James 'Paraffin' Young established his first paraffin works in 1851. Bathgate's stone-built, largely Victorian town centre, the nearby Neolithic interest of **Cairnpapple Hill**, the Torphichen Preceptory and Bathgate's pleasant location at the foot of the Bathgate Hills offer more than the town's industrial reputation would imply. With the arrival of new high-tech industries in the area, Bathgate is seeing new growth.

BEDRULE CHURCH
Bedrule, Borders

Off A698 near Denholm. D. Free (0450 506).

As well as the immediate appeal of the church's environment – it sits high above the Rule Water – Bedrule Church is visited for its fine stained glass and its armorial bearings. Despite its contemporary tranquillity, the area was once the stronghold of the so-called 'fighting Turnbulls'.

BEECRAIGS COUNTRY PARK
near Linlithgow, Lothian

2m S of Linlithgow on Preston Road. All year. Visitor centre 0830–1700. D (A/P). Free (0506 844516).

The 1000 acres at Beecraigs easily accommodate a fish farm, a deer farm, woodland walks and space for several outdoor activities.

BEN LAWERS VISITOR CENTRE
Ben Lawers, Tayside

Off A827 14m SW of Aberfeldy. Easter–30 Sept, 1000–1700. D (A/P). NTS (05672 397).

This building is without doubt one of Scotland's most controversial visitor centres. Critics claim that its non-indigenous architecture despoils the landscape, that its high-tech displays spoonfeed visitors with an inappropriate interpretation of the mountain and that it acts as a magnet, encouraging floods of people (often badly equipped) up beyond it, towards the top of Ben Lawers. The path to the summit is becoming badly eroded and the mountain's rare alpine plants are threatened. So it is that the centre's critics tussle with the access-for-all versus conservation conundrum.

The narrow twisting road that leads up from the north side of Loch Tay to the centre gives car-borne visitors the opportunity to enjoy incredible panoramic views across the loch. The road continues to **Glen Lyon**.

BIRNAM
Tayside

Just off A9 10m N of Perth.

Birnam is a smallish settlement which has been enlarged in recent years by a number of new bungalows. The village, with its seasonal B and Bs, is a useful touring base and caravans and chalets supply visitor accommodation. The village is best known for the mention of Birnam Woods in Shakespeare's *Macbeth*. The popular Birnam Circular Walk and the Beatrix Potter Garden are local outdoor attractions. Birnam is separated from **Dunkeld** by the **River Tay** and a fine stone bridge which was built by Thomas Telford in 1809.

BLACKNESS CASTLE
near Linlithgow, Lothian

On B903 4m NE of Linlithgow. Apr–Sept, Mon–Sat 0930–1900, Sun 1400–1900; Oct–Mar Mon–Wed 0930–1600, Thurs 0930–1300, Sun 1400–1600. HS (031–244 3101).

Blackness Castle, which dates from the 15th century and sits on a **Firth of Forth** promontory, has had a varied career. It began as one of Scotland's most important fortresses, one that under the 1707 Articles of Union was allowed to be left fortified. It served as a prison during the time of the Covenanters, a powder magazine in the late 19th century, and, more recently, as a youth hostel.

BLAIR ATHOLL
Tayside

Off A9 6m N of Pitlochry.

A pleasant Highland village, Blair Atholl lies at the meeting point of several glens and is on the River Garry. Although best known for **Blair Castle**, the seat of the chief of Clan Murray, Blair Atholl also has a distillery and visitor centre, a meal and flour mill and the Atholl Country Collection which tells the history of life in the area and in the village.

BLAIR CASTLE
Blair Atholl, Tayside

Blair Atholl. 1 Apr–late Oct, Mon–Sat 1000–1700; Apr, May, Oct, Sun 1400–1700. D (P) (079681 207).

A white, turreted baronial castle in extensive grounds, this seat of the Duke of Atholl, chief of Clan Murray, is frequently the venue for public events and activities from Highland Games and country fairs to pony-trekking. As a result, it is Scotland's most visited privately owned home. Even without the bonus of laid-on entertainment, the castle has much to commend it. Its oldest part is Cumming's Tower which was built in 1269. It has played host to **Mary Queen of Scots**, Bonnie Prince Charlie and Queen Victoria. Visitors can walk through 32 fully furnished rooms; it has collections of furniture, china and armour; and it has a licensed restaurant and a resident piper. It also has a caravan park just inside its gates. The Dukes of Atholl were, by the special privilege of Queen Victoria, allowed to retain a private army and the Atholl Highlanders are thus the last private army in Britain.

BLAIRGOWRIE
Tayside

At junction of A93 and A926 15m N of Perth.

A bustling market town of red sandstone buildings in north-east Highland Perthshire, Blairgowrie is known as the agricultural hub of Scotland's soft fruit industry. It is a well-heeled, tweed-wearing and prosperous commuter town for **Perth** and also has a wintertime role as a ski centre for the nearby slopes at Glenshee. The town lies on the A93, which travels northwards through the Ericht Gorge and then ascends up through the Cairnwell, Britain's highest main road pass, and the Glenshee ski area before descending to Braemar.

BOLFRACKS GARDEN
near Aberfeldy, Tayside

On A827 2m W of Aberfeldy. Early Apr–mid Oct, 1000–1800 (0887 20207).

Rising up the southern side of the Tay valley between **Aberfeldy** and **Kenmore**, Bolfracks Garden shows a broad sweep of daffodils in spring. Otherwise, the owners of the garden, which is a member of Scotland's Gardens Scheme,

list trees, peat banks, herbaceous borders, shrubs and perennials as specialities.

BONNYRIGG, see LASSWADE.

BORDERS WOOL CENTRE
Galashiels, Borders

Wheatlands Road, Galashiels. Apr–Oct, Mon–Sat 0930–1700; Nov–Mar, Mon–Fri 0930–1700. Free (0896 4293 or 4774).

Although most of the space within the low stone building is given over to the retailing of woollen products from rugs to sheepskin mittens, the centre does have live sheep, hand spinning, wool sorting and weaving demonstrations. A sign reading 'Wear British wool: 41 million sheep can't be wrong' provides a lighthearted sales pitch, while photographs of several different breeds of sheep (Shetland, Black Welsh, Jacob) offer some educational substance.

BORTHWICK CASTLE AND BORTHWICK CHURCH
near Edinburgh, Lothian

Off A7 13m SE of Edinburgh. Castle: viewing from outside only. Church: all year. D (0875 20653).

The double-towered, twin-winged castle, constructed in the 15th century was visited by **Mary Queen of Scots** and Bothwell after their marriage in 1566. Shortly afterwards, when surrounded by her enemies, the queen was forced to escape from the castle disguised as a page in order to rejoin her husband. In 1650 Borthwick Castle, the strongest and largest of Scotland's tower-houses, was surrendered to Cromwell. Borthwick Church is largely Victorian although it has an apse which dates from the 12th century and a vault dating from the 15th century.

BOWDEN, see **ST BOSWELLS**.

BOWHILL
near Selkirk, Borders

Off A708 3m W of Selkirk. Grounds open end Apr–end Aug, Mon–Sat 1200–1700, Sun 1400–1800. House open July, Mon–Sat 1200–1700, Sun 1300–1630. D (0750 20732).

The home of the Scotts of Buccleuch for two hundred years, the house at Bowhill was built by the 3rd Duke of Buccleuch. Of particular note is the celebrated collection of paintings, including works by Van Dyck, Reynolds and Gainsborough, and portrait miniatures. The grounds contain an adventure play area, a riding centre, nature trails and a tea room. Bicycles can also be hired.

BRANKLYN GARDEN, see
PERTH.

BRECHIN
Tayside

At junction of A935 and A933 8m W of Montrose.

With the eastern Grampian Mountains at its back, the steep-streeted market town of Brechin sits beside the River South Esk. Its two particularly notable features are the cathedral, now the parish church, and the **Brechin Round Tower**. The squat cathedral dates from the 12th century, was partly destroyed during the Reformation but was restored in the early 20th century. Beside the cathedral is the **Brechin Round Tower**, an earlier structure which is one of only two examples of its type on the Scottish mainland (the other is at **Abernethy**). The **Caterthuns**, prehistoric hill forts, are five miles north-west of Brechin.

BRECHIN ROUND TOWER
Brechin, Tayside

In Brechin. All year. Viewed from the churchyard. Free. HS (031–244 2903).

Dating from about the 11th century, the Brechin Round Tower was built by Irish masons to an Irish model (around 80 such towers survive in Ireland). The stone roof was added in the 14th century. The tower stands 87 feet tall and has a narrow doorway which is positioned six feet above ground. The tower is adjacent to Brechin Cathedral.

BRITISH GOLF MUSEUM, see
ST ANDREWS.

BROUGHTON
Borders

On A701 12m W of Peebles.

On the western edge of Borders region, the pretty village of Broughton lies on the Biggar Water just before it joins the **River Tweed**, to the south-east of Broughton. A Scottish ale, Greenmantle, is brewed in the village. Here the author of thrillers and the creator of Richard Hannay, John Buchan, grew up. There is a **John Buchan Centre** in the village. On the outskirts of Broughton is Broughton Place, a Scottish baronial-style mansion by Sir Basil Spence which was built in 1938. It incorporates a summertime art gallery. In the village, at the corner of the Biggar road, is a much-admired private garden containing over 14 000 bedding plants.

BROUGHTY FERRY
Tayside

On A930 just E of Dundee.

Broughty Ferry, now really a suburb of **Dundee**, was once a booming fishing harbour on the Firth of Tay. The angling life of Broughty Ferry declined rapidly after the advent of the steam trawler since the large boats were too big for passage into the small harbour. Broughty Ferry was then adopted by affluent Dundee citizens, who came in search of wholesome air and built grand houses in which to stay. The 15th-century Broughty Castle is now a museum, displaying exhibits related to Dundee's maritime history and the whaling industry. Also nearby is **Claypotts Castle**.

BROXBURN
Lothian

On A899 9m W of Edinburgh.

Broxburn is fairly typical of many ex-**shale** oil mining towns in West Lothian – nondescript yet lying in a strange landscape which is peppered with the hummocks of shale bings. Obstinately red despite hopes that, with landscaping, these shale refuse tips would heal over, many of the bings are now protected by law as industrial monuments.

MICHAEL BRUCE'S COTTAGE
near Milnathort, Tayside

Kinnesswood, off A911 4m E of Milnathort. Apr–Sept, 1000–1800 (keys at the garage, Kinnesswood). D (A). Admission by donation (059284 255).

This is a low-key museum in the cottage where Michael Bruce (1746–67), the Gentle Poet of **Loch Leven**, was born. Bruce is probably best known for 'Ode to a Cuckoo'.

JOHN BUCHAN CENTRE
Broughton, Borders

S end of Broughton. Easter–mid Oct, 1400–1700. D (A) (0899 21050).

Housed in the former United Free Church, the John Buchan Centre is devoted to the life and works of local boy Buchan who became a lawyer, writer, historian and politician. Buchan's successful writing career was followed by a successful political one: as 1st Lord Tweedsmuir, he went on to become the Governor-General of Canada. His thrillers, among them *The Thirty-Nine Steps*, have been out of fashion for some years, charged with being racist and of promoting intolerance – a charge refuted by Buchan fans.

BURKE AND HARE see
panel p74.

BURLEIGH CASTLE
near Kinross, Tayside

Off A911 2m NE of Kinross. Apr–Sept,
Mon–Sat 0930–1900, Sun 1400–1900;
Oct–Mar, Mon–Sat 0930–1600, Sun
1400–1600. Key-keeper at farm opposite.
Free. HS (031–244 3101).

Frequented by James IV, the ruined
Burleigh Castle was the 16th-century
tower-house seat of the Balfours of
Burleigh. The castle is roofless but
is otherwise complete and includes
a section of defensive wall and a
corner tower.

BURNTISLAND
Fife

On A921 5m SW of Kirkcaldy.

Lying on the **Firth of Forth** facing
Granton across the water, the former
coaling port of Burntisland is

commonly called 'the playground
of Fife'. Visitors flock to the town in
summer, attracted by Burntisland's
sands, its verdant links and a busy
programme of organized events.
In contrast to this festive, pleasure-
based image, the town's history is
less frivolous. Its harbour is reputed
to have been used by Agricola in AD
83. Visitors of renown included **Mary
Queen of Scots** in 1563 and James VI
in 1601 (when he remarked on the
need for a new translation of the
Bible, which became the Authorized
Version of 1611). Burntisland was
reputedly occupied by Cromwell
during the Civil War. The town's
16th-century church is highly
regarded as an unusual example
of a post-Reformation church. Its
especially attractive features are
the canopied central pew and the
Trades' Lofts.

**BUTTERFLY AND INSECT
WORLD**, see **EDINBURGH**.

William Burke and William Hare

William Burke (1792–1829) and William Hare (1790–1860) came independently to Scotland from Ulster to work on the **Union Canal**. They met in 1827, when Burke and his Scottish mistress, Helen MacDougal, became the lodgers of Hare and his wife. Partners in murder, Burke and Hare killed 16 people for profit, supplying the Edinburgh medical establishment with bodies upon which to practise anatomy.

Despite popular belief, historians have found no evidence that the gruesome duo actually robbed graves – although this was undoubtedly another source of bodies used by others. Instead Burke and Hare murdered by suffocation, which left no trace and which allowed unquestioning anatomists, blind with ambition, to accept the bodies as dead from natural causes.

Their first body-sale appears to have been the corpse of an old man, lodging with the Hares, who did die naturally. They arranged to deliver the body to Edinburgh University, where no questions were asked. A sum of seven pounds, ten shillings was paid. Knowing of the city's thriving 'resurrectionist', or grave-robbing businesses, Burke and Hare were only too aware of the demand for bodies. The murder of other lodgers – Joseph the miller, an old lady, and Englishman from Cheshire – followed. A method – stifling the victim by covering their mouth and nose – evolved, later to be called 'burking'. Payment for corpses was now ten pounds. The murders of the prostitute Mary Paterson, another old woman, yet another and her grandson, a cinder-gatherer, a drunk woman and a washerwoman added to their gory total.

(continued)

Burke and Hare *(continued)*

Only when an informant betrayed them were they arrested. The body of an old Irishwoman was recovered and the Hares were persuaded to give evidence against Burke and his mistress. Burke and Helen MacDougal were brought to trial late in 1828; Burke was found guilty and was sentenced to death.

Hare, his wife and Helen MacDougal are said to have fled independently from Scotland. Burke was hanged on 21 January 1829 and, ironically, his own body was dissected at Edinburgh University. Under pressure from a belligerent crowd, a viewing of the body was arranged and a reputed 30 000 people passed before it. With the punishment of apparently unending irony, Burke's remains can still be seen in the Anatomy Museum of Edinburgh University.

As in the cases of murderers through the centuries, public fascination lies with motive. Did Burke and Hare enjoy the killing? Were their motives purely financial? Was the Edinburgh medical and intellectual establishment really to blame? Twentieth-century academics have devoted a surprising amount of time to these questions, sifting the evidence and speculating, some keen to damn the duo, others determined to prove them humane and simply needy. Whatever, interest in Burke and Hare is abiding – they linger in the public imagination, strolling through the shadows of Ghost Walking Tours of Edinburgh, and are remembered in the name of an Edinburgh pub.

CAIRNPAPPLE HILL
Lothian

Off B792 3m N of Bathgate. Apr–Sept, Mon–Sat 0930–1900, Sun 1400–1900; Oct–Mar, closed Mon (am) and Fri. HS (031–244 3101).

The prehistoric Cairnpapple Hill site was used as a place of burial and ritual from 3000 to 1400 BC. Today, a display documents the site's structural changes and the changes of use, from its beginnings as a Neolithic sanctuary. In about 1800 BC, it was transformed into a vast open-air temple comprising a stone circle surrounded by a ditch. Three hundred years later, Cairnpapple became a burial cairn, which was enlarged several centuries later to accommodate cremations and more burials. The site has been reconstructed and is considered one of the most important prehistoric monuments in Scotland.

CAITHNESS GLASS
near Perth, Tayside

Inveralmond, Perth on A9 north of the town. Factory shop: all year, Mon–Sat 0900–1700, Sun 1100–1700 (Easter–end Sept). Factory viewing: all year, Mon–Fri 0900–1630, open till 1800 every day in Jul and Aug. D. Free (0738 37373).

A combined factory, shop and visitor centre, Caithness Glass is about the strange business of the humble paperweight. Visitors are guided through paperweight-making, from glass-blowing to design. The world of the paperweight opens up – worldwide sales, collectors' items, limited editions, each year's special designs – and a remarkable specialist industry is uncovered. The Perth factory opened in 1979 and is a branch of the Wick-based company of the same name. A Caithness Paperweight Collectors' Club was started in 1976 and membership currently stands at around 3000.

CAMBO COUNTRY PARK
Kingsbarns, near Crail, Fife

Kingsbarns, 3m N of Crail. Easter–end Sept, daily 1000–1800. D (P) (0333 50810).

This estate offers a full family day out, with a wide range of activities and terrains, including a pets' corner, a wooded glen, a woodland adventure area, nature trails, a live bee display, a children's BMX track and sea frontage.

CAMPERDOWN HOUSE AND COUNTRY PARK
near Dundee, Tayside

Off A923 near junction with A972 3m NW of city centre. End Mar–beginning Nov, 1000–1645. D (A) (0382 621993).

The 19th-century estate mansion (which now houses a self-service restaurant) resides in 395 acres of parkland. That acreage also accommodates a caravan park, an adventure playground and the **Camperdown Wildlife Centre**.

CAMPERDOWN WILDLIFE CENTRE
near Dundee, Tayside

Off A923 nr junction with A972 3m NW of city centre. All year. Daily 1000–1600. D (0382 623555).

Animals present in the wildlife centre include indigenous species – deer, wildcats, pheasants and pinemarten – as well as a large collection of domestic stock. There are also wildfowl ponds.

CANAL MUSEUM
Linlithgow, Lothian

The Basin, Union Canal, Linlithgow. Apr–Sept, Sat–Sun 1400–1700. D. Free (0506 842575).

Former canal stables, built around 1822, have been converted into a museum which tells of the life and times of the **Union Canal** from its 1822 opening (when it ran from **Edinburgh** to Falkirk and there joined the Forth and Clyde Canal) to its current recreational role.

CARLOPS
Borders

On A702 12m SW of Edinburgh.

A small village, on the North Esk River, Carlops is a popular base for walkers heading into the **Pentland Hills**.

CARLUNGIE EARTH-HOUSE, see ARDESTIE AND CARLUNGIE EARTH-HOUSES.

ANDREW CARNEGIE, see panel p78.

CARNOUSTIE
Tayside

On A930 10m E of Dundee.

Perhaps best known for its golf course, used for the British Open, Carnoustie doubles up as a summer seaside resort.

CARRINGTON
Lothian

Off A7 10m S of Edinburgh

The small, attractive settlement of Carrington won the accolade of 'the best-kept village in Britain' in 1978. Cottages with pantiled roofs and the 18th-century parish church give Carrington its intrinsic appeal.

CARTER BAR
Borders

On A68 8m S of Jedburgh.

Considered by many as the most scenically spectacular of Scotland's front doorsteps, Carter Bar lies on the summit ridge of the Cheviots. Views extend to the Lowlands and to the **Eildon Hills**. In winter, the Border crossing point pays the price for its views and its altitude, for the A68 is often blocked by snow. The last Border battle (the Redeswire, or Reidswire Raid) between the English and the Scots took place here in 1575 and is commemorated by the Stone of Reidswire. Nearby, Roman earthworks can be seen.

CASTLEJAIL
Jedburgh, Borders

Castlegate, Jedburgh. All year. Mon–Sat 1000–1700, Sun 1300–1700. D (P) (0835 63254 or 0450 73457).

Andrew Carnegie

On 25 November 1835, Andrew Carnegie (1835–1919) was born the son of a weaver in a tiny cottage in **Dunfermline**. In later years Carnegie felt himself fortunate in his place of birth: 'All is redolent of the mighty past,' he wrote. In 1848, facing poverty, the Carnegie family sold all their possessions to buy their passage to America. Along with two million other British immigrants, the Carnegies went to the land of opportunity to escape bankruptcy.

They settled in Allegheny City, near Pittsburgh. Andrew Carnegie was employed by a series of Scotsmen in the cotton industry and then as a messenger boy. He began to read at night, educating himself until he was promoted to telegraph operator. He went to work for the Pennsylvania Railroad, buying shares with loans and his earnings. Successful investment in the railways led to investment in iron and steel manufacturing where he made his fortune. By the time he retired in 1901, Carnegie owned the largest private fortune in the world. For the man who wrote 'to die rich is to die disgraced', this presented something of a problem. He had begun his philanthropic works many years before, and was not forgetful of his home town. He opened the first free British Carnegie Library, which was to be one of over 2000 worldwide, in Dunfermline in 1881.

Before his death in 1919, having sold his company, Carnegie gave his entire fortune away – over 350 million dollars. He set up trust funds for education, peace, social welfare and research. Those funds have financed diverse projects – Carnegie Hall in New York, the children's television show *Sesame Street*, 7000 church organs, village halls and pre-school playgroups are just a small selection. During his lifetime, Carnegie was accused of and was satirized for being numerous things, among them hypocritical and hopelessly idealistic. What is certain is that he was a pacifist (and was one of the first people to conceive of the idea of a League of Nations), he was anti-imperialist (and tried to prevent the US acquisition of the Philippines), he was anti-racist and he was definitely philanthropic. At the end of his life, his hope remained that 'the wealth that came to me to administer as a sacred trust for the good of my fellow men, is to continue to benefit humanity for generations untold'.

He left his mansion and grounds, Pittencrieff, to the town. A statue of Carnegie looks out across the well-tended Pittencrieff public park. Of Scots he said: 'Touch his head, and he will bargain and argue with you to the last; touch his heart, and he falls upon your breast.'

In 1825, on the site of Jedburgh Castle which had been demolished in the 15th century, a jail was built. It was designed to embody new ideas of penal reform. Today visitors can enter reconstructed rooms to gain an impression of this era of reform and of prisoners' changing fortunes.

CASTLELAW FORT
near Edinburgh, Lothian

Off A702 7m S of Edinburgh. Apr–Sept, Mon–Sat 0930–1900, Sun 1400–1900; Oct–Mar, Mon–Sat 0930–1600, Sun 1400–1600. Free. HS (031–244 3101).

Two banks and ditches comprise this small Iron Age hill fort. One contains an earth-house. The site was occupied during the second century AD.

CASTLE MENZIES
near Aberfeldy, Tayside

On B846 1m W of Aberfeldy. Apr–mid Oct, Mon–Sat 1030–1700, Sun 1400–1700. D (P) (0887 200982).

An imposing grey stone 16th-century fortified tower-house, Castle Menzies began a programme of renovation in the mid-1970s which is still continuing. The castle's interior is impressively sparse, freed of the artefacts that too often clutter fine buildings. Nooks and crannies include small bedrooms, one of which was the sleeping place of Charles Edward Stuart, or Bonnie Prince Charlie. A broad stone staircase twists to the upper floors and a large hall, the scene of Clan Menzies reunions.

CATERTHUNS
near Brechin, Tayside

5m NW of Brechin near Menmuir. All year. Free. HS (031 244 3101).

Two large Iron Age hill forts, one called the Brown Caterthun, the other named the White Caterthun, lie on either side of a road. The structure of the Brown Caterthun includes four concentric ramparts and ditches, while the White fort features a massive stone rampart, a ditch and outer ramparts.

CERES
Fife

On B939 7m SW of St Andrews.

Ceres is an attractive village which is home to the **Fife Folk Museum,** housed within the 17th-century Weigh House. The village's parish church, with its horseshoe-shaped gallery, dates from 1806. Beside the church is a medieval mausoleum belonging to the Crawford family.

CHESTERS HILL FORT
near Haddington, Lothian

1m SW of Drem on unclassified road to Haddington. All year. Free. HS (031–244 3101).

The Chesters Hill Fort is one of the best-preserved examples in Scotland of an Iron Age fort, protected by a system of multiple ramparts.

CLAN TARTANS, see panel
p80.

Clan tartans

Like so many things that are perceived as quintessentially Scottish, even the innocuous-seeming subject of tartan is riven by dispute. Is the system of clan tartans, whereby kinship can be identified by cloth, an old tradition, the practice of centuries, or is it a relatively new phenomenon, an invented gimmick? Some have seen the answer to that question as crucial, believing that the Highland sense of identity and a not insignificant amount of credibility hinge upon it.

Those who argue that the system of clan tartans is a verifiable and ancient part of Highland heritage burrow deep into old books to find proof of the cloth's status. They quote Virgil's reference to Celts 'in striped garments', pointing out that the Romans had no word for 'checked' and that 'striped' was their closest approximation. The defenders argue that after the 1745 Rebellion, when tartan was banned, the clan tartan system was forgotten and had to be reinvented – yet the prohibition only lasted for 37 years. A 1819 patternbook prepared by Wilson's of Bannockburn indicates that the move to link tartans with family names had begun. Clan tartans took off in the 1880s, when, in the wake of a flood of romanticism about Scotland – fostered by **Sir Walter Scott** and Queen Victoria – clan societies were founded. Clans selected their own tartan, and tartans became an identity badge. Since then, clanship has been watered down to include anyone, related or not, of the same surname. It is not unusual to see two complete strangers clad in the same tartan embracing like long-lost friends.

However old the system of clan tartans is, perhaps the most important aspect is the role of tartan today. Kinship (whether with strangers or not), ready-made associations and a sense of tradition are three of the pleasures available to clan members through tartan. For Scotland, it means a thriving weaving industry and an irresistible tourist magnet.

There are consolations for those left on the outside of all the clannishness: you can invent your own tartan. You will need to design it, order 300 yards of it from a Scottish woollen mill, prepare a thread count and register it with the Highland Society of London and the Scottish Tartans Society in **Comrie**.

CLAPPERTON DAYLIGHT PHOTOGRAPHIC STUDIO
Selkirk, Borders

Scott's Place, E of Selkirk town centre. Apr–Oct, Sat–Sun 1400–1630; other times by arrangement. D (0750 20523).

Still family-owned, this is one of the oldest original daylight photographic studios in existence. The displays of photographs, dating back to the 1860s, are changed regularly.

JIM CLARK MEMORIAL TROPHY ROOM
Duns, Borders

44 Newtown Street, Duns. Easter–end Oct, Mon–Sat 1000–1300, 1400–1700, Sun 1400–1700. D (0361 82600, ext 36/37).

Trophies and other motor-racing memorabilia form a tribute in the midst of Duns housing estates to the late Jim Clark, twice world motor racing champion, who lived in **Duns**. The room was set up after Clark's death on a racing track in Germany in 1968.

CLATTO COUNTRY PARK
Dundee, Tayside

Dalmahoy Drive, off A972 from Dundee city centre. All year. Daily 1000–dusk. Free (0382 89076).

Twenty-four acres of reservoir water has been turned into a watersports centre, where windsurfing, canoeing and dinghy sailing can be practised. An area of mixed woodland, an adventure playground and barbecue facilities complete the package.

CLAYPOTTS CASTLE
Dundee, Tayside

S of A92 3m E of city centre. 1 Apr–30 Sept, Mon–Sat 0930–1900, Sun 1400–1900. Free. HS (031–244 3101).

A tall, angular, late 16th-century tower-house, Claypotts is notable because of its completeness. It bears the dates 1569 and 1588 and was built for the Strachan family.

CLOVENFORDS
Borders

On A72 2m W of Galashiels.

Nestling in Borders hills, Clovenfords lies on the Caddon Water. The village is often noted for the literati who lived here (poet John Leyden) or who briefly stayed here (**Sir Walter Scott** and the Wordsworths).

COCKBURNSPATH
Borders

On A1 18m N of Berwick-upon-Tweed.

On the edge of the **Lammermuir Hills**, the village of Cockburnspath has within its boundaries the ruined Cockburnspath Tower, a 17th-century mercat cross and a church with a 16th-century round beacon tower. Nearby are Pease Bridge, built in 1780 and then said to be the highest bridge in the world (over 100 feet), and the baby-blue futuristic-looking nuclear **Torness Power Station**.

COCKENZIE
Lothian

Off A198 10m E of Edinburgh.

Now dominated by two-chimneyed Cockenzie Power Station, the coal-fuelled, electricity-generating station with pylons striding away from it, Cockenzie was formerly a **Firth of Forth** fishing village. Port Seton, also once a fishing village, has merged with Cockenzie. Pink and honey sandstone, satellite dishes and a 'swimming pond' are town features. Further along the coast is Seton Sands, given over to a caravan park and leisure complex.

COLDINGHAM
Borders

On A1107 15m SE of Dunbar.

Sited just inland of Coldingham Bay, the buildings of Coldingham are mainly 18th century. The town's parish church incorporates the remains of a 12th-century abbey. The discovery of a female skeleton embedded upright in its south transept in the 19th century was adopted by **Sir Walter Scott** in *Marmion*. The **John Wood Collection**, a photographic exhibition of Borders life, is displayed in the town.

COLDSTREAM
Borders

On A697 8m NE of Kelso.

Divided from England by the **River Tweed**, the ford at Coldstream was used for many forays into the enemy's camp by both the English and the Scots. The bridge over the river, designed by James Smeaton, was opened in 1766. Coldstream subsequently became another Gretna Green – the marriage place of several eloping, under-age English couples. In 1659, the famous Coldstream Guards were assembled here. Their original headquarters, amongst the town's honey sandstone, is now the Coldstream Museum. Another feature of Coldstream is the Majoribanks Monument, an obelisk with a stone figure of Charles Marjoribanks, elected first member of parliament for Berwickshire after the passing of the 1832 Reform Act.

COMMON RIDINGS, see
panel p83.

COMRIE
Tayside

On A85 22m W of Perth.

Set amidst the splendour of rolling hills and divided by the fine River Earn, Comrie is a popular holiday and weekend destination. In summer, visitors can enjoy the outdoor life, the scenic beauty and watersports of nearby Loch Earn. In winter, people come to watch the New Year Flambeaux Procession parading through the town's typically Highland main street. Lying right over the **Highland Line**, a geological fault line, picturesque Comrie is Scotland's earthquake

Common ridings

Throughout the summer, Borders towns hold their individual 'riding the marches' ceremonies and festivals. These Common Ridings – often involving the checking and patrolling of the boundaries of town-owned common lands on horseback – are said to have their origin in the Middles Ages. Then, with raiding parties crossing frequently from England to Scotland (and vice versa), defensive exercises, a fierce territorial sense and keen vigilance developed. Other commentators attribute the Ridings to a later practice of demarcating public lands before the eyes of landowners. Whatever their source, the ceremonial Ridings of today, with their stringent sequences and precise rules, recall the centuries of Borders' territorialness.

Although different in character from town to town, the Common Ridings, which may last for several days, share some ceremonial features. The horse – horse-riding is a staple activity in the Borders – is pivotal to the festivities and the centrepiece of the celebrations is often the 'Ride-Out', a procession of horsemen and bands.

There is also a vocabulary which is unique to the Ridings: souter (the standard bearer), cornet (the youngest cavalry leader in a troop), callant (the finest of the young men), bussin the colours (displaying and waving flags).

Of the many Borders towns – **Peebles, Duns, Galashiels, Jedburgh, Hawick**, Langholm and **Lauder** among them – that hold Common Ridings, the Selkirk Gathering in June is the oldest. A local young man is chosen to lead the 500-year-old Riding as the souter. The most momentous part of his role is to 'cast the colours', to unfurl the flag and wave it in set manoeuvres. Then he represents Fletcher, the sole survivor after Scotland's crushing defeat at the Battle of Flodden in 1513.

Hawick's Common Riding, also held in June, focuses on a post-Flodden event, when some callants attacked an English raiding party and captured the Hexham Pennant. The Hawick celebration is led by the cornet, again a young man chosen from the local community. He is accompanied by the 'cornet's lass' on his tour of duties which includes a fast gallop up the Nip Knowes, the cornet's horse race and the cornet's ball.

Another variation on the theme is Jedburgh's Common Riding, which is called the Jethart Callants' Festival. Each Common Riding is different, yet all participants share two things – a fervent respect for tradition and a vigorous desire to enjoy themselves.

centre. Attractions include the **Scottish Tartans Museum** and the **Melville Monument**, which sits atop Dunmore Hill and can be reached by prepared walking trails.

CORSTORPHINE,
see **EDINBURGH VILLAGES** panel p116.

COWDENBEATH
Fife

On A909 5m NE of Dunfermline.

Cowdenbeath is one of a number of communities in southern Scotland to be economically boosted and physically ravaged by the coal-mining of the 19th century. The 20th-century decline of the industry left more debris in its wake: physical scars and unemployment. Some efforts have been made in Cowdenbeath to revitalize the community and its environment, in particular the reclamation of wasteland to create Lochore Meadows Country Park.

CRAIGMILLAR CASTLE
near Edinburgh, Lothian

Off A68 3½m SE of city centre. Apr–Sept, Mon–Sat 0930–1900, Sun 1400–1900; Oct–Mar, Mon–Sat 0930–1600, Sun 1400–1600, closed Thurs (pm) and Fri in winter. HS (031–244 3101).

On the outskirts of **Edinburgh**, the handsome Craigmillar Castle is comprised of the ruins of a massive 14th-century keep, enclosed by a 15th-century curtain wall, within which lie the remains of the 16th- and 17th-century apartments. **Mary Queen of Scots** was a frequent guest here, and it is believed that it was during her period of residence in 1566 that the plot to murder Darnley was hatched.

CRAIGTOUN COUNTRY PARK
near St Andrews, Fife

2½m SW of St Andrews. Easter–early Oct, daily 1030–1830. D (P) (0334 73666.)

Several day-out, outdoor activities are available at Craigtoun, including a miniature railway, crazy golf, trampolines, boating, bowling green, putting green and picnic areas. There are also an open-air theatre, gardens and glasshouses.

CRAIL
Fife

On A917 9m SE of St Andrews.

Orange pantiles, crow-stepped gables, cobbled, tree-lined streets and the fine, restored 17th- and 18th-century buildings in Crail contribute to the town's overall attractiveness. Crail's roots are very firmly in the fishing industry: from the ninth century onwards, the harbour traded in fish, selling abroad as well as to home markets. Curing and smoking became special skills in the area and today 'Crail Capon', a locally smoked haddock, is the contemporary fishy speciality. The 16th-century Collegiate Church of St Mary, with its eighth-century Pictish cross slab and a stone, reputedly hurled in rage by the devil from the nearby Isle of May, are of interest as are the Crail Museum, Crail Tolbooth and **Lochty Private Railway**.

CRAMOND, see EDINBURGH VILLAGES panel p116.

CRICHTON CASTLE
near Dalkeith, Lothian

On B6367 7m SE of Dalkeith. Apr–Sept, Mon–Sat 0930–1900, Sun 1400–1900; Oct–Mar, Sat 0930–1600, Sun 1400–1600. HS (031–244 3101).

Sitting atop a hillock, Crichton is a large and imposing castle which shows a range of transitional stages from the plain 14th-century keep to the more elaborate ruins dating predominantly from the 15th to 17th centuries. The 16th-century upper frontage of faceted stonework was erected by the Earl of Bothwell. Half a mile away is the small Crichton Collegiate Church, dating from the 15th century and still in use today.

CRIEFF
Tayside

On A85 16m W of Perth.

'Welcome to Crieff – the Holiday Town' says the roadside sign. As one of the many 'gateway' towns to the Highlands, Crieff's situation on the very edge of the Highlands has màde it a busy holiday town and the principal shopping centre for the area. Well-heeled and handsome,

the town is mostly unspoiled, retaining all the appeal that made it a health resort at the beginning of the 20th century. Traditional shops and enormous houses (many now hotels) in pink and plum sandstone give Crieff its warm atmosphere of comfortable affluence. The River Earn winds around its feet. The town itself rises up the hill from the valley floor. Among its catchment visitor attractions are **Stuart Strathearn, Crieff Visitors' Centre**, the **Weaver's House**, the Melville Monument,**Tullibardine Chapel**, **Glenturret Distillery** and **Drummond Castle Gardens**.

CRIEFF VISITORS' CENTRE
Crieff, Tayside

On the A822 leading south from Crieff on Muthill Road. All year. Daily 0900–late (winter 0900–1600). Factories only on working days. D Free. (0764 4014).

The purpose-built job-creating visitors' centre contains a 180-seat restaurant, showrooms with two walk-round craft factories which explain the arts of paperweight-making and of pottery. The statutory factory shop sells products made on the premises.

CROMBIE COUNTRY PARK
near Newbigging, Tayside

On B961 3½m NE of Newbigging. All year. 1000–dusk. D (P). Free (02416 360).

The 250 acres of Crombie Country Park incorporate a Victorian reservoir, woodland, wildlife hides, trails, a children's play area and an interpretation centre.

CROSS KIRK
Peebles, Borders

*Peebles. Apr–Sept, Mon–Sat 0930–1900,
Sun 1400–1900; Oct–Mar, Mon–Sat
0930–1600, Sun 1400–1600. Key from
custodian in nearby house. Free. HS
(031–244 3101).*

The nave and the West Tower are
all that remain of a late 13th-century
Trinitarian Friary in **Peebles**. The
foundations of the domestic
buildings have been exposed beside
the kirk.

CULROSS
Fife

Off A985 7½m W of Dunfermline.

On the north shore of the **Firth
of Forth**, Culross (pronounced
'Cooross') flourished in the 16th and
17th centuries, trading in salt and in
coal. It has survived almost intact
since that time, dominated today, as
are many villages along the western
part of the Forth estuary, by the oil
refinery at Grangemouth. The old
part of Culross consists of a large
picturesque collection of harled,
often white-washed buildings. They
have been taken under the wing
of the National Trust for Scotland
which has laboured to preserve and
restore the buildings, just as it has
in Tayside's **Dunkeld**, another model
settlement. As in other harbour
towns, several wynds and closes
run down towards the water. These
narrow, flagstoned and cobbled
alleyways join the older lower and
the newer upper parts of the village.
Sites of special interest in Culross
which have been restored since the
1940s by the NTS are the **Study**,

Culross Abbey, Town House and
Culross Palace.

CULROSS ABBEY
Culross, Fife

Culross. Free. NTS (031–226 5922).

The remains of a Cistercian
monastery, founded in 1217,
lie alongside the ruins of other
domestic buildings. The choir of the
abbey church is the present parish
church.

CULROSS PALACE
Culross, Fife

*Culross. Closed until spring 1993. NTS
(031–226 5922).*

The small 'palace', or mansion, was
built between 1597 and 1611 by
the local laird and industrialist Sir
George Bruce, who considerably
expanded Culross's salt and
coal trade. A lovely elongated
building, now painted in a warm,
pale mandarin, the house is an
outstanding example of its type. Its
interior boasts fine painted ceilings
and pine panelling.

CUPAR
Fife

On A91 8m W of St Andrews.

Although it lays claim to a
long history via its scattering
of monuments (a 17th-century
mercat cross, a 1785 church with
1415 sections), Cupar is decidedly
modern, a busy shopping and
administrative centre which sports

some sense of its own importance. Several of the town's houses (18th and 19th century) add to Cupar's standing. Nearby are the **Hill of Tarvit** and the **Scotstarvit Tower**.

CURRIE (AND BALERNO)
near Edinburgh, Lothian

On A70 4m SW of Edinburgh.

Lying on **Edinburgh**'s **Water of Leith**, Currie and Balerno were both important paper-making centres. Today, their purpose is wholly residential.

DALKEITH
Lothian

On A68 7m SE of Edinburgh.

A former cattle market town and a
shopping centre today, Dalkeith was
an important hub of 19th-century
industries – coal, bricks and textiles.
The older parts of the town, where
careful restoration is evident, sit
uncomfortably beside the Central
Area Redevelopment project.
Dalkeith is the administrative centre
for Midlothian, and also on one of
the main routes south and therefore
suffers from severe congestion,
which the planned by-pass is
intended to resolve. The town sits
on a high peninsula between the
North and South Esk rivers, which
finally join beyond Dalkeith Palace
in **Dalkeith Park**.

DALKEITH PARK
Dalkeith, Lothian

At E end of Dalkeith High Street.
Easter–end Oct, daily 1100–1800. D (P)
(031–663 5684 (1100–1800) or 031–665
3277 outwith these hours).

The extensive grounds of Dalkeith
Palace (which is itself not open to
the public) offer woodland walks
beside the river, a tunnel walk,
an adventure playground, nature
trails, an 18th-century bridge and an
orangery.

DALMENY HOUSE
by South Queensferry, Lothian

By South Queensferry, 7m W of Edinburgh.
May–Sept, Sun–Thurs 1400–1730. Open all
year for groups by arrangement. D (A/P)
(031–331 1888).

Dalmeny House, for over 300 years
the seat of the Primrose family
(Earls of Rosebery), stands in
grounds beside the **Firth of Forth**.
One of the first Scottish neo-Gothic
designs, the house was built in
1815-17 by William Wilkins. The
hammer-beamed hall is a fine
example of Tudor Gothic style.
Vaulted corridors and classical
main rooms are complemented
by a considerable collection of
18th-century French furniture,
tapestries, porcelain from the
Rothschild Mentmore collection,
the Napoleon collection and other
notable works of art.

DAMSIDE GARDEN HERBS
AND ARBORETUM
near Montrose, Borders

Off the A92 between Montrose and
Stonehaven by Johnshaven. May–Oct,
Tues–Sun 1100–1900; Apr, Nov and Dec
weekends only 1100–1900; D (0561 61498).

This unusual eight-acre herb garden
displays the history of Celtic,
Roman, Monastic and Formal herbs.
An arboretum, an information area,
a tearoom and a shop accompany
the garden.

DAWYCK BOTANIC GARDEN
near Peebles, Borders

On B712 8m SW of Peebles. 15 Mar–22
Oct inclusive, daily 1000–1800. D (P)
(07216 254).

This outstation of **Edinburgh's Royal
Botanic Gardens** contains rare trees,
shrubs, Chinese rhododendrons and
narcissi along its woodland walks.
Within the woodland is Dawyck
Chapel, designed by William Burn.

JOHN DEWAR & SONS
Perth, Tayside

Dunkeld Road, Inveralmond, Perth. All year except holidays. Tours: Mon–Thurs 1000, 1115, 1400 and 1515, Fri 1000 and 1115. Free (0738 21231).

Beside the roundabout which leads to the northern stretch of the A9, hundreds of whisky casks lie stacked behind wire fences. This is the site of Dewar's whisky bottling plant, where over 300 000 bottles are filled each day. Conducted tours (you have to be over eight years old) guide visitors around the plant.

DIRLETON
Lothian

On A198 3m W of North Berwick.

Dirleton is one of a number of picturesque East Lothian villages. Its special appeal lies in the village green. Fronted by well-kept hedges, fences and trees, behind which sit several fine houses with crow-stepped gables. Particular attractions are **Dirleton Castle**, just off the village green, and the local sandy beaches and golf courses.

DIRLETON CASTLE
Dirleton, Lothian

On A198 3m W of North Berwick. Apr–Sept, Mon–Sat 0930–1900, Sun 1400–1900; Oct–Mar, Mon–Sat 0930–1600, Sun 1400–1600. D (P). HS (031–244 3101).

The ruins of Dirleton Castle lie within verdant gardens, established in the late 16th century. The castle dates back to 1225, although it was rebuilt in the 14th century and extended in the 16th century. It was first besieged by Edward I in 1298 and was finally destroyed in 1650. A dovecot and a 17th-century bowling green surrounded by yews survive within the gardens.

DOGTON STONE
near Kirkcaldy, Fife

Off B922 5m NW of Kirkcaldy. All reasonable times. Entry by Dogton Farm. D. Free. HS (031–244 3101).

A weathered, ancient Celtic cross with traces of animal and figure sculpture upon it stands within the farm boundaries.

DRUMELZIER
Borders

On B712 8m SW of Peebles.

Drumelzier (pronounced 'Drum-elyer') is a popular picnic spot. Its fame, however, rests on its supposed connections with the Scottish version of the Arthurian legends. Near the junction of the Drumelzier Burn and the **River Tweed** is the reputed burial place of Merlin, King Arthur's wizard, for story has it that he was stoned to death at Drumelzier.

DRUMMOND CASTLE GARDENS
near Crieff, Tayside

Off A822 3m S of Crieff. May–Aug, daily 1400–1800; Apr and Sept, Wed and Sun 1400–1800. Last admission 1700. D (P) (076481 257).

Through wrought-iron gates off the Muthill to Crieff road lie the gardens of Drummond Castle (not open to the public). The gardens were established in about 1630 by John Drummond, 2nd Earl of Perth. Around 1830, the parterre was Italianized and embellished with fine figures and statues from Italy. Sundial enthusiasts will be keen to see the one in the grounds, which was designed and built by John Mylne, Master Mason to King Charles I.

DRYBURGH ABBEY
Dryburgh, Borders

Off A68 6m SE of Melrose. Apr–Sept, Mon–Sat 0930–1900, Sun 1400–1900; Oct–Mar Mon–Sat 0930–1600, Sun 1400–1600. HS (031–244 3101).

Dryburgh Abbey, perhaps the most spectacular of the four famous Border abbeys, is situated in a magnificent wooded setting beside the **River Tweed**. Founded in the reign of David I by Hugh de Morville, Constable of Scotland, little, apart from the transepts, remains of the church itself. None the less, the ruins still give an idea of the incredible scale of the abbey. The cloister buildings have survived in a more complete state than in any other Scottish monastery (bar Iona and **Inchcolm**). **Sir Walter Scott**, his wife, daughter and son-in-law John Lockhart lie in a pink and black speckled granite tomb in the North Choir Chapel. Also buried here is Field Marshal Earl Haig (1861–1928).

DRYHOPE TOWER
near Selkirk, Borders

Off A708 near St Mary's Loch 15m W of Selkirk. All reasonable times. Free.

Sitting at the east end of St Mary's Loch, this squat 17th-century tower was originally four storeys high. The tower was the birthplace of Mary Scott, the Flower of Yarrow, who married the freebooter Auld Wat of Harden in 1576 and who was an ancestor of **Sir Walter Scott**.

DUDDINGSTON, see EDINBURGH VILLAGES
panel p116.

DULL
Tayside

On B846 3m E of Aberfeldy.

A hamlet on the north side of the **River Tay**, Dull is reputed to have been an ancient seat of monastic learning. St Adamnan, the biographer of St Columba, was supposed to have been buried near Dull where a religious college was founded in his memory.

DUNBAR
Lothian

Off A1 27m E of Edinburgh.

A solid town of red sandstone, Dunbar grew up around the fishing industry. Today its harbour, neighbouring beaches like Belhaven and record-breaking hours of sunshine attract holidaymakers, many of whom make the short trip from Edinburgh for their summer sojourn. Bordered to the south by the **Lammermuir Hills**, the town has on its doorstep East Lothian's fertile agricultural land, upon which grow Dunbar Red potatoes.

Dunbar appears in Scottish history books as the location of the Battle of Dunbar of 1650, when Cromwell defeated the Covenanters, although the battle actually took place to the south-east of the town. It was to Dunbar Castle (now visible as ruins by the harbour) that the Earl of Bothwell supposedly abducted **Mary Queen of Scots** in 1576 before their subsequent marriage. The **John Muir House**, the birthplace of the founder of American national parks, is open to the public. Other local places of interest include **Traprain Law** and **Torness Power Station**.

DUNDEE
Tayside

Commercial, industrial Dundee, one of Scotland's four major cities, is often overlooked by visitors to Scotland. Ask someone who has passed through Dundee for their impressions, and they may say, slightly incredulously, 'Housing estates, miles and miles of housing estates'. In the city centre, many historic buildings have been torn down over the years to make way for modern commercial structures. Decried by some commentators, others have argued that the marriage of modern and Victorian at least speaks of the city's prosperity and of its continuing commercial importance. However, only the 15th-century Old Steeple, the **Howff Burial Ground** and the East Port are of interest to the visitor in search of the distant past. Little else remains to tell the tale of Dundee's turbulent 800-year history. In 1547 the army of King Henry VIII of England held the city for a week; in the 17th century, it was stormed by the Duke of Montrose; and in 1745 it was held by the Jacobites.

From the visitor's point of view, despite what the 20th century and misguided city fathers may have done architecturally to Dundee, the city has some enormous natural advantages. Not least of these is its situation on the edge of the Tay estuary, easily viewed from Dundee's road and rail bridge approaches. On three sides of the city there are wide tracts of fertile farmland which certainly lessen the impact of its less visually attractive points.

For city promoters, perhaps Dundee's two best assets are its fascinating trade history – fishing, wool, linen, whaling and the so-called three 'j's', **jute, jam and journalism** (see panel p93) – and its water frontage. The harbour ensured the city's wealth and its place in world trade from the 13th century onwards. Recently, efforts have been made to capitalize on these two aspects of the city – trade and water – to attract visitors and improve amenities. Waterside refurbishments and such floating attractions as the *Discovery*, the Antarctic expedition ship of Captain Scott, and HMS *Unicorn*, the oldest British warship, are working towards a change in the city's fortunes. Other places of interest in and around Dundee are Barrack Street Museum, the McManus Galleries, **Camperdown House and Country Park, Camperdown Wildlife Centre, Clatto Country Park, Tealing Earth-Houses** and **Claypotts Castle**. See also the panel on the **River Tay** (p.178) for reference to the Tay bridges.

DUNDEE, RRS DISCOVERY

On waterfront, Victoria Dock. June–Aug, daily 1000–1700; Apr–May, Sept, Mon–Fri

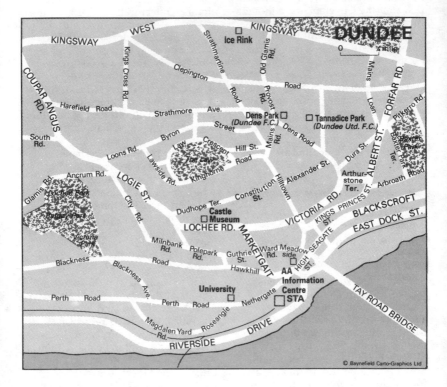

Town plan of Dundee

Dundee's jam, jute and journalism

Dundee, a vibrant trading port since the 13th century, has long been associated with three industries which have become become a catchphrase – 'the three js: jam, jute and journalism'. Whatever the levity implied by the catchphrase, the three industries have contributed in no mean way to the city coffers. Jute has been almost non-existent since the 1960s, but jam and journalism continue.

Dundee's jute industry developed from the linen industry. By the 1830s, experiments were taking place with raw jute – the fibre from plant barks. Jute production is thought to date from 1833, when the process of softening the fibre with a mixture of water and whale oil to produce jute yarn developed. The jute industry flourished with the onset of the Crimean War and the American Civil War when tents and soldiers' clothing were in high demand. In 1895, over 40 000 people were employed in Dundee mills. By the early 20th century, looms in India were taking over. Rescue for the Scottish industry came with World War I, when Dundee's mills were said to be producing a million sandbags a day for the government. After the war the Jute Control, which restricted imports, was introduced to protect the industry from Indian competition. Despite this, decline was imminent.

A better survivor has been Dundee marmalade which was developed in the city by accident. In 1797, John Keiller, a grocer, bought a cargo of Seville oranges, which proved too bitter to sell. His wife saved the day. She boiled them with sugar, gave the resultant marmalade to friends and family and eventually sold

(continued)

Dundee's jam, jute and journalism *(continued)*

it in their shop. Its rapid success led to the founding of the firm of James Keiller and Son in 1797. Although marmalade was the major product, by the end of the 19th century the company was producing confectionery and chocolate. In 1951, Keiller was acquired by Crosse and Blackwell Ltd which in turn was acquired by Nestlé. By the 1970s, Keiller sales were slumping, and in 1981 Nestlé announced the closure of the company. Fortunately, the Okhai family bought Keiller and marmalade production continued. Barker and Dobson took over the factory in 1986, and the future of Keiller marmalade, still sold in its distinctive white pot, seems assured. Many might say that D.C. Thomson, the Dundee-based publishing house, has made the greatest Dundonian contribution to British culture by creating such national institutions as Denis the Menace, Korky the Cat and Desperate Dan. The company began in the 1870s when William Thomson, a Dundee ship owner, invested in the *Dundee Courier and Argus* (founded 1816). In 1886 he gained full control of the paper, and brought in his son D.C. Thomson as his partner. Today, the company has over 30 publications, among them the teenage magazine *Jackie*, the old-fashioned but enormously popular *People's Friend*, the *Scots Magazine* and the *Sunday Post*.

The three js have had mixed fortunes: all had significant impact on a much wider world than Dundee, and all have brought, at some time, wealth, employment and status to the city.

1300–1700, Sat–Sun, bank holidays
1100–1700. D (A/P) (0382 201175 or
0382 25282).

The Royal Research Ship *Discovery*,
a triple-masted square rigger,
was purpose-built in Dundee in
1901 and served as Captain Scott's
Antarctic exploration vessel from
1901 to 1904. It was brought back to
Dundee in 1986 to its new home on
the Firth of Tay. A guided tour of
the ship, which tells of penguin and
huskies, ice and cold, evokes the
heroic nature of Scott's expeditions
and gruelling experiences of
Scott's team.

DUNDEE, HOWFF BURIAL GROUND

Meadowside. Daily, closes 1700 or dusk if
earlier. D (0382 23141.)

The Howff Burial Ground, formerly
the gardens of the Greyfriars
Monastery, was gifted to the city
by **Mary Queen of Scots** in 1564. It
operated as a burial ground from
the 16th to the mid 19th centuries
and still contains many finely
carved tombstones. Until 1778, the
graveyard doubled as a meeting
place (or howf) for Dundee's
Incorporated Trades. Several
gravestones are engraved with the
symbols of the old craft guilds.

DUNDEE, MILLS OBSERVATORY

Balgay Hill, north side of the city.
Apr–Sept, Mon–Fri 1000–1700, Sat
1400–1700; Oct–Mar, Mon–Fri 1500–2200,
Sat 1400-1700. D (A/P). Free (0382 23141).

Constructed in 1935 for the people
of Dundee, the Mills Observatory

is Britain's only full-time public
observatory with an astronomer in
residence. Perched up above the
River Tay in wooded surroundings,
it has telescopes, displays on
astronomy and space exploration
and a small planetarium. As in all
matters skyward, viewing is subject
to the right weather conditions.

DUNDEE, SHAW'S SWEET FACTORY

Fulton Road, west end of the Kingsway,
by NCR factory. Mid June–mid Aug,
Mon, Tues, Thurs, Fri 1330–1630; mid
Aug–Christmas, Mar–mid June, Thurs
1330–1630. D. Free (0382 610369).

A mini-museum of sweet-making
and a 1950s-style sweet factory,
producing old-fashioned sweets
(fudge, humbugs, fruit drops) using
traditional methods and equipment
which dates from 1936 to 1956, are
the offerings at Shaw's. A sweet-
maker also gives demonstrations
and there is a factory shop.

DUNDEE, HMS UNICORN

Victoria Dock, just E of Tay Road Bridge.
1 Apr–mid Oct, Sun–Fri 1000–1700,
Sat 1000–1600. Opening in winter, daily
1000–1600. D (P) (0382 200900).

In Dundee's harbour floats HMS
Unicorn, a 46-gun frigate which was
commissioned by the navy in 1824.
It is the oldest British warship still
on water, one of only four frigates
left in the world and is a Royal
Naval Museum. Visitors can enter
the captain's quarters and the main
gun deck to get an idea of naval life
19 years after the Battle of Trafalgar.

DUNDEE, UNIVERSITY BOTANIC GARDEN

Off Riverside Drive. Mar–Oct, 1000–1630; Nov–Feb 1000–1500. D (P). Free (0382 66939).

A pleasant interlude from the city's hubbub, these 22 acres of landscaped gardens include a collection of conifers, native and exotic plants, temperate and tropical planthouses and a visitor centre. The gardens were established in 1971, with the principal intention of supplying plant material to the University of Dundee for research.

DUNFALLANDY STONE
near Pitlochry, Tayside

Just off A9 1m S of Pitlochry. All reasonable times. Free. HS (031–244 3101).

This fine Pictish cross is reached via a short hillside path. Encased in a stone shelter with a glass front is the cross, thought to have been carved in the ninth century. A figure on horseback, surrounded by a selection of tools, is visible.

DUNFERMLINE
Fife

Just W of M90 16m NW of Edinburgh.

The one-time capital of Scotland and seat of Scottish kings has long been associated with industry – coal-mining and linen-weaving – and is well known for **Dunfermline Abbey and Palace** and as the birthplace of the great philanthropist **Andrew Carnegie**. Contemporary Dunfermline is a large, sprawling town which has a retail park to the east, and housing estates on all sides. Its busy centre – largely pedestrianized – is an attractive combination of narrow streets and the lovely ruins of the abbey and palace.

DUNFERMLINE ABBEY AND PALACE

Monastery Street, Dunfermline. Apr–Sept, Mon–Sat 0930–1700, Sun 1400–1700; Oct–Mar, Mon–Sat 0930–1600, Sun 1400–1600. D (P). HS (031–244 3101).

Side by side, the two structures were once both part of abbey life. The Benedictine abbey was founded in the 11th century by Queen Margaret. The foundations of her church lie beneath the nave, which dates from the 12th century. Robert the Bruce was buried in the choir (although his heart supposedly lies at **Melrose Abbey**). Monastic buildings still visible include the refectory, the pend and the guest house. The palace, of which only the dramatic blond sandstone façade remains, was constructed from the monastery guest house in the 16th century for James VI. Charles I was born here in 1600, the last monarch to be born in Scotland. Nearby is the large, well-tended public Pittencrieff Park.

DUNKELD
Tayside

Off A9 15m N of Perth.

Against a dramatic backdrop of Highland hills, Dunkeld lies beside the **River Tay** and the A9. Dunkeld's main street (Atholl Street) is an

unspoilt Highland high street
of traditional, privately owned
shops, teashops and stern stone
buildings. Atholl Street forms a 'T'
with Cathedral Street which leads
to **Dunkeld Cathedral** and **Dunkeld
Little Houses**, making the town easily
negotiable on foot. An unlikely
surprise is the sign beside the
Scottish Horse Regimental Museum
which reads 'MOD property – keep
out'. Outdoor sights include closes
which run down to the river and the
Dunkeld Bridge, built in 1809 and
considered one of Thomas Telford's
finest. It spans the Tay linking
Dunkeld with **Birnam**. Pleasant
riverside walks, strolls within the
abbey grounds and the longer
hike around the nearby **Hermitage**
provide active options.

DUNKELD CATHEDRAL
Dunkeld, Tayside

*Cathedral Street, Dunkeld. Apr–Sept,
Mon–Sat 0930–1900, Sun 1400–1900;
Oct–Mar, Mon–Sat 0930–1600, Sun
1400–1600. Free. HS (031–244 3101).*

Begun in 1318 and ruined during the
Reformation, the cathedral enjoys
a tranquil location between fields
and the **River Tay**. The choir was
reroofed in 1660 and now serves
as the parish church. Information
plaques tell of continuing repairs to
the cathedral's eroded, precariously
balanced stonework.

DUNKELD LITTLE HOUSES
Dunkeld, Tayside

*Dunkeld. Tourist Information Centre with
audio-visual presentation open 1 June–31
Aug, Mon–Sat 1000–1700, Sun 1400–1700;*

*early Apr–end May, 1 Sept–Christmas,
Mon–Sat 1000–1300 and 1400–1700. D.
Free. NTS (03502 460).*

Since 1954, the National Trust for
Scotland has owned 20 houses in
Dunkeld. Cathedral Street's white-
washed Little Houses (not open
to the public but viewed from the
outside) date from the time after the
1689 Battle of Dunkeld when their
predecessors were burned down. An
NTS shop, the Ell shop, is close by.

DUNS
Borders

On A6112 13m W of Berwick-upon-Tweed.

Somehow a plain town, despite
the contribution made by its
pleasant town square, Duns is best
known for its famous sons. It was
reputedly the birthplace of the
medieval philosopher Duns Scotus
(as are at least two other towns
in Europe) who is commemorated
by a statue in the town's public
park. The motor-racing champion
Jim Clark grew up in Duns, and
is remembered in the **Jim Clark
Memorial Trophy Room**. Local points
of interest are **Edin's Hall Broch,
Edrom Norman Arch** and **Manderston
House**, a lavish Edwardian mansion.

EARLSHALL CASTLE AND GARDENS
near Leuchars, Fife

1m E of Leuchars, 6m from St Andrews.
Easter weekend, every Sunday in April,
May–end Sept 1400–1800. D (P)
(033483 9205).

The interior of this 16th-century
tower-house, the home of the Baron
and Baroness of Earlshall, features a
long gallery with a painted ceiling,
timber panelling, a display of
weapons and a number of furnished
public rooms. The gardens include
yew topiary, a nature trail, picnic
facilities and a tearoom.

EARLSTON
Borders

On A68 3m NE of Melrose.

Earlston is situated in the
Lauderdale valley by the Leader
Water. A tower on the outskirts
of the town is associated with the
13th-century poet and prophet
Thomas the Rhymer.

EASSIE SCULPTURED STONE
Eassie, Tayside

In Eassie Kirkyard, 7m SW of Forfar.
All reasonable times. Free. HS
(031–244 3101).

Lying in Eassie's churchyard, the
sculptured stone is an elaborately
carved monument with a decorated
Celtic cross on one side and Pictish
symbols on the other.

EAST CALDER, see MID CALDER.

EAST LINTON
Lothian

Just off A1 or B1407 6m E of Haddington.

This pretty East Lothian village
on the River Tyne is much visited
because of its **Preston Mill and
Phantassie Doocot**. In its own right,
East Linton is well worth a visit
– the warm hue of red sandstone
and the carefully kept houses
and gardens make it enormously
picturesque. Of interest in the
immediate vicinity are the small
1770 Church of Prestonkirk with its
13th-century chancel, **Traprain Law**
and the dramatic **Hailes Castle**.

EAST SALTOUN, see PENCAITLAND.

EDDLESTON
Borders

On A703 3m N of Peebles.

The earthworks of the Iron Age
fort of Milkieston Rings and the
monument to George Meikle Kemp
who designed **Edinburgh's Scott
Monument** are the points of interest
around Eddleston, which lies on the
Eddleston Water.

EDINBURGH
Lothian

On his 1769 tour of Scotland Thomas
Pennant described Edinburgh as

'a city that possesses a boldness and a grandeur of situation beyond any that I had ever seen'. Indeed, Edinburgh has never been short of admirers and has not been obliged to court visitors. Without fail, people come to see the dramatic skyline of the city centre, as the jagged profile of **Edinburgh Castle** and the castle rock stand aloof from the more prosaic commercial life of the streets below.

The easily defensible rocky volcanic spine, now called **Edinburgh's Old Town**, was the where the city began, probably with a Pictish settlement. Edinburgh's growth and development hinged for many centuries on the castle. In the 11th century, King Malcolm moved the royal court from **Dunfermline** to Edinburgh. His successor and son, David I, founded the abbey at Holyrood, which inevitably stimulated building along what is now the Royal Mile, and he built Edinburgh Castle's St Margaret's Chapel in memory of his mother. In the following centuries Edinburgh remained the capital of an independent Scotland, thriving and surviving despite attack and threat of attack. The Act of Union in 1707 meant the loss of the Scottish capital's power base: London would now dominate.

Somehow, Edinburgh has retained its dignity: the sudden flash of brilliance in the arts, medicine, law, the sciences and in philosophy during the late 18th and early 19th centuries that became known as the Scottish Enlightenment ensured the city's respected status. Political power base or not, Edinburgh is still held in high regard.

The construction of **Edinburgh's New Town** in the late 18th century, the survival in the subsequent centuries of the vast majority of the city's fine buildings and the photogenic natural advantages enjoyed by the city have guaranteed its future as a tourist destination. As a place in which to live, it is fortunate in its amenities; as a place to visit, it is manageable and can cater for all interests.

Whether pursued in the crisp darkness of winter late afternoons or in the clear, bright light of summer, the business of sightseeing, gallery-viewing, eating out, theatre-going and shopping will be time- and energy-consuming enough for even the most active visitors. Further attractions and subjects of interest related to Edinburgh are **Craigmillar Castle, Edinburgh's Villages, Edinburgh's Green Spaces, Edinburgh's Festivals, Pentland Hills, Forth Bridge, Forth Road Bridge** and **Hopetoun House.**

EDINBURGH, BUTTERFLY AND INSECT WORLD

On A7 towards Dalkeith 5m S of Edinburgh. Open mid Mar–end Oct, daily 1000–1730. D (031–663 4932).

Beside a busy garden centre, Europe's largest Butterfly and Insect World resides in hothouses which recreate rain-forest and tropical conditions. Butterflies from different parts of the world flutter around visitors as they walk past plants, waterfalls and lily ponds. Insects such as scorpions, tarantulas, stick insects and leaf-cutting ants can also be seen.

EDINBURGH, CALTON HILL
see **EDINBURGH, GREEN SPACES** panel p105.

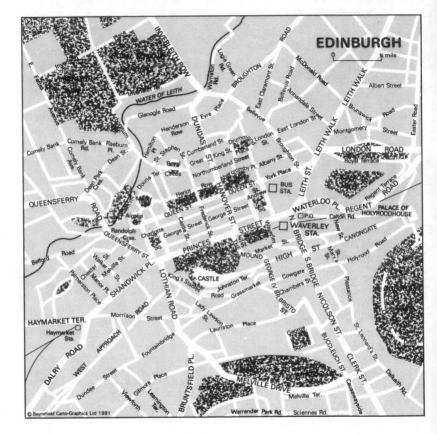

Town plan of Edinburgh

EDINBURGH, CANONGATE KIRK

On the Canongate, Royal Mile.
If closed apply to the Manse, Reid's Close,
near the church. D (031–556 3515).

Built by order of James VII in 1688 and restored in 1951, Canongate Kirk is the parish church of Canongate, indicating Canongate's one-time status as an independent burgh, and is the Kirk of Holyroodhouse and Edinburgh Castle. Its burial ground contains the graves of economist Adam Smith, of 'Clarinda', the friend/lover of Robert Burns and the grave of the poet Robert Fergusson.

EDINBURGH, EDINBURGH CASTLE

Castle Rock, top of the Royal Mile.
Apr–Sept, Mon–Sat 0930–1700, Sun
1100–1700; Oct–Mar, Mon–Sat 0930–1620,
Sun 1230–1530. D (P). HS (031–244 3101).

Undoubtedly the best-known feature of Edinburgh, the castle frowns down upon all the hustle and bustle of city life. Certainly, when you visit the castle you find a pocket of tranquillity and a fine perspective, in both senses of the word. Panoramic views across the city in all directions are perhaps the castle's finest offering, with the tiny, enchanting St Margaret's Chapel, reputedly the oldest building in Edinburgh, coming a close second. Also within the castle walls are the Scottish War Memorial, the Crown Room (the Scottish crown jewels were rediscovered after a search initiated by **Sir Walter Scott**), the Scottish United Services Museum, Queen Mary's Apartments (where **Mary Queen of Scots** gave birth to James VI, or James I of England), the handsome Old Parliament Hall, a graveyard for regimental mascot dogs and the barracks of the Royal Scots and the Royal Scots Dragoon Guards. The castle esplanade is the stage of August's Military Tattoo. Another popular castle tradition is the one o'clock gun, fired on weekdays. Edinburgh Castle is perhaps at its most magnificent at night, when even the orange glow of its floodlights cannot remove the sense of its dour, brooding bulk.

EDINBURGH, EDINBURGH ZOO

On A8 (Corstorphine Road) 4m W of city
centre. All year. Daily, summer 0900–1800,
winter 0900–1700 (or dusk if earlier), Sun
opening 0930. D (A) (031–334 9171).

Still a popular family attraction despite anti-zoo sentiment, Edinburgh Zoo places considerable emphasis on its educational role. Animal-handling classes, where children can touch and learn about small animals, brass-rubbing and a variety of animal-related activities are organized for school holidays. The zoo is Scotland's largest animal collection and houses about 2000 animals in 80 acres. Especially popular is the daily penguin parade which occurs from March to October at 2.30 pm.

EDINBURGH, FESTIVALS, see panel p102.

EDINBURGH, THE GEORGIAN HOUSE

Edinburgh's festivals

E dinburgh's biggest visitor attractions are the International Edinburgh Festival and the Edinburgh Festival Fringe. Each August, the city's population increases by over 500 000 as the world's largest arts festival moves into town. For three weeks, the city is given over to performance – in pubs, on street corners, in theatres and concert halls, on buses, in parks, in churches, in tents. Every corner provides a venue for the thousands of performers who flood to Edinburgh in search of an audience and recognition during Edinburgh Festival fever.

Just as the city is today dominated by visitors during Festival time, the first Festival of 1947 was the inspiration of outsiders. Rudolf Bing, then manager of Glyndebourne Opera, wanted to start an annual festival and first approached Oxford and Cambridge. The two cities were unenthusiastic. Encouraged by Edinburgh supporters, among them the Lord Provost, Sir John Falconer, and Harry Harvey Wood of the British Council, who rallied and assembled a powerful pool of backers, Bing's idea took shape and the Edinburgh International Festival was born. Sunshine and Italian opera, French theatre, the Vienna Philharmonic and prima ballerina Margot Fonteyn were the order of the day. In what was no doubt a flash of much-needed post-war extravagance, **Edinburgh Castle** was floodlit, by special dispensation of the Ministry of Power.

Rudolf Bing's successors as Festival directors included his assistant Ian Hunter, Robert Ponsonby, Lord Harewood, Peter Diamand, John Drummond, Frank Dunlop and, most recently, Brian MacMaster. The Edinburgh Festival Fringe also started in

(continued)

Edinburgh's festivals *(continued)*

1947, when eight theatre companies who had been excluded by the selection process of the International Festival banded together and performed anyway. The Fringe has stuck faithfully to its 'open-door' policy, welcoming all groups and individuals who wish to perform, regardless of talent. So it is that, while critics of the 'Official' Festival harp on about sliding standards, critics of the Fringe complain that there are no standards. The Fringe's administrative body, the Fringe Society, is unapologetic about its all-comers approach. The Fringe, its supporters say, is about risk-taking – financial and artistic risk-taking for performers and ticket-buying risk-taking for audiences. The Fringe, because it is fraught with pitfalls and dud shows, is full of possibilities too. It is, eulogize the fans, a perennially exciting leap into the unknown. This unknown now comprises around 1000 shows and sales of over 400 000 tickets. The Edinburgh Military Tattoo, the biennial Edinburgh Book Festival, the Television Festival, the Film Festival and the Jazz Festival jumped on to the Festival bandwagon at different stages, giving the city's arena more diversity, more colour and even more appeal.

Beyond the August jamboree, Edinburgh has added other festivals to its calendar – the Spring Fling, the Science Festival and the popular Children's Festival. By diversifying into activities which involve local people, the city's arts organizations have ensured that, for residents and for visitors, Edinburgh lives up to its title, the Festival City.

No 7 Charlotte Square. 1 Apr–31 Oct,
Mon–Sat 1000–1700, Sun 1400–1700. Last
admission 30 minutes before closing. D
(A/P). NTS (031–225 2160).

Situated in what has been described
as the most perfect Georgian square,
Charlotte Square in **Edinburgh's**
New Town, the Georgian House,
restored by the National Trust for
Scotland, recreates an Edinburgh
town house of around 1800. Interior
fittings evoke the life suggested by
the building's external appearance,
while the kitchen quarters give an
insight into below-stairs life.

EDINBURGH, GLADSTONE'S LAND

Lawnmarket, Royal Mile. 1 Apr–31 Oct,
Mon–Sat 1000–1700, Sun 1400–1700. Last
admission 30 minutes before closing. D
(A/P). NTS (031–226 5856).

Acquired by the National Trust for
Scotland in 1934 and restored as
the typical house of a 17th-century
merchant, this remarkable six-storey
tenement retains its original façade.
Completed in 1620, it was the home
of Edinburgh burgess Thomas
Gledstanes. With a narrow frontage,
cramped between its neighbours,
and like a building which is holding
its breath, the house was none the
less a prestigious and relatively
spacious Old Town home. Its
arcaded ground floor and painted
ceilings are particularly notable.

EDINBURGH, GORGIE CITY FARM PROJECT

51 Gorgie Road. All year. Daily including

public holidays 0900–1630. D. Free
(031–337 4202).

A complete contrast with many
of the sights around Edinburgh,
Gorgie City Farm is a low-key
and unpretentious centre. It is
designed for local schoolchildren
and urbanites keen to meet farm
animals. The farm inhabits 2½ acres
to the west of the city centre.

EDINBURGH'S GREEN SPACES, see panel p105.

EDINBURGH, GREYFRIARS BOBBY

Corner of George IV Bridge and
Candlemaker Row. All times. D. Free.

The small statue of Greyfriars
Bobby, the loyal Skye terrier who
watched over his master's grave in
Edinburgh's Kirk of the Greyfriars for
14 years, marks the Hollywoodized
story of man's best friend.
Paradoxically, the statue is subject to
occasional vandalistic attacks.

EDINBURGH, HILLEND SKI CENTRE

Biggar Road, S outskirts of Edinburgh.
Apr–Sept, daily 0930–2100; Oct–Mar, daily
0930–2200. D (P) (031–445 4433).

Set on the edge of the **Pentland Hills**,
the largest artificial dry ski slope
in Britain is served by a chairlift,
T-bars and tows. Tuition, boots
and ski hire are all available. The

Edinburgh's green spaces

The most central of Edinburgh's green spaces is Princes Street Gardens, which lie below **Edinburgh Castle**. Once the site of the Nor' Loch, which was drained as part of **Edinburgh's New Town** improvements, the gardens have been a guaranteed source of visual and recreational pleasure for the public since 1850. Until that time, the gardens were for the exclusive use of Princes Street residents, just as other city centre gardens such as Queen Street Gardens and Charlotte Square Gardens are today.

In spring, daffodils carpet the Princes Street Gardens slope which rises up to the castle crag; concerts are held in the sometimes canopied Ross Bandstand; street theatre, face-painting and puppet shows are commonplace during the Edinburgh Festival; the Flower Clock is a summertime crowd-puller; picnics, ice-cream vans and lunch-hour sandwiches are standard fare. Perhaps the highlight of the year is the Festival Fireworks display, when the gardens are the prime location for fireworks-viewing and the auditorium for the accompanying concert. Much-sought-after tickets provide the only access to the gardens for this event.

Smaller patches of green in the city's New Town are provided by private gardens such as those in Moray Place and Ainslie Place which are communally owned by the residents of neighbouring streets. Some, like an extensive area next to the Water of Leith, are not obvious to the eye. On the opposite, public bank is a very pleasant walkway which runs beside the river under a canopy of trees.

(continued)

Edinburgh's green spaces *(continued)*

Along with Princes Street Gardens, the Meadows, an elongated tree-edged park to the south of the city, Holyrood Park to the east, Calton Hill and the Royal Botanic Garden to the north are the most popular public recreational areas. The Meadows, much used by Edinburgh's student population, was once the South, or Borough Loch, drained in 1740. Its contemporary role is as the venue for tennis, jogging, frisbee, picnics, dog-walking, fairs and summer afternoon dozing.

Activities at Holyrood Park, reached from the bottom of the Royal Mile and formerly called the King's or Queen's Park, are much the same. Holyrood's special event is the Fringe's family fun day, when performers gather to give free tasters of their skills at a day-long jamboree. The park's main appeal is the craggy volcanic welts of Arthur's Seat and Salisbury Crags, dramatic to look at and excellent vantage points for views of the city.

Views from Calton Hill, the monument-littered mound at the east end of the city, are similarly spectacular. By contrast, the 70-acre Royal Botanic Garden provides an escape from the city. Large and leafy, the scene at the Botanic Garden is one of pram-pushing, of reading books and of lingering at duckponds. Half a million people visit the garden and its magnificent hothouses annually, returning frequently to watch the changing seasons and the changing beds and borders.

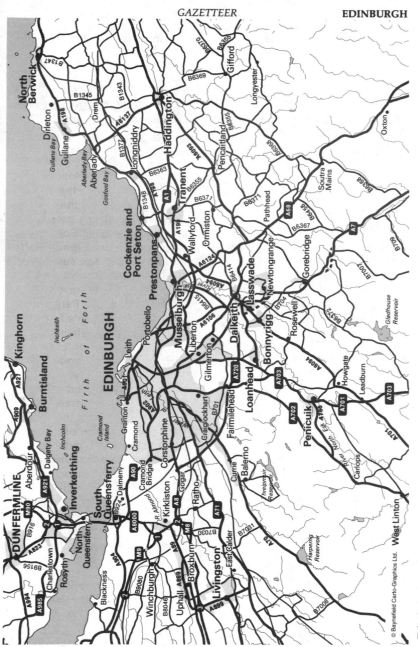

Edinburgh and environs

© Bayrefield Carto-Graphics Ltd.

chairlift can also be used by non-skiers in search of Pentland walks or views of Edinburgh.

EDINBURGH, HOLYROOD ABBEY, see EDINBURGH, PALACE OF HOLYROODHOUSE.

EDINBURGH, HUNTLY HOUSE

Canongate, Royal Mile. Jun–Sept, Mon–Sat 1000–1800; Sun during Festival 1400–1700; Oct–May, Mon–Sat 1000–1700. D (P). Free (031–225 2424 ext 6689).

This 1570 house, once the town residence of the Marquis of Huntly, is now a city museum, illustrating Edinburgh through the ages and exhibiting a collection of Edinburgh silver, glass and pottery.

EDINBURGH, KIRK OF THE GREYFRIARS

Greyfriars Place, S end of George IV Bridge. Easter–Sept, Mon–Fri 1000–1600, Sat 1000–1200. D. Free (031–225 1900).

A place of considerable interest for fans of **Greyfriars Bobby** is the grave of his master, John Gray, who died in 1858 and is buried in the churchyard. Historically, the church is of great importance for it was the place where the National Covenant was signed in 1638. In the religious struggle that followed, 1400 Covenanters were held in the churchyard in 1679. There are memorials to the Covenanting martyrs within the church walls and the graveyard contains an important collection of 17th-century monuments.

EDINBURGH, JOHN KNOX HOUSE

45 High Street, Royal Mile. All year. Mon–Sat 1000–1700. Last admission 1630. D (A) (031–556 9579/2647).

The exterior of this picturesque 15th-century house is its most charming aspect, while the interior contains an exhibition on the life of **John Knox** and a painted ceiling. It is unclear whether Knox ever lived in the house, but he is believed to have stayed there from 1561 until his death in 1572.

EDINBURGH, LADY STAIR'S HOUSE

Off Lawnmarket, Royal Mile. June–Sept, Mon–Fri 1000–1800, Sun during Festival 1400–1700; Oct–May, Mon–Fri 1000–1700; Free (031–225 2424 ext 6593).

The only surviving 17th-century building in Lady Stair's Close, the house contains a museum of relics associated with Robert Louis Stevenson, **Sir Walter Scott** and Robert Burns.

EDINBURGH, LAMB'S HOUSE

Burgess Street, Leith. By prior arrangement all year. D. Free. NTS (031–554 3131).

Near the end of **Leith**'s busy thoroughfare, Leith Walk, is Lamb's House, the restored former residence and warehouse of a prosperous merchant of the late 16th or early

17th century. It is now used as a day centre for senior citizens.

EDINBURGH, LAURISTON CASTLE

N of A90 at Cramond Road South, 4m NW of city centre. Apr–Oct, daily except Fri 1100–1300, 1400–1700; Nov–Mar, Sat–Sun 1400–1600. D (A) (031–336 2060 or 031–225 2424 ext 6678).

Held in trust by the City of Edinburgh District Council, Lauriston Castle was first built as a tower, which was considerably extended in the 1820s by William Burn. The interiors are Edwardian, the work of W.R. Reid, its last owner, who refurbished the castle in 1903.

EDINBURGH, MUSEUM OF CHILDHOOD

38 High Street. All year. Mon–Sat 1000–1700, until 1800 June–Sept, Sun during Festival, Sun 1400–1700. Free (031–225 2424).

Noisy and invariably bustling with children, the museum displays, behind glass, several antique and old toys arranged in themes. The mass of colour and the reminders of well-worn or long-lost childhood friends prove irresistible to all ages.

EDINBURGH'S NEW TOWN,
see panel p110.

EDINBURGH'S OLD TOWN,
see panel p112.

EDINBURGH, OUTLOOK TOWER AND CAMERA OBSCURA

Castle Hill, between the Castle and Lawnmarket. Apr–Oct, Mon–Fri 0930–1730, Sat–Sun 1000–1800; Nov–Mar, Mon–Fri 0930–1700, Sat–Sun 1030–1630. Last admission 45 minutes before closing.

The white turret of the Camera Obscura stands on top of the Outlook Tower next to the castle esplanade. Over 100 years old, the Victorian optical device still gives visitors a revolving, living picture of Edinburgh, projected via a sort of periscopic action on to a viewing table.

EDINBURGH, PALACE OF HOLYROODHOUSE

Foot of the Royal Mile. Apr–Oct, Mon–Sat 0930–1715, Sun 1030–1630; Nov–Mar, Mon–Sat 0930–1545. The palace is closed during royal visits (which usually occur May to July) and for periods before and after royal visits.
D (P) (031–556 7371).

A guide leads sightseers, often at an alarmingly rapid pace, through selected rooms and state apartments of the palace (rebuilt in its present form between 1671 and 1680) which is the Queen's official residence in Scotland. You are taken past paintings (portraits of over 80 Scottish kings), tapestries and furniture, and on to the upstairs room where a supposed blot of blood on the floor marks the place where Riccio, **Mary Queen of Scots'** secretary, was murdered. The guide's narration tells of the palace's history, of the brief but

Edinburgh's New Town

Between 1760 and 1840, Edinburgh's elegant neo-classical New Town was conceived and constructed. Until that time, the medieval, cramped **Old Town** had been home for the people of Edinburgh.

In 1767, architects were invited to enter a competition to design 'a New Town marking out streets of a proper breadth, and bylanes and the best situation for a reservoir, and any other public buildings which may be thought necessary'. The site was to be fields to the north of the Old Town, across the Nor' Loch, which lay below the Old Town ridge (now Princes Street Gardens).

The competition was won by 23-year-old James Craig (1744–95). His design, a simple grid-iron system of wide avenues, was based on the parallel streets of Princes Street, George Street (with the counterbalances of Charlotte Square and St Andrew Square) and Queen Street. The well-to-do inhabitants of these new streets, which ran at different levels, would be assured a spacious environment and, in some cases, fine views – of **Edinburgh Castle** from Princes Street, and of the **Firth of Forth** from Queen Street and from points on George Street.

Today, Princes Street and George Street are busy shopping streets, the former (whose façades have been considerably corrupted) being host to chain stores and mainstream shops, the latter offering more exclusive, rather genteel shopping. Few people now live in the buildings that line the three streets: offices have supplanted residents, although there are still fine flats in Queen Street.

The residential areas of the New Town are mostly north of

(continued)

Edinburgh's New Town *(continued)*

Queen Street. Wide cobbled streets, tall honey sandstone houses, leafy communal gardens and an impressive residential alumni list have ensured that many New Town addresses (Heriot Row, Moray Place) carry with them enormous prestige. Recently, several of these residential streets have been bollarded off to stop through traffic.

James Craig was by no means responsible for all of the New Town; to his section, Robert Reid and William Sibbald added the second, parallel New Town, descending to the north: Great King Street, Drummond Place and Royal Circus. To the west of these, James Gillespie Graham devised a third New Town in the 1820s, heavily using crescents and circles.

As well as these three phases, additions were designed by W.H. Playfair (Calton Hill terraces) and James Milne (Stockbridge). The north side of the highly prestigious Charlotte Square was the design of **Robert Adam**, who also gave Edinburgh some of its most notable public buildings, among them Register House on Princes Street.

Playfair's public buildings are on particularly prominent city centre sites. His is the Royal Scottish Academy (1826) and his too are several of the motley assortment on Calton Hill, including the unfinished replica of the Parthenon.

While the most central parts of it have enjoyed continual popularity, its outer edges have been less loved, but in recent years, the New Town has been revitalized. Now, all New Town buildings are being scrubbed free of Victorian soot and are being restored to their former grandeur.

Edinburgh's Old Town

'Time has piled up the Old Town, ridge on ridge, grey as a rocky coast washed and worn by the foam of centuries; peaked and jagged by gable and roof ... The New [Town] is there looking at the Old ... There is nothing in Europe to match that, I think,' eulogized the 19th-century poet Alexander Smith. Edinburgh's Old Town, so prominent and such a contrast to **Edinburgh's New Town**, invariably begs comment.

In 1769 the Welsh writer Thomas Pennant wondered at its extraordinarily cramped nature. He concluded that the shoulder-to-shoulder sardine houses of the Old Town had evolved 'on a principle of security', as the buildings squeezed as close as they could to the protection of **Edinburgh Castle**. Until recently, many parts of the Old Town were in a dilapidated, ruinous state. This led the poet Edwin Muir to write of the Canongate as 'a mouldering obnoxious ruin'.

Before the construction of the New Town, late medieval Edinburgh, squashed on to the spine of rock running down from the castle, was a heady social mishmash. Judges, shopkeepers and prostitutes lived side by side, enjoyed a not inelegant, decidedly democratic environment.

After the wholesale departure (called 'the Great Flitting') from the Old Town of the wealthy and the aristocratic to the New Town from 1760 onwards, the former became the run-down domain of the poor and of impoverished immigrants. Two centuries of neglect are now being rectified and the 17th- century tenements,

(continued)

Edinburgh's Old Town *(continued)*

revamped and cleaned up, are proving to be desirable city centre homes once again.

Along the spine of rock which is topped by the castle and tailed by the **Palace of Holyroodhouse** is the Royal Mile, a thoroughfare which confusingly consists of named sections: Castlehill, Lawnmarket, the High Street and the Canongate. The Royal Mile has within its length all the features that a visitor might look for in any city – theatre, galleries, specialist shops, restaurants and a number of attractions. Among the latter, **Parliament House**, **Gladstone's Land**, a restored 17th-century tenement, the **Camera Obscura**, **Lady Stair's House** and the **Museum of Childhood** cater for a wide variety of interests.

A number of walking tours, some of them after dark, traverse the Old Town, guiding the hapless up the narrow, badly-lit wynds and closes that lead off the Royal Mile. In these alleyways, you will hear tales of murder and dark doings, of the Old Town's long-dead criminal element (**Burke and Hare**, Deacon Brodie, the inspiration for Robert Louis Stevenson's *The Strange Case of Dr Jekyll and Mr Hyde*).

This is perhaps the greatest charm of the Old Town – here, for centuries, the colourful morass of humanity has lived, worked and played. Unlike the pristine New Town, where everything has always been done behind closed doors, the Old Town has traditionally bared all.

eventful six years Mary spent here, of Cromwell's occupation in 1650, of Bonnie Prince Charlie's six-week court at the palace in 1745, of visits and sojourns by most members of the British royal family from Victoria onwards. The tour of the palace completed, visitors find themselves let loose in the pleasant grounds, to discover the ruins of the abbey, against which the oldest part of the palace is built. The abbey was founded by David I in 1128. During the 15th century the abbey was used as the court of James I, II and III. David II, James II, James V and Darnley, **Mary Queen of Scots'** second husband, were buried here. The abbey was desecrated in 1688 and their bodies were moved to the royal vault.

EDINBURGH, PARLIAMENT HOUSE

Parliament Square, behind the High Kirk of St Giles, Royal Mile. All year. Tue–Fri 1000–1600. D (P). Free (031–225 2595).

Built between 1632 and 1639, this was the seat of the Scottish parliament from 1639 until the Act of Union in 1707. It now houses the supreme law courts of Scotland. Parliament Hall, where bewigged advocates warm themselves at the coal fire in winter months, is of particular interest because of its hammer-beam roof. In the square beside Parliament House is **St Giles Cathedral**.

EDINBURGH, ROYAL BOTANIC GARDENS see

EDINBURGH'S GREEN SPACES panel p105.

EDINBURGH, ROYAL OBSERVATORY

Blackford Hill. All year. Mon–Fri 1000–1600, Sat–Sun and public holidays 1200–1700. D (P) (031–668 8405).

Scotland's largest telescope resides in the Royal Observatory on the south side of Edinburgh. The fine views from the public park on Blackford Hill add to the merits of the observatory, which has a visitor centre with space displays, an astronomy shop and photographs relating to the observatory's work in Hawaii, the Canary Islands and Australia.

EDINBURGH, ST GILES HIGH KIRK

On the Royal Mile. All year. Mon–Sat 0900–1700 (1900 in summer), Sun (pm). D (A). Free (031–225 4363).

The High Kirk of Edinburgh, St Giles, stands next to **Parliament House**. Many additions were made to it and a considerable number of alterations, including a refacing of the exterior in the 19th century. The tower or crown spire which dominates the building is late 15th century. Among the points of interest inside the church are marble monuments, the Thistle Chapel (built in 1910), the royal pew, the burial place of the Marquess of Montrose (who was a Covenanter campaign leader turned Royalist) and a relief of Robert Louis

Stevenson. The cobbled area to the front of St Giles features a heart shape, which marks the site of the old Tolbooth, or town prison, made famous by **Sir Walter Scott** in *The Heart of Midlothian*.

EDINBURGH, ST MARY'S CATHEDRAL

Palmerston Place, West End. D (A) (031–225 6293).

Recently cleaned, repaired and floodlit as part of a project to illuminate many of Edinburgh's major buildings, the three-towered St Mary's dominates the west end of Edinburgh's fine Melville Street. Building started on the Sir Gilbert Scott design in 1874, but work was not completed until 1917. The grass apron fronting the neighbouring choir school and some deciduous trees add a welcome touch of vegetation to the otherwise stern, imposing aspect of the cathedral.

EDINBURGH, SCOTCH WHISKY HERITAGE CENTRE

358 Castlehill, the Royal Mile. All year. 1 June–30 Sept, 0900–1830; 1 Oct–31 May, 1000–1700. D (031–220 0441).

Visitors are invited to take a seat in a whisky barrel to journey through a display which describes (in a choice of seven languages) the turbulent history of whisky in sight, sound and smell. Robert Burns (or his model) reads his lament on the closure of his favourite distillery; smugglers flee the excisemen and a scientist labours over attempts to advance whisky-making technology.

The whisky-making regions, a model of a Speyside distillery and a blender's laboratory are also featured in the centre.

EDINBURGH, SCOTT MONUMENT

Princes Street. Apr–Sept, Mon–Sat 0900–1800; Oct–Mar, Mon–Sat 0900–1500.

The pinnacled, neo-Gothic spire which strikes skyward at the eastern end of Princes Street was funded by public donation following an appeal after **Sir Walter Scott**'s death in 1832. Erected between 1840 and 1844, the 200-foot structure was designed by George Meikle Kemp, who did not live to see its completion. A marble statue of Scott and Maida (his dog) is accompanied by niches filled with statuettes of over 60 of his fictional characters, and the busts of 16 Scottish poets. Fit members of the public can climb the long, narrow staircase (287 steps) to the top of the monument for fine views of the city.

EDINBURGH VILLAGES, see panel p116.

EDINBURGH, WATER OF LEITH

A programme of repair, path building and scrub clearing has resulted in a pleasant walkway which can be joined at various points throughout the city. The narrow ribbon of a river which rises in the **Pentlands** once provided paper mills, corn mills and snuff

Edinburgh villages and suburbs

Stockbridge, the Dean Village, Cramond Village, **Leith**, Swanston, **Portobello**, Colinton, Juniper Green, Duddingston Village, Morningside and Corstorphine are just a handful of the villages and separate settlements which have now been largely subsumed by the general sprawl of the city of Edinburgh. Once quite distinct geographically (the Dean Village was surrounded by fields) or politically (Leith was an independent royal burgh), they are now often reduced to a suburban role.

But their inhabitants would argue otherwise. Most villages, they would say, have retained their own identity. Many have their own busy main streets, with a full complement of shops and facilities. Some have become fashionable, while others are merely functional, just pied-à-terres for city workers.

If typecasting and generalizing are evidence of a distinct local identity, Edinburgh in-jokes are often about the specific sorts of people that inhabit the different villages. Morningside is reputed to be full of well-heeled, slightly superior retired couples (especially ladies); Stockbridge is for young professionals; and Colinton is for middle-of-the-road families.

Tired clichés may not convince, but the existence of an extraordinary number of local amenity groups must. The architectural and historical merits of these Edinburgh settlements are protected by a range of self-appointed groups. Every village has one: the Duddingston Preservation Society, the Corstorphine Trust and the

(continued)

Edinburgh villages *(continued)*

Dean Village Association are among them. Such bodies are very much committed to their local environment and, like small-town church committees, they voluntarily undertake a variety of tasks from organizing fetes to campaigning against proposed building developments.

Colinton, the Dean Village and Stockbridge are threaded together by the Water of Leith. The Dean Village, a conservation rag-bag area of 800-year-old, Georgian, Victorian and late 20th-century buildings has in its oldest stone part, below the Dean Bridge, a picturesque, cobbled street charm. Its newer parts, built on the sites of a skinnery and a distillery, are, like Corstorphine's and Colinton's, less appealing.

The walkway beside the Water of Leith leads from the Dean Village to Stockbridge, a busy shopping centre coupled with elegant Georgian homes, and the Stockbridge Colonies, rows of tiny back-to-back Victorian terraced houses.

Cramond, pretty but under the flight path of Edinburgh airport, lies on the north-western outskirts of Edinburgh on the **Firth of Forth**. Duddingston, the cramped but endearing village beside Arthur's Seat, evinces the olde worlde village atmosphere.

Different in almost every other way, the villages share one thing: their inhabitants think that they are the best places in Edinburgh in which to live.

mills with water, becoming as a result severely polluted. Efforts have been made in recent years to clean the water, and anglers can now often be seen trying for trout. In some stretches the Water of Leith is still used as a dumping ground: supermarket trolleys and traffic cones are fished from the river bed from time to time. A particularly pleasant walk runs from the Dean Village to Stockbridge (see **Edinburgh Villages** and **Edinburgh's Green Spaces**).

EDIN'S HALL BROCH
near Duns, Borders

On the NE slope of Cockburn Law, off A6112 4m N of Duns. All times. D. Free. HS (031–244 3101).

A mile's walk takes you to this large Iron Age broch, unusual for Lowland Scotland, which was inhabited during Roman times too.

EDRADOUR DISTILLERY
near Pitlochry, Tayside

On unclassified road 2½m E of Pitlochry. Mid Mar–Oct, daily 0930–1700; Nov–mid Mar Sat 1000–1600 (shop only). Otherwise this by prior arrangement. D (P) (0796 2095).

Established in 1825, this is Scotland's smallest whisky distillery. In the hills above **Pitlochry**, a single-track road takes you to a cluster of low white-washed buildings, surrounded by pleasant gardens, from which comes a 'handcrafted malt'. The distillery's copper vats are the smallest allowed under excise regulations.

EDROM NORMAN ARCH
near Duns, Borders

Off A6105 3m NE of Duns. All reasonable times. Free. HS (031–244 3101).

The richly carved, early 12th-century doorway of the old Edrom parish church now stands behind the current church.

EDZELL CASTLE
Edzell, Tayside

Off B966 6m N of Brechin, 1m W of Edzell. Apr–Sept, Mon–Sat 0930–1900, Sun 1400–1900; Oct–Mar, Mon–Sat 0930–1600, Sun 1400–1600 except closed Tues am and Thurs am D (P). HS (031–244 3101).

The ruined castle (dating from the early 16th century) was incorporated into a large courtyard mansion of 1580. Most celebrated at Edzell is the pleasance, or walled garden, complete with bath-house and summer-house, which was created by Sir David Lindsay in 1604. The carved decorations on the garden walls are unique in Britain.

EILDON HILLS
Borders

The strange lumpy hills (from 1216 feet to 1385 feet) which rise above **Melrose** are in fact one hill with three peaks. Formed by lava pushed up through the ground from volcanoes a mile north-west of them, the Eildons alone in the area managed to survive the flattening effect of glaciers. Their prominence on the landscape can be best seen from **Scott's View**. The Eildons are the site of the largest Roman camp

in southern Scotland, Trimontium.
Often climbed by **Sir Walter Scott**,
a granite block giving details of the
view on the Mid Hill is dedicated
to him.

ELCHO CASTLE
near Perth, Tayside

On River Tay 3m SE of Perth.
Apr–Sept, Mon–Sat 0930–1900, Sun
1400–1900. D (P). HS (031–244 3101).

Sitting beside the **River Tay**, Elcho
Castle is a handsome and complete
16th-century fortified mansion.
Its four projecting towers and
the wrought-iron grilles over the
windows, which are original, are of
particular interest.

ELIE
Fife

On A917 S of St Andrews.

A pleasant seaside resort with good
sands which are popular with
Edinburgh residents, the traditional
fishing village of Elie also tempts
rock-hunters, for garnets have been
found on its beach in the past.

ETTRICK
Borders

Off B709 28m SW of Selkirk.

Famed as the home of James Hogg
(1770–1835) (also dubbed the Ettrick
Shepherd), poet and protégé of **Sir
Walter Scott**, Ettrick remembers its
son with a monument on the site of
his birthplace. Hogg's grave lies in
the churchyard.

EYEMOUTH
Borders

Off A1107 8m N of Berwick-upon-Tweed.

Eyemouth is a small, working
fishing harbour and summer resort
which lies at the estuary of the Eye
Water. A crescent of pale mandarin
sand, some lovely traditional
houses and the red sandstone
headland make the village extremely
picturesque. Hotels and pubs
called the Contented Sole and the
Whale Hotel and a local museum
emphasize Eyemouth's long fishing
heritage. The museum's centrepiece
is the Eyemouth Tapestry,
made by local people in 1981 to
commemorate the terrible disaster of
1881 when 189 Eyemouth fishermen
were drowned within sight of
the land.

FAIRWAYS HEAVY HORSE CENTRE
near Perth, Tayside

Walnut Grove, by Perth, 2m E of Perth, off A85. All year. Daily 1000–1800. D. Free (0738 32561/25931).

A working and breeding centre for Clydesdale horses where visitors can simply watch the Roman-nosed horses (mares, stallions and foals) or can ride in a Clydesdale-drawn wagon. There are also videos which show the horses at work and being shod.

FALKLAND
Fife

On A912 11m N of Kirkcaldy.

At the foot of the Lomond Hills, the picturesque village of Falkland, made a royal burgh in 1458, has been carefully preserved and is a conservation area. Lintels above many of the doors of the 17th-century houses still carry the initials of the couples for whom the houses were built, as well as a heart and the date. Falkland is famed for Falkland Palace, the favourite palace and hunting grounds of the Stuart (Stewart) kings.

FALKLAND PALACE AND GARDENS
near Kirkcaldy, Fife

In Falkland. 1 Apr–31 Oct, Mon–Sat 1000–1800, Sun 1400–1800. Last admission 1700. NTS (033 757 397).

Still owned by the Queen, Falkland Palace was built between 1501 and 1541 by James IV and James V, on the site of an earlier castle which dated from the 12th century. The Stuarts used the palace as their country seat, taking full advantage of the hunting and hawking in Falkland Forest and on the Lomond Hills. Guides lead visitors on a 40-minute tour of the palace. The east range contains the king's bedchamber and the queen's room, both of which were restored by the National Trust for Scotland. The NTS manages the property. As well as herbaceous borders and a wide lawn, the garden also contains the original royal, or real, tennis court, built in 1539 for James V and the oldest in Britain.

FAST CASTLE
Coldingham, Borders

Off A1107 4m NW of Coldingham (08907 71280).

Only ruins remain of this one-time stronghold which stands stark and deserted on a crag looking out at the North Sea.

FERNIEHIRST CASTLE
near Jedburgh, Borders

1½m S of Jedburgh. May–Oct, Wed 1330–1630. D (A/P) (0835 62201).

The 16th-century Borders castle on the Jed Water is the ancestral home of the Kerr family and has recently been restored and refurbished by the Marquis of Lothian, Chief of the Kerrs. An information centre, giving details of Border families and Border history, is housed in the former stables.

FIFE FOLK MUSEUM
Ceres, Fife

At Ceres 3m SE of Cupar.
Apr–Oct, daily (except Tues) 1415–1700. D
(P) (033 482 380).

Two weavers' cottages and the
17th-century Weigh House have
been combined to form a museum
devoted to the domestic and
agricultural past of Fife.

FIRTH OF FORTH, see panel
p122.

FLOORS CASTLE
near Kelso, Borders

On B6089 2m NW of Kelso. Castle and
grounds open Easter–Oct: Apr–June, Sept,
Sun–Thur, 1030–1700; July–Aug, daily,
1030–1700; Oct, Sun and Wed, 1030–1600.
D (P) (0573 23333).

Bold wrought-iron gates lead up
to the 1721 William **Adam** mansion,
built for the 1st Duke of Roxburghe,
which was altered in 1839–1840
by William Playfair. Among the
mansion's internal curiosities,
alongside the more usual sitting
rooms and drawing rooms is a bird
room, designed by Playfair to house
a collection of stuffed birds. Of
particular note is the mansion's roof
– a mêlée of chimneys, battlements,
turrets and cupolas. A holly tree
in the grounds is said to mark the
place where James II was killed in
1460 when a cannon misfired.

FORFAR
Tayside

Off A94 14m N of Dundee.

Lying on flat ground between the
lochs of Forfar and Fithie, Forfar is
a busy town given some old-world
charm by a number of narrow,
cobbled streets.

FORTH BRIDGE
near Edinburgh, Lothian

By South Queensferry, 10m W of
Edinburgh. D (031–331 1699).

In 1990, to mark the centenary of
the Forth Bridge, the red Victorian
cantilever structure which carries
trains northwards over the **Firth
of Forth**, a visitor centre opened
in **South Queensferry**, a massive
fireworks display was held and the
bridge was spectacularly floodlit by
Scottish Power. The Forth Bridge's
statistics are impressive: its painted
surface is the equivalent of 135
acres, it takes 49 940 gallons of paint
to redecorate, the railway track is
157 feet above the water, and the
bridge's span is just over one mile.
Behind the engineering phenomenon
of the bridge lies the human stories
of the men who worked on it,
and the men who died building it.
Perhaps the worst tale is of three
men trapped during construction
who could not be freed. To put them
out of their misery, they were fed
poison and the bridge's structure
became their tomb.

FORTH ROAD BRIDGE
near Edinburgh, Lothian

By South Queensferry, 10m W of
Edinburgh. D (031–331 1699).

The modern road counterpart of
the **Forth Bridge** was opened by
the Queen in 1964. A toll bridge,

The Firth of Forth

On a warm summer evening, motorists crossing the **Forth Road Bridge** will see below them the broad spectrum of water-borne Firth of Forth life. White sails billow in the notorious wind as **Edinburgh's** yachters tack and turn about; waterskiers slice through the waves; an oil tanker may be loading at Hound Point in the middle of the firth; a pleasure-boat cruises towards one of the islands, **Inchcolm** or Inchkeith. The odd fishing trawler might be a speck on the seaward horizon, travelling perhaps from one of the Firth of Forth harbours – Granton, Newhaven, **Portobello**, Fisherrow, **Cockenzie**, Port Seton or **Prestonpans** – where the fishing industry, if it survives at all, hangs on by its fingernails. Another decline, mourned by some and celebrated by others, is that of Rosyth Naval Dockyards, once the safe haven of the many sleek but ominous navy frigates which entered the Firth of Forth.

Maritime life as a whole has dwindled in the area. **Leith**, on the southern shore of the estuary, was once the thriving port for Edinburgh. Whalers frequented Leith; ships docked with loads of grain, timber, wine and building material and left with cargoes of coal, salt, fish, paper and ale. Today, the shipping industry and its support services (engineering works, repair yards, drydocks) are all but gone.

As elsewhere, the tourist industry has been replacing traditional ones. The Firth of Forth laps several sandy beaches, **Aberdour** being one of the most popular. There are numerous visitor attractions: **Blackness Castle**, Bo'ness and Kinneil Railway and **Dalmeny House**. The three large Firth of Forth bridges are magnets in themselves. People come to see Kincardine Bridge, with its once record-holding 364-foot-long swing section which is now shut fast. The **Forth Bridge**, which celebrated its centenary in 1990 and was floodlit for the occasion, is one of the most familiar images in the world. The **Forth Road Bridge**, one of the longest suspension bridges in Europe, commands excellent if gusty views down the Forth estuary. It made the ferry between **South Queensferry** and **North Queensferry** redundant in 1964.

Many visitors to Edinburgh remain unaware, and Edinburgh citizens often forget, that the city is a coastal one, with nearby beaches, fishing and watersports at its disposal. Warmer weather might help, but the hardy waterskiers under the bridges at South Queensferry seem unperturbed.

it is 1½ miles long, it bears road carriageways, cycle paths and footpaths, the towers which carry the suspension cables are 512 feet high, while the cables themselves consist of 12 000 galvanized high-tensile steel wires. When the Forth Road Bridge opened, it was the largest suspension bridge in Europe. Today, although an incredible piece of engineering and a fine sight on the skyline from many points in Edinburgh, the bridge can be a frustrating bottleneck for commuters during the rush hour. Plans have been afoot to build another road bridge over the Forth for some time, although the siting remains under discussion.

FORTINGALL
Tayside

Off A827 9m W of Aberfeldy.

A pleasant village near the foot of the lovely **Glen Lyon**, Fortingall consists of not much more than a roadside of pretty thatched-roof houses, a hotel and a church. The famed Fortingall yew, reputed to be over 3000 years old and the oldest living tree in Europe, grows beside the church, propped up with supports and walled in for its own protection. Rumour has it that Pontius Pilate was born in a Pictish fort above the village, the son of a Pictish woman and a Roman legionary, and that he later returned to die here.

GALASHIELS
Borders

On A7 34m S of Edinburgh.

A hub of the textile industry in the Borders, and the home of the renowned Scottish College of Textiles, Galashiels is a mishmash of warehouses, car showrooms and older steel-grey stone buildings. Visually compromised by interloping flat-roofed, red or yellow brick modern buildings, the town is far less appealing than its Borders neighbours. Housing estates climb up a hillside in unremitting ranks, and not even the town's location in a valley crease beside the Gala Water can save Galashiels from an impression of industrial greyness. There are, however, a number of tourist attractions related to the textile industry, including the **Peter Anderson Woollen Mill** and the **Borders Wool Centre**. Nearby is **Torwoodlee House**. The town's unusual motto 'Soure Plums' recalls the deaths of some English soldiers in a Border foray of 1337 after gathering plums.

GIFFORD
Lothian

On B6355 4m S of Haddington.

Gifford is a neat, planned 17th- and 18th-century village, now a conservation area and a commuter village for Edinburgh, which was built around Yester House. A plaque in **Yester Parish Church** commemorates the birth of the Reverend John Witherspoon in 1723, one of the signatories of the American Declaration of Independence.

GLAMIS
Tayside

Near junction of A94 and A928 10m N of Dundee.

The pleasant village of Glamis (pronounced 'Glahms') is best known for **Glamis Castle**, but it has much to recommend it in its own right, including the Angus Folk Museum which is housed inside a row of single-storey 17th-century cottages.

GLAMIS CASTLE
Glamis, Tayside

On A94 5m SW of Forfar. Easter, mid Apr–mid Oct, daily 1200–1730, other times by prior arrangement. D (P) (030 784 242).

Glamis Castle was the childhood home of the Queen Mother and the birthplace of Princess Margaret. The building dates from 1675 to 1687, although sections of it are much older. The architectural extravagance and the considerable size of the castle, combined with the added spice of legend – Shakespeare's Macbeth was the Thane of Glamis – and a ghost, make Glamis a popular castle to visit. Its setting against the backdrop of the Grampian Mountains is also particularly fine. Guided tours lead visitors through the castle, which is the family home of the Earls of Strathmore and Kinghorne. A self-service restaurant, a garden produce shop and a gallery are also within the grounds.

GLENEAGLES
Tayside

Off A9 15m SW of Perth.

Gleneagles, home of the renowned Gleneagles Hotel, whose ever-expanding luxury leisure facilities now include a prestigious golf course, a riding school and a shooting range, draws its name from the glen in which it sits.

GLENGOULANDIE DEER PARK
near Aberfeldy, Tayside

On B846 9m NW of Aberfeldy.
Daily 0900 to 1 hour before sunset. D (A/P) (08873 261/306).

One of the places in this area where you can see shaggy auburn Highland cattle, as well as red deer, out on the hills. The red deer are farmed. There is also a caravan park here.

GLEN LYON
Tayside

Off A827 12m W of Aberfeldy.

The beautiful Glen Lyon, said to be the longest glen in Scotland, is dotted with wild primroses in spring and glows with russets and auburns in autumn. The narrow road which twists up the glen from **Fortingall** passes MacGregor's Leap, an impossibly wide jump across the River Lyon made by a MacGregor trying to escape the Campbells, and the so-called Roman Bridge before arriving at Bridge of Balgie and a single-track road which climbs up the back of **Ben Lawers**. Further up Glen Lyon is the bleak Loch Lyon and a hydro-electric dam.

GLENROTHES
Fife

On A92 5m N of Kirkcaldy.

A Scottish 'new town', built to serve collieries that never materialized, Glenrothes boasts, like a fitted kitchen, all mod cons. The town's Kingdom Centre is one of Europe's largest shopping malls, and there are various 1960s buildings which are of some architectural interest: St Columba's Church (by Wheeler and Sproson), St Paul's Church and the High School. Several pieces of sculpture – the result of appointing an artist in 1968 to contribute to the environment – dot the town.

GLENTURRET DISTILLERY
near Crieff, Tayside

Off A85 5m W of Crieff. Mar–Dec, Mon–Sat 0930–1630. D (P) (0764 2424).

The Glenturret Distillery is Scotland's oldest distillery. Its visitor centre incorporates an audio-visual display, a museum, a souvenir shop, two restaurants and a whisky-tasting bar. Guided tours explain the whisky-making process.

GOLF, see panel p126.

GOSFORD HOUSE
Longniddry, Lothian

Off A198 15m E of Edinburgh.
June and Jul, Wed, Sat and Sun 1400–1700. D (A/P) (08757 201).

Golf

G olf in Scotland is not the exclusive sport it often is in in other countries. From its fabled, probably fictional, beginning when a Scottish shepherd hit a stone into a rabbit hole with his stick and then tried it again, to the present day, it has remained a democratic sport, open to all-comers. Novices, experts, children and adults can all take advantage of the inexpensive municipal courses present in almost every town.

Scotland has 400 courses – more, pro rata with the population, than in any other country in the world. There are the famous ones – Muirfield, **Carnoustie**, **St Andrews** Old Course, Royal Troon, Turnberry – of which Carnoustie and St Andrews are municipal courses. Other big names are more exclusive and may be owned by private interests and managed as clubs.

A large number of club and public courses in Scotland are links courses – a Scottish phenomenon. These courses are laid on the strip of sandy, undulating terrain which lies between the beach and sea and the firmer inland ground. As a result, Scottish golf is often portrayed as a breezy pastime for the hardy, with sea gusts hindering shots and reddening cheeks.

Along the north shore of the **Firth of Forth** is a reputable string of Fife coastal courses – **Elie**, Leven, Lundin Links and **Crail** – which concludes with St Andrews Old Course. Although the Royal and Ancient Golf Club of St Andrews is acclaimed as the true home of golf, it is in fact superseded in age by the Honourable Company of Edinburgh Golfers, which was formed in 1744 and is supposedly the oldest golf club in the world. This club plays at Muirfield Course, **Gullane**. Reflecting their golfing history, both St Andrews (**St Andrews, British Golf Museum**) and Gullane (**The Heritage of Golf**) have museums and displays.

Tayside inland courses much enjoyed by the golfing cognoscenti include Carnoustie, one the British Open courses, the King's at **Gleneagles** and the Rosemount course at **Blairgowrie**. None the less, when visitors think golf, they invariably think St Andrews. For St Andrews has long been the golfing city, a reputation of which Robert F. Murray (1863–94) in 'The City of Golf' was scornful:

> Would you like to see a city given over,
> Soul and body, to a tyrannising game?
> If you would, there's little need to be a rover,
> For St Andrews is the abject city's name.

The central part of the mansion, which sits beside the **Firth of Forth**, was designed by **Robert Adam** in 1800. Ninety years later, the north and south wings were added by architect William Young. The centrepiece of his work is the marble hall in the south wing. The grounds of the house include ornamental waters.

GREAT SCOTS VISITOR CENTRE
Auchterarder, Tayside

Abbey Road, Auchterarder.
Easter–June, daily 1300–1700; July–Oct, Mon–Sat 1000–1700, Sun 1300–1700. D (0764 62079).

The centre combines a weaving display and Scotland's last steam-powered factory machine with local history, the story of Scotland told by computerized lighting and a mill shop.

GREENKNOWE TOWER
near Kelso, Borders

On A6089 9m NW of Kelso. Apr–Sept, Mon–Sat 0930–1900, Sun 1400–1900; Oct–Mar, Mon–Sat 0930–1600, Sun 1400–1600. Free. HS (031–244 3101).

Built in 1581, Greenknowe is an L-plan tower, still retaining its iron gate and turrets.

GREENLAW
Borders

On A697 8m N of Kelso.

Originally situated on a low green hill (law) from which the town takes its name, Greenlaw lies on the Blackadder Water in the foothills of the **Lammermuirs**. The ruined 13th-century Hume Castle sits two miles south of the town.

GULLANE
Lothian

On A198 14m E of Edinburgh.

A well-heeled commuter town for Edinburgh, Gullane (pronounced 'Gillan' by those in the know) is also popular with beach-goers in summer because of its fine sands. It boasts several golf courses, chief among them the championship Muirfield course, home of the Honourable Company of Edinburgh Golfers, to the north-east of the town. The **Heritage of Golf** exhibition is in Gullane.

HADDINGTON
Lothian

Off A1 16m E of Edinburgh.

A handsome town beside the River Tyne, Haddington is dominated by the fine red sandstone **St Mary's Collegiate Church** in its pleasant riverside setting. Haddington, negotiated via dignified 17th- to 19th-century streets, has been the site of a settlement since at least the 12th century. It was the birthplace of Alexander II and it is believed that **John Knox** was born here too – he was educated at a local school. The town flourished during the 18th century, when it, as an agricultural market town, benefited from the success of East Lothian farming. Places of interest in and around Haddington include **Hailes Castle, St Mary's Pleasance, Lennoxlove House, Traprain Law** and **Stevenson House**.

HAILES CASTLE
near Haddington, Lothian

Off A1 5m E of Haddington.
D (A). HS (031–244 3101).

The dramatic aspect of the ruined Hailes Castle, as it sits upon a rock and grass knoll above the River Tyne, makes it a popular Sunday excursion. Of the remaining sections, which date from the 13th to the 15th centuries, perhaps the most disturbing is the gloomy pit prison.

HALLIWELL'S HOUSE MUSEUM AND GALLERY
Selkirk, Borders

In Selkirk town centre. Apr–Oct, Mon–Sat 1000–1700, Sun 1400–1600; Jul–Aug daily till 1800; Nov–Dec, daily 1400–1600. D (P). Free (0750 20096/20054).

A row of 18th-century houses has been renovated and refurbished to house a local history museum with a gallery and a video. The buildings' former connections with the ironmongery trade have been used in the refurbishment.

HAWICK
Borders

On A7 42m S of Edinburgh.

The largest Border town and the self-dubbed 'home of knitwear', Hawick's honey sandstone buildings give some elegance to the contrary mixture of small clothes boutiques and derelict warehouses. Still an important textile manufacturing centre, Hawick is also an agricultural market town and a shopping centre. The monument in Hawick (pronounced 'Hoik') High Street commemorates the capturing of a banner by local youths from the English in 1514, an event which is remembered in Hawick's **Common Riding**. Local attractions include the **Hawick Museum** and **Hermitage Castle**.

HAWICK MUSEUM
Hawick, Borders

In Wilton Lodge Park, on western outskirts of Hawick. Apr–Sept, Mon–Sat 1000–1200 and 1300– 1700, Sun 1400–1700; Oct–Mar, Mon–Fri 1300–1600, Sun 1400–1600. D (A/P) (0450 73457).

As well as the former estate house which now acts as a local history museum, art gallery and a natural history museum, the 107 acres of Wilton Lodge Park also contain gardens, greenhouses, playing fields, riverside walks and a café.

HERITAGE OF GOLF
Gullane, Lothian

West Links Road, Gullane
Open by appointment. D. Free
(08757 277).

Set up by Archie Baird, local golfer and collector, this **golf** museum explains the development of golf in Scotland (while attributing its origins to Holland) and has displays on the methods of the early makers of golf equipment.

THE HERMITAGE
near Dunkeld, Tayside

Off A9 2m W of Dunkeld. All reasonable times. D. NTS (0796 3233 or 03502 667).

A looped walking trail leads visitors beside the River Braan and through a lush area of mixed woodland, which has as its centrepiece a 1758 folly called the Hermitage or Ossian's Hall. A second folly, called Ossian's Cave, has been built around a natural formation of rocks. What is reputed to be the tallest tree in Britain, a 200-foot Douglas fir, can also be seen on the trail.

HERMITAGE CASTLE
Liddesdale, Borders

Off B6399 in Liddesdale, 5½m NE of Newcastleton. Apr–Sept, Mon–Sat 0930–1900, Sun 1400–1900; weekends only in winter. D (P). HS (031–244 3101).

A vast and eerie ruin, the 13th-century Hermitage Castle was the stronghold of the de Soulis family and subsequently of the Douglases. The castle walls and the four towers are almost complete, restored in part in the 19th century. It was to this dour castle, lying on moorland beside the Hermitage Water, that **Mary Queen of Scots** travelled from **Jedburgh** to visit the wounded Bothwell in 1566.

HIGHLAND LINE, see panel p130.

HIGHLAND MOTOR HERITAGE CENTRE
near Perth, Tayside

Off A9 at Bankfoot 6m N of Perth. Mon–Fri 0830–2030, Sat 0830–2300; Nov–Easter, Mon–Fri 0930–2030, Sat–Sun 1000–1800. D (0738 87696).

Classic and vintage cars, historic costumes and motoring memorabilia have as their backdrop period settings. Motor heritage videos and the ubiquitous shop and restaurant are also part of the centre.

HILLEND SKI CENTRE, see **EDINBURGH.**

HILL OF TARVIT
near Cupar, Fife

On A916 2m S of Cupar. House: Easter weekend and Apr, Sat–Sun 1400–1800; 1 May–30 Sept, daily 1400–1800.

The Highland line

A relief map of Scotland reinforces what you can clearly see from the ground – that the country is geologically split in several places. One of these divisions, slicing across from Bute through Helensburgh in the west towards Stonehaven in the north-east, is the Highland Line, a fault or geological fracture. The geological and physical significance of its mountainous wall is paralleled by a cultural boundary – the Highland Line is often perceived as the traditional dividing line between Lowland Scotland of the south and Highland Scotland of the north.

In popular mythology and in visual representation, 'Highland' usually means mountains swathed in mist, tartan and bagpipes. The Southern Highlands, which lie in the most northerly section covered by this book, do meet the familiar Highland criteria. In geological jargon, the area of clear-eyed lochs and craggy mountains is primarily comprised of Dalradian rocks, a hotchpotch of gneiss, granite, sandstone, schist, limestone, shale, quartzite and serpentine.

Geologists would point out other particulars of the Southern and Central Highland scenery. A very evident one is the 'U'-shaped glens or valleys, which were carved by glaciers during the Ice Age, when melting ice caused them to move through the landscape, gouging it beneath them. A classic example is the lovely **Glen Lyon** near **Fortingall**, Tayside.

Another distinctive feature, on mountain summits and long spines, is the topping of rubble – scree or schist – loosened by the violent weather extremes at high altitudes. Corries (basins or half-basins scooped out of the high sides of mountains), are a further Highland phenomenon. Much of Scotland's skiing takes place in such snow-filled corries.

The Southern Highlands are reached, along the mountainous wall of the Highland Line, by a string of towns and cities which promote themselves, quite legitimately, as 'gateways' to the Highlands. Among them are Stirling, **Dunkeld**, **Perth**, **Comrie** and **Crieff**. Of the five, Comrie is perhaps the most conscious of the Highland Line, for it stands immediately over the fault and is, as a consequence, Scotland's earthquake centre. In the innocuous-looking Highland town, which nestles in amongst rolling sheep-dotted hills, occasional (and usually mild) tremors ripple, sending shivers down spines and sizemometers jiggling.

Last admission 1730. Garden: all year, 1000–sunset. D (P). NTS (0334 53127).

Designed by Sir Robert Lorimer for Frederick Boner Sharp, art collector, this Edwardian country house features Sharp's collection of French, Chippendale and vernacular furniture, Dutch paintings, tapestries and Chinese porcelain as well as a restored Edwardian laundry, the Lorimer-designed grounds and a potting shed.

Bruce and was enlarged between 1721 and 1754 by William Adam and his son John, is the seat of the Marquesses of Linlithgow. Among the rooms visited on tours of the house are the pine-panelled library, the Bruce bedchamber, the yellow and red drawing rooms and the state dining room. The grounds, which lie on the south bank of the **Firth of Forth**, include woodland walks, deer parks and a nature trail.

THE HIRSEL
near Coldstream, Borders

On A697 immediately W of Coldstream. All year. All reasonable daylight hours. D (P) (0890 2834).

The museum, housed in farm steadings, tells of the history of the estate and of local natural history, while a craft centre includes furniture, leatherwork, pottery and weaving workshops. Visitors can also walk in the grounds of Hirsel House (not open to the public) and through the rhododendron wood.

HOUSE OF THE BINNS
near Linlithgow, Lothian

Off A904 4m E of Linlithgow. Easter, Sat–Mon and 1 May–Sept, Sat–Thurs 1400–1700. Last tour 1630. D (P). NTS (050683 4255).

The historic home of the Dalyell family, parts of the House of the Binns date from the early 17th century. With its small towers and its windowed castle walls, it reflects the transition from heavily fortified stronghold to more accommodating mansion.

HOLYROOD,
see **EDINBURGH, PALACE OF HOLYROODHOUSE**

HOPETOUN HOUSE
near Edinburgh, Lothian

W of South Queensferry. Easter–Sept, daily 1000–1700. Last admission 1645. D (A/P) (031 331 2451).

Hopetoun House, an impressive **Adam** mansion which was started in 1699 to the designs of Sir William

HOUSE OF DUN
near Montrose, Tayside

On A935 4m W of Montrose. Easter weekend and 28 Apr–21 Oct, daily 1100–1730. D (A/P). NTS (067481 264).

This William **Adam**-designed Palladian house overlooks the Montrose Basin. It was bequeathed to the National Trust for Scotland in 1980 and visitors can now use marked woodland paths and see weavers using a traditional loom, as well as view the house. Of particular note in the house is the plasterwork in the saloon by Joseph Enzer.

HUNTINGTOWER CASTLE
near Perth, Tayside

*Off A85 3m W of Perth. Apr–Sept,
Mon–Sat 0930–1900, Sun 1400–1900;
Oct–Mar, Mon–Sat 0930–1600, Sun
1400–1600. HS (031–244 3101).*

Two complete towers, dating from
the 15th and 16th centuries, linked
by a 17th-century range, comprise
this castellated mansion. It was
formerly known as Ruthven Castle
and was the location in 1582 of
the Raid of Ruthven when James
VI, then 16 years old, was held
by a group of conspirators who
demanded the dismissal of favoured
royal advisors. After some months,
the coup failed and the leader of the
conspiracy was beheaded.

INCHCOLM ABBEY
Inchcolm Island, Firth of Forth

On Inchcolm Island in the Firth of Forth, boat trips from Aberdour or South Queensferry. Apr–Sept, Mon–Sat 0930–1900, Sun 1400–1900; Oct–Mar, Mon–Sat 0930–1600, Sun 1400–1600; closed Wed (pm) and Thurs in winter. D (A/P). HS (031–244 3101).

The atmospheric and unusual setting on the wind-battered island of Inchcolm heightens the impressiveness of the best-preserved group of monastic buildings in Scotland. Founded in about 1123, the buildings include an octagonal chapter house, upper floors and inner courtyards. The abbey was the scene of two memorable productions of Shakespeare's *Macbeth* in the Edinburgh Festivals of 1988 and 1989 – Inchcolm is mentioned in the play itself.

INCHCOLM ISLAND
Firth of Forth

In the Firth of Forth.

Although visited primarily for its abbey, the island and the boat journey to the island make it a pleasant day trip for picnickers and for those interested in a different view of the Firth of Forth.

INNERLEITHEN
Borders

On A72 5m E of Peebles.

The springs of Innerleithen, among them St Ronan's Well, made the town something of a health resort in the 19th century. A mill town with a full quota of mills and mill shops, Innerleithen lies at the confluence of the River Tweed and the Leithen. Its setting is dramatic – on the valley floor between two hulking, forested hills and a hill scarred with schist. With something of the feel and scale of a Highland town, Innerleithen describes itself as 'a centre for hill-walking'. Robert Smail's Printing Works are in the town and Traquair House is nearby.

INNERPEFFRAY
Tayside

On B8062 4m SE of Crieff.

Innerpeffray is on the touring route of bibliophiles, for Innerpeffray Library is the oldest library in Scotland. Founded in 1691 by David Drummond, it was originally housed in the attic of the neighbouring chapel. The collection of books was moved between 1750 and 1758 to its present home. The oldest book is dated 1508 and the borrowers' ledger dates from 1747.

INVERESK LODGE GARDEN
near Musselburgh, Lothian

On A6124 S of Musselburgh, 7m E of Edinburgh. All year, Mon–Fri 1000–1630, Sun 1400–1700. D (A). NTS (031–226 5922).

The garden, attached to a 17th century house which is not open to the public, specializes in plants for small gardens. A shrub-rose border and climbing roses are particular features.

INVERKEITHING
Fife

Just before start of M90 13m N of Edinburgh.

Built on a ridge which juts out into the **Firth of Forth**, Inverkeithing is that common cocktail – modern, unattractive housing estates surrounding an old town centre and a broad main street of more pleasing buildings. To the east of the town, beside the Forth, is a shipbreaker's yard, all cranes and shipping clutter. Beyond that, the workings of an enormous quarry seem to dig into the peninsula upon which the town sits. The railway line which comes across the **Forth Bridge** serves Inverkeithing – from where a short and magnificent train journey over the Forth takes commuters into **Edinburgh**.

JEDBURGH
Borders

On A68 40m SE of Edinburgh.

Jedburgh Abbey and **Mary Queen of Scots House** are the main tourist magnets for Jedburgh, a Border town which lies only ten miles from England and which, as a result of its position, was always of considerable strategic importance in cross-Border warfare. Despite the violence of its history, Jedburgh's situation, in the valley of the Jed Water, is pleasant and the town's centre, with examples of Scottish vernacular architecture, is considered one of the most attractive in the region. Jedburgh's past guest list includes Bonnie Prince Charlie, **Mary Queen of Scots**, Robert Burns, William and Dorothy Wordsworth. **Sir Walter Scott** practised as an advocate here. Contemporary Jedburgh, like its Borders neighbours, is involved in the textiles industry. Also of interest in the Jedburgh area are the **Woodland Visitor Centre** and **Castlejail Museum**, which occupies the site of Jedburgh Castle.

JEDBURGH ABBEY
Jedburgh, Borders

High Street, Jedburgh. Apr–Sept, Mon–Sat 0930–1900, Sun 1400–1900; Oct–Mar, Mon–Sat 0930–1600, Sun 1400-1600, closed Thurs (pm) and Fri. D (P). HS (031–244 3101).

Founded around 1118 by David I for Augustinian monks from France, Jedburgh Abbey was built on a site which had been used for Christian worship since the ninth century. The red sandstone ruin, standing above the Jed Water, is remarkably complete. Foundations of domestic buildings can also be seen. A viewing route and a visitor centre help explain the abbey's layout.

KAILZIE GARDENS
near Peebles, Borders

On B7062 2m E of Peebles. Daily,
1100–1730. D (P) (0721 20007).

As well as its early spring speciality
of 'Snowdrop Days' and its
collection of shrub roses, Kailzie
Gardens also boasts an 1812 walled
garden, a laburnum alley, waterfowl
and woodland and burnside walks,
all spread over 17 acres.

KELLIE CASTLE AND GARDENS
near Pittenweem, Fife

On B9171 3m NW of Pittenweem, 10m S
of St Andrews. Castle: Easter weekend, Apr,
Sat–Sun 1400–1800; 1 May–31 Oct, daily
1400–1800. Last admission 1730. Gardens:
all year, daily 1000–sunset. D (P). NTS
(03338 271).

The present castle is mainly 16th
and early 17th century – building
work was completed about 1606 –
although the oldest part is believed
to date from 1360. The interior is
largely Victorian, the result of a
comprehensive restoration around
1878 by its owners, the Lorimer
family, and features ornate plaster
ceilings, furniture, painted panelling
and a Victorian nursery. The walled
garden is a late Victorian layout,
and contains old-fashioned roses
and fruit trees.

KELSO
Borders

At junction of A6089 and A698 23m SW of
Berwick-upon-Tweed.

A veritable forest of signs points
the way to Kelso's rugby ground,
emphasizing the importance of this
sport in the Borders, while other
signs show the route to Kelso's
racecourse – horses too are very
much a part of Border culture.
A market town lying on the **River
Tweed** and on the Teviot, Kelso itself
is somehow hearty and brawny: flat,
spacious with a cobbled Georgian
town square, it has a plain, unfrilly
but substantial air. Kelso was one
of **Sir Walter Scott**'s favourite places:
'the most beautiful, if not the most
romantic village in Scotland'. Of
especial interest in and around
Kelso are **Floors Castle, Kelso Abbey,
Mellerstain House** and **Smailholm
Tower**. The five-arch stone bridge
over the Tweed, built by John
Rennie in 1803, was modelled on the
old Waterloo Bridge which used to
span the Thames. The Turret House,
one of Kelso's oldest buildings
which is now owned by the
National Trust for Scotland, contains
the Kelso Museum.

KELSO ABBEY
Kelso, Borders

Bridge Street, Kelso. Apr–Sept, Mon–Sat
0930–1900, Sun 1400–1900; Oct–Mar,
Mon–Sat 0930–1600, Sun 1400–1600. Free.
HS (031–244 3101).

Once the largest of the Border
abbeys, which suffered almost
total destruction at the hands of
the English Earl of Hertford in
1545, Kelso Abbey was also one
of the earliest completed by David
I. Founded in 1128, the remaining
portion – the west façade, transepts
and tower of the abbey – is still
considered a remarkable piece of
architecture.

KENMORE
Tayside

On A827 5m W of Aberfeldy.

A picturesque white-washed estate village which inhabits a slight promontory at the north-east end of Loch Tay, Kenmore is a popular visitor spot. A caravan site, a hotel, the lovely grounds and golf course of Taymouth Castle, the nearby Croft-na-Caber watersports centre, fishing on the **River Tay**, hill-walking on **Ben Lawers** and loch fishing provide a wide range of holiday options. The overall appeal of this mellow, green part of the Highlands is confirmed by the fact that Taymouth Castle was reputedly one of the contenders for Queen Victoria's Highland home. It was defeated, of course, by Balmoral.

KERR'S MINIATURE RAILWAY
Arbroath, Tayside

In Arbroath on the seafront. Apr–Sept, Sat–Sun 1400–1700; Jul and first half of Aug, daily 1400–1700 (0241 79249).

Four locomotives (steam or petrol-powered) shunt along 400 yards of track beside the main Edinburgh to Aberdeen line. A tunnel, a footbridge and miniature platforms complete the railway experience. There is also a small-scale bus and a tiny fire-engine to give children rides along the seafront.

KILLIECRANKIE
Tayside

Off A9 2m N of Pitlochry. D (P). NTS. (0796 3233).

A National Trust for Scotland visitor centre explains the Scottish significance of the Pass of Killiecrankie, a wooded gorge where in 1689 Jacobite forces overcame government troops. The leader of the Jacobites, Viscount Dundee (or 'Bonnie Dundee' as **Sir Walter Scott** had him) died at the moment of victory. In the heart of the pass is the Soldier's Leap, where two rocks almost bridge the gorge. The pass is a point on a network of walks around the area, which also includes **Pitlochry Power Station and Dam** with its famous salmon ladder. The village of Killiecrankie is now by-passed by a spectacular viaduct which carries the A9.

KINCARDINE
Fife

At junction of A985 and A977 8m E of Stirling.

Notable primarily because it is dominated by the Kincardine Bridge which spans the western end of the **Firth of Forth**, Kincardine is a small port which formerly thrived as the departure point of a Firth of Forth ferry. Like all settlements along the narrower part of the Forth, Kincardine's environment is dominated by Grangemouth's oil refinery. The nearby power station is said to have the tallest chimney in Europe.

KINROSS
Tayside

Just off M90 12m S of Perth.

With large houses at its northern approach and the smaller ones of the original village to the south, Kinross is a solid, well-kept town on the shore of the lovely **Loch Leven** – although the layout of the town makes little of this. A wool factory and a car auction compound loom largest on the industrial and commercial front as you drive south through Kinross, before giving way to views of the loch and of **Loch Leven Castle**. Also nearby are **Kinross House Gardens**.

KINROSS HOUSE GARDENS
Kinross, Tayside

Kinross. May–Sept, 1000–1900 (0577 63416).

Formal gardens surround Kinross House (which is not usually open to the public), and feature yew hedges, roses and herbaceous borders.

KIRKCALDY
Fife

At junction of A907, A915 and A917.

A principal town in Fife which combines its industrial role with that of a coastal resort, Kirkcaldy's economic base was, from 1847 onwards, the linoleum industry. Kirkcaldy (pronounced 'Kirkcawdy') was the birthplace of economist and philosopher Adam Smith in 1723, and of architect **Robert Adam** in 1728. Kirkcaldy's parks and the small group of 17th-century houses, Sailors' Walk (restored by the National Trust for Scotland), are the main scenic areas of the town. Of particular interest is Kirkcaldy Museum which houses a collection

of Wemyss Ware china. Kirkcaldy's Links Market fair is the largest of its kind in Scotland. It is held in April.

KIRKLISTON
Lothian

Just off M8 and M9 8m W of Edinburgh.

Visited primarily for its church which dates from the 12th century, Kirkliston lies on the River Almond. During the construction of the **Forth Bridge**, Kirkliston was an accommodation centre for the workforce. Because of the large amount of cheese that had to be imported, reputedly to feed Irish labourers, the town earnt itself the nickname 'Cheesetown'. Nearby are **Niddry Castle, Hopetoun House** and **Dalmeny House**.

KIRRIEMUIR
Tayside

At junction of A926 and A928 15m N of Dundee.

Kirriemuir's narrow, winding streets and a number of fine red sandstone buildings give the picturesque town a well-to-do air. Its situation, on slopes looking across the wide sweep of Strathmore, is particularly pleasant. A former jute manufacturing town, Kirriemuir is today a good touring base for the Braes of Angus. Another attraction is **Barrie's Birthplace**, the cottage where J.M. Barrie, the creator of *Peter Pan*, was born in 1860, now a museum to the author and playwright.

JOHN KNOX, see panel p139.

John Knox

John Knox (c.1513–72) was born to an East Lothian farmer, it is thought in either **Gifford** or **Haddington**. He was certainly educated in Haddington and went on to the University of **St Andrews**. By 1540 Knox had completed his studies and had started work as a notary and tutor in East Lothian. Over the next few years it seems that he either became a Protestant or was inclining publicly in that radical direction. Certainly, East Lothian was then a hotbed of reformist movement: people were tired of what they perceived to be a corrupt Roman Catholic Church run by the aristocracy for their own financial gain. The English 'rough wooing' of Scotland's Catholic child-queen Mary for Henry VIII's heir, Edward, failed and Scotland was divided: pro-France and pro-Roman Catholic versus pro-England and pro-Protestant. The division is over-simplistic, for there were many who found themselves unwittingly in both camps. Violence and conflict increased.

George Wishart emerged as a Protestant leader and began to preach his 'heresy' across Scotland. Knox acted as his bodyguard in Lothian and when Wishart was finally captured, tried by the Roman Catholic Church in St Andrews and burned in March 1546, Knox was deeply affected. **St Andrews Castle** was subsequently captured by a Protestant group who murdered Cardinal Beaton, the man responsible for Wishart's death.

From the pulpit, Knox preached his doctrine to the people of St Andrews until the French Catholics recaptured the castle. Knox was condemned to life as a galley-slave on French ships. Somehow, during his captivity, he wrote a Protestant manifesto which he addressed to his congregation at St Andrews. After 19 months in captivity, Knox was freed and in 1549 landed

(continued)

John Knox *(continued)*

in England. He was appointed pastor of Berwick and became increasingly involved in the workings of the Church of England, entering into theological controversy and argument. He then spent some years in Europe where he completed several pamphlets and doctrinal theses, including his notoriously misogynistic *The First Blast of the Trumpet against the Monstrous Regiment of Women.*

In 1559 Knox returned to Scotland. Recognizing the rapid growth of Protestantism, Scotland's Queen Regent, the French Roman Catholic Mary of Guise, mother of the future **Mary Queen of Scots**, had just outlawed Protestant preachers. Knox preached his famous sermon in **Perth** against the idolatry of Mass, and riots and the looting of churches spread. A political and ecclesiastic power struggle ensued between the Protestant Lords of the Congregation and the Scottish monarchy. The Lords looked to England for help. In 1560 a treaty was signed, providing for a peace between England, Scotland and France, and the Scottish Reformed Church took centre-stage.

However, on 19 August 1561, Mary Queen of Scots returned and Knox was confronted by Mary's Roman Catholicism and her wish to restore it. Knox spent the next six years defending the new Scottish Reformed Church and Scottish Protestantism against Mary's manoeuvres. The death of Darnley, Mary's subsequent marriage to Bothwell, her abdication in favour of her son and her conference of the regency on to the Protestant Earl of Moray finally accomplished what Knox had worked for: the Reformed Kirk seemed safe. Knox was himself not to live in peace – more power struggles led to another period in exile before his death in November 1572.

LADY VICTORIA COLLIERY
Newtongrange, Lothian

Newtongrange, on A7 past Dalkeith.
All year. Tues–Fri 1000–1600, Sat–Sun
1200–1700. D (031–663 7519).

Now reopened as an industrial
heritage attraction, the Victorian
colliery enables visitors to gain
an insight into mining life. A tour
of the pithead is combined with
tableaux, designed to evoke life in
a mining community, in the visitor
centre. Lady Victoria Colliery, in the
midst of this one-time coal- mining
heartland which has had its
economic base removed, is on a
self-drive coal heritage trail which
includes the **Scottish Mining Museum**
at Prestongrange.

LAMMERMUIR HILLS

Straddling and forming the eastern
half of the boundary between
Lothian Region and Borders
Region, the Lammermuirs contain
the sources for several tributaries
that feed the **River Tweed** and
nourish the fertile Tweed valley.
The hills themselves are primarily
sheep-farming country.

LARGO
Fife

On A915 10m SW of St Andrews.

Like many of the fishing villages
which lie on the **Firth of Forth**, Largo
once enjoyed boom years of herring
catches, and now scant fishing
takes place at all. Divided into

Upper and Lower Largo, the Lower,
the picturesque part of the village
which is on the waterfront, is famed
as the birthplace of the original
Robinson Crusoe, Alexander Selkirk
(1676–1721). A rather shaggy statue
of Selkirk dressed in goatskins
inhabits a niche in the wall of his
birthplace.

LASSWADE
Lothian

Off A7 5m S of Edinburgh.

The home of **Sir Walter Scott** for
six years, Lasswade is situated
in the valley of the North Esk
River. The villages of Bonnyrigg,
Redrow, Polton Street, Hillhead and
Broomieknowe, merged in 1865,
were joined to Lasswade in 1929.
Thomas De Quincey, the Victorian
author and opium addict, lived in
what is now De Quincey Cottage at
nearby Polton for 19 years until his
death in 1859.

LAUDER
Borders

On A68 28m SE of Edinburgh.

A sedate, pleasant town, Lauder
lies on the Leader Water, a tributary
of the **River Tweed**. Of historical
note are the cruciform Church of
St Mary, thought to be the work
of Sir William Bruce, which dates
from 1673, and the Lauder Bridge,
now no longer standing. It was from
this bridge that Archibald, the Earl
of Angus, hanged the favourites
of James III in 1482, earning
himself the nickname 'Bell-the-Cat'.
Thirlestane Castle is nearby.

LAURISTON CASTLE, see EDINBURGH.

LEITH
Lothian

On A199 just NE of Edinburgh city centre.

Because Leith was once a royal burgh in its own right, there is a strong tradition of the citizens of Leith differentiating themselves from those of Edinburgh. Leith was in fact incorporated into the boundaries of Edinburgh in 1920, and was subsequently known as Edinburgh's port. In its heyday, Leith was a bustling fishing harbour and a thriving docks, backed up by ship repair yards, engineering works and drydocks. Today, Leith's maritime life is subdued. Its shore life has, however, livened up considerably in recent years, as buildings have been restored, fashionable restaurants opened and streets tidied up.

LENNOXLOVE HOUSE
near Haddington, Lothian

On B6369 1m S of Haddington. Easter weekend, May–Sept, Wed, Sat, Sun 1400–1700. D (P) (062 082 3720).

The family house of the Maitlands (one of whom was a secretary to **Mary Queen of Scots**) for several centuries, Lennoxlove House was originally called Lethington. It was renamed by the Duchess of Lennox (who was the model for Britannia on English coins) in memory of her devotion to her husband. Rooms

visited on the tour of Lennoxlove House include the front hall, the china hall, the blue room, the petit point room (with its writing cabinet, a gift from Charles II), the yellow room and the great hall (where a death mask of Mary Queen of Scots is kept). The house is currently the home of the Duke and Duchess of Hamilton.

LEUCHARS
Fife

On A919 5½m NW of St Andrews.

Famous for **Leuchars Norman Church**, the town is also host to the nearby RAF station, which was the base of a Norwegian squadron during World War II. **Earlshall Castle** lies a mile to the east of Leuchars.

LEUCHARS NORMAN CHURCH
Leuchars, Fife

Leuchars. Mar–Oct, all reasonable times. D. Free.

This 12th-century church is considered by some to be the loveliest Norman fragment in Britain because of the richly carved chancel and apse. The 17th-century bell-tower, at one end of the church, is also notable.

LINLITHGOW
Lothian

Just off M9 16m W of Edinburgh.

Linlithgow's attractions for the visitor are many, but the town's centrepiece is the wonderful **Linlithgow Palace**, visible on its grass plateau from the M9. The town's broad, assured main street leads towards a small square. From the cobbled square, Kirkgate leads in turn to the palace and to **St Michael's Parish Church** with its spiky modernist crown of thorns. A popular commuter town for Edinburgh, Linlithgow offers an appealing blend of history, amenities and a sense of community. Other attractions in the Linlithgow vicinity are the **Canal Museum, Blackness Castle**, the **House of the Binns** and **Beecraigs Country Park**.

LINLITHGOW PALACE
Linlithgow, Lothian

S shore of loch, Linlithgow. Apr–Sept, Mon–Sat 0930–1900, Sun 1400–1900; Oct–Mar, Mon–Sat 0930–1600, Sun 1400–1600. D (P). HS (031–244 3101).

Viewing the pale auburn stone of Linlithgow Palace from the outside is, in itself, a pleasurable experience. Its position, beside the loop of the loch and in extensive public parkland, means that it is somehow very local. Around the palace's walls dog-walkers and pram-pushers have acoustic accompaniment from the loch – the clink of sailing dinghies' masts and the honk of ducks. There has been a royal residence on the site from the 12th century. All the Stuart kings lived here, and it was here, in 1542, that **Mary Queen of Scots** was born. The chapel and great hall are late 15th century. The palace was ruined by a fire in 1746. In the centre of the palace's quadrangle is an ornate fountain, which was a wedding present from

James V to Mary of Guise. It is said to have flowed with wine on their wedding day.

LIVINGSTON
Lothian

Just off M8 12m W of Edinburgh.

Reputedly named after a merchant, Leving, who made his home here in the 12th century, Livingston's 20th-century expansion has been far less coincidental. Decreed Scotland's fourth new town in 1962, Livingston, formerly a centre for **shale** mining, was deliberately developed as a centre for new industry and as the non-organic home for thousands of families. Despite the element of risk involved in such pre-planned growth, Livingston has enjoyed considerable success for modern industries with specific space and building-design requirements. There is also a broad spread of amenities for residents. **Livingston Mill Farm** is one of the town's few historical visitor attractions.

LIVINGSTON MILL FARM
Livingston, Lothian

Off A705 Kirkton, Livingston Village. Apr–Sept, daily 1000–1700; Oct–Mar, first Sat and Sun each month 1300–1600. D (P) (0506 41495).

This restored 18th-century farm steading and water mill has been turned into a family recreation area offering a small agricultural museum, a children's farm and play area, a picnic and barbeque site and riverside walks.

LOANHEAD
Lothian

On A768 6m S of Edinburgh.

A Lothian coal-mining community economically stranded by pit closures, Loanhead has been struggling out of its depression via two industrial estates.

LOCH OF KINNORDY NATURE RESERVE
near Kirriemuir, Tayside

On B951 1m W of Kirriemuir. Daily except Sat in Sept and Oct. D (031–557 3136).

Two observation hides enable ornithologists to look across marshland which has a large number of nesting birds.

LOCH LEVEN
near Kinross, Tayside

Off M90 just before Kinross.

Visible from the M90, Loch Leven always appears misty and dreamy. Even on a clear day, the loch is comprised of silhouettes – of two-man fishing boats, islands and the Lomond Hills. For anglers, the loch means trout: the special Loch Leven trout which are not found anywhere else. For historians, the loch, because it surrounds **Loch Leven Castle** on its island, was the real prison of **Mary Queen of Scots** for a year before she escaped. It is a National Nature Reserve and is an important freshwater area for migratory and breeding wildfowl.

LOCH LEVEN CASTLE
near Kinross, Tayside

On an island on Loch Leven, Kinross. Apr–Sept, Mon–Sat 0930–1900, Sun 1400–1900. HS (031–244 3101).

Reached by boat from Kinross, this castle was the prison of **Mary Queen of Scots** from 1567 until her escape in 1568. It was within the walls of the castle, now just a square tower, dating from the late 14th century or early 15th century, that Mary had a miscarriage, reputedly losing twins. Here also Mary signed a deed of abdication in favour of her infant son. She was helped to very temporary freedom by 16-year-old William Douglas, who stole the castle keys, placed the queen in a boat, locked the castle gates behind him and threw the keys into the loch. They were later recovered.

LOCH OF THE LOWES
near Dunkeld, Tayside

Off A923 2m NE of Dunkeld. Visitor centre open Apr–Sept; observation hide open permanently. D (03502 337).

A sheltered loch with surrounding woodland, the Loch of the Lowes is used for watching wildlife (there is an observation hide), especially waterfowl and ospreys. A visitor centre carries appropriate educational material.

LOCHTY PRIVATE RAILWAY
near Crail, Fife

On B940 7m W of Crail. Mid June–early Sept, Sun 1345–1700. Steam-hauled passenger service is operated on a

*half-hourly basis (approx). D. Free
admission to site.*

Volunteers from the Fife Railway
Preservation Group operate and
service the railway, running a
steam-hauled passenger train service
between Lochty and Knightsward.

LOWER CITY MILLS, see
PERTH.

LUFFNESS CASTLE
near Aberlady, Lothian

*On A198 1m E of Aberlady. By
arrangement. Free (087 57 218).*

The 16th-century castle and its
13th-century keep were built on
the site of a Viking camp. Gardens,
extensive old fortifications and an
old moat also lie within Luffness's
grounds.

MALLENY HOUSE GARDENS
Balerno, Lothian

*Off A70 7½m SW of Edinburgh in
Balerno. All year. Daily 1000–sunset. D
(A). NTS (031–226 5922).*

The National Bonsai Collection
for Scotland is housed at Malleny
Gardens which also have a fine
selection of shrub roses and a
woodland walk. The house to which
the gardens belong was built in
1635, with 19th-century additions. It
is not open to the public.

MANDERSTON
near Duns, Borders

*Off A6105 2m E of Duns. Mid May–Sept,
Thurs and Sun 1400–1730. D (A/P)
(0361 83450).*

The so-called 'silver staircase'
at Manderston is perhaps the
best-known structural eccentricity of
the house, although what is meant is
that the stair rails are silver-plated.
Marble floors and lavish soft
furnishings add to Manderston's
internal opulence. Externally it
is considered to be a magnificent
example of a large Edwardian
country house. A number of estate
buildings, including a fine stable
block, a dairy, gardens, a tearoom
and a shop add to Manderston's
visitor appeal.

MARY QUEEN OF SCOTS, see
panel p147.

MARY QUEEN OF SCOTS HOUSE
Jedburgh, Borders

*Queen Street, Jedburgh. Easter–mid Nov,
daily 1000–1700. D (P) (0835 63331/0450
73457).*

This 16th-century fortified house
is reputed to be where **Mary Queen
of Scots** stayed in 1566. It was from
here that she journeyed to **Hermitage
Castle** to visit the Earl of Bothwell,
her lover, who was wounded. Upon
her return to Jedburgh, she fell
dangerously ill and was, in later,
more despairing days, reputed
to have wished that she had died
at Jedburgh. The house is now a
museum devoted to Mary, with
relics and artefacts (her watch and
thimblecase). The room where she
and her ladies-in-waiting slept can
still be seen.

MEGGINCH CASTLE GARDENS
near Perth, Tayside

*On A85 10m E of Perth. Apr–Jun
and Sept, Wed only 1400–1700; Jul
and Aug, Mon–Fri 1400–1700. D (P)
(08212 222).*

A wide range of gardening history
can be seen in the grounds of
15th-century Megginch Castle.
A 16th-century rose garden,
an 18th-century physic garden
and a 19th-century flower
parterre span the centuries. Other
features include 1000-year-old
yews, a double-walled kitchen
garden, a Gothic courtyard with
a pagoda-roofed dovecote. An
astrological garden has recently been
created.

Mary Queen of Scots

Was she a murderess, a lustful power-broker, a tragic heroine or a deceived woman? Was she the perpetrator or the victim? Was she a Scottish leader or was she an agent for French Roman Catholicism? These are some of the unanswered and unanswerable questions about Mary Queen of Scots (1542–87) that have transfixed historians and public alike. The facts of her life are largely known, but it is the unknowns – motive and political machination – that keep her story alive. The gaps in that story are glaring and compulsive, loaded as they are with that irresistible cocktail of sex, religion and murder.

For her safety, the infant Scottish sovereign Mary was sent by her countrymen to France. She remained there over ten years, marrying the Dauphin in 1558. The following year, her husband became King of France. Meanwhile, a power struggle between Roman Catholics (of which Mary was one) and Scottish Protestants ensued.

In 1561, the recently widowed Mary returned to Scotland. Her principal residence was Edinburgh's **Palace of Holyroodhouse**, and it was from here that she began her struggle to get Roman Catholicism tolerated. In 1565 she married her cousin Henry, Lord Darnley.

The first in a series of intrigues – an attempted rebellion by Mary's half-brother, the Earl of Moray which failed – soon followed. Darnley, his ambitious eye fixed on royal status for himself, was reputedly next. Mary had refused to bestow upon him the Crown Matrimonial and he took revenge by allying himself with Mary's enemies and participating in the murder of Riccio, Mary's Italian secretary, at Holyrood in 1566.

(continued)

Mary Queen of Scots *(continued)*

The Earl of Moray returned to Scotland, but Darnley apparently changed sides again and fled with Mary to **Dunbar**. Escorted by the Earl of Bothwell and a small army, the couple marched on Holyrood and the conspirators fled once more. Shortly afterwards, Mary gave birth to a son, James (later James VI of Scotland and James I of England).

Politically, Mary and Darnley's marriage was doomed. Mary became involved with Bothwell. In 1567, the house at Kirk O' Field where Darnley was staying was blown up, and Darnley's body was recovered. He had been strangled. Some commentators argue that Mary was deeply implicated in the plot against Darnley; others lay responsibility at the feet of Bothwell.

He married Mary in late spring of 1567. Threatened by rebellion and suspected of Darnley's murder, Mary and Bothwell escaped to **Borthwick Castle** and then to Dunbar. In June she surrendered, as Bothwell again fled, and was imprisoned in **Loch Leven Castle** by Protestant forces. From there, she abdicated in favour of her son.

An escape attempt in 1568 backfired when she went to her cousin Elizabeth I for assistance. She was imprisoned by Elizabeth in the Tower of London when she was still only 26. She remained a captive there for almost 20 years before she was beheaded at Fotheringhay on 8 February 1587.

MEIGLE
Tayside

On A94 12m SW of Forfar.

Of special interest in the small village of Meigle is the Meigle Museum, a former school, which houses 25 sculptured stones dating from the seventh to the tenth centuries. It is the largest collection of Dark Age stones in western Europe. A leaflet explains the elaborate carvings on each stone in detail.

MEIKLEOUR BEECH HEDGE
Meiklour, Tayside

On A93 just S of Meikleour 12m NE of Perth.

The beech hedge was planted in 1746 and is now 580 yards long and 100 feet high – as such, it is the highest beech hedge of its kind in the world.

MELLERSTAIN HOUSE
near Kelso, Borders

Off A6089 7m NW of Kelso. Easter, 1 May–30 Sept, Sun–Fri 1230–1630. D (A/P) (057 381 225).

An **Adam** family-designed mansion, Mellerstain was begun in around 1725 by William Adam and was completed about 50 years later by his son Robert. Impressive externally and internally, the house is the home of the Earls of Haddington. The pale green, ivory and pink library is held in especially high regard and is thought to be

one of the finest Adam rooms in Scotland. Several of the 11 areas and rooms which can be viewed have decorative ceilings, with extensive plaster reliefs. Terraced gardens, a lake and a tearoom can also be visited.

MELROSE
Borders

On A6091 just E of Galashiels.

Large sandstone houses and an impression of more brasseries and dried flower shops than is usual give Melrose a well-heeled, self-satisfied atmosphere. Its town square and traditional shop fronts make Melrose a pretty, unspoilt town. Its cluster of interesting attractions – **Melrose Abbey**, **Melrose Motor Museum**, **Melrose Station** and **Priorwood Gardens** – are conveniently within comfortable walking distance of one another. Rising above the town are the strange, lumpy **Eildon Hills**.

MELROSE ABBEY

Main Square, Melrose. Apr–Sept, Mon–Sat 0930–1900, Sun 1400–1900; Oct–Mar, Mon–Sat 0930–1600, Sun 1400–1600. D. HS (031–244 3101).

The roofless abbey church, all arches and flushed red sandstone, with patches of honey stone, is still striking and is perhaps one of the best-known ruins in Scotland. Founded in 1136 by David I for Cistercian monks, it was damaged by 14th-century raids, repaired by Robert the Bruce (whose heart is reportedly buried here), and subsequently fell into decay until

Sir Walter Scott worked to preserve the remaining ruins between 1822 and 1826. The elaborate stonework and the figure of a pig playing the bagpipes on the roof are the abbey's most commented-on features. A museum at the abbey entrance gives something of the abbey's history. Next to the abbey grounds are **Priorwood Gardens**.

MELROSE MOTOR MUSEUM

Near Melrose Abbey. Mid May–mid Oct, daily 1030–1730 or by arrangement; part-time from Easter to mid May. D (089 682 2424 or 0835 22356).

A collection of vehicles from 1909 to the late 1960s is combined with motorcycles, bicycles, old signs and other motoring memorabilia. Display cases also show the minutiae of the automobile world – toy cars and cigarette cards.

MELROSE STATION

Melrose. All year except 25–26 Dec and 1–2 Jan. Daily 1 Apr–31 Oct 1000–1800; 1 Nov–31 Mar 1000–1700. D (P) (089 682 2546).

Pretty, slightly bijoux Melrose Station is a remnant from a bygone age. It is the only town station remaining on the closed-down Edinburgh to Carlisle 'Waverley Route'. When the station opened in 1849, it was described as 'the handsomest provincial Station in Scotland'. As such, it is a fitting home for a visitor centre which remembers the Waverley Route in displays. The station combines its heritage role with a more contemporary one: craft workshops,

a craft shop and a restaurant are also accommodated here.

MELVILLE MONUMENT
near Comrie, Tayside

Visible from A85 1m N of Comrie, 6m W of Crieff, access by footpath from parking place on Glen Lednock Road. All times. Free.

Standing high on the 840-foot Dunmore Hill above **Comrie**, the Melville Monument, an obelisk memorial to Lord Melville (1742–1811), can be reached on the Glen Lednock Circular Walk, which departs from Comrie. Views from the monument of the beautiful countryside around Comrie are spectacular.

MERTOUN GARDENS
St Boswells, Borders

St Boswells. Apr–Sept, Sat, Sun and Mon public holidays 1400–1800. Last admission 1730. D (P) (0835 23236).

The circular dovecot, believed to be the oldest in the area, a walled garden, 20 acres of trees, herbaceous borders, flowering shrubs, open ground and walks are available at Mertoun.

MID CALDER
Lothian

Off A71 10m W of Edinburgh.

Mid Calder, East Calder and West Calder were all communities which served the once-booming **shale oil** industry. Today Mid Calder, lying like its neighbours amidst the shale oil bings, has little of historical note to recommend it apart from a church which dates from 1541. Calder House was where John Knox administered the first Protestant Communion.

MONIKIE COUNTRY PARK
near Newbigging, Tayside

Off B961 1m N of Newbigging, 10m N of Dundee. All year, 1000–dusk. D (P) (082 623 202).

Situated around three areas of water – Victorian reservoirs built by the Dundee Water Company – the 185 acres of parkland accommodates watersports (canoeing, sailing, windsurfing, rowing) and woodland walks. There are also picnic and play areas and a summertime tearoom.

MONTROSE
Tayside

On A92 30m NW of Dundee.

Montrose is situated on a tongue of land which pokes down into the Montrose Basin. Medieval wynds and closes, substantial 17th- and 18th-century buildings and the 220-foot Gothic steeple of the old church put Montrose on the map of Scottish settlements with inherent visual appeal. Its vast stretch of golden sand has ensured the town's popularity as a summertime resort. It enjoys year-round prosperity as a market town for the area, as a major shopping centre and as a port. North Sea oil has brought further income, with the construction of an oil base on the Ferryden side of the River South Esk. The House of Dun,

a William Adam building, lies just to the west of Montrose.

MOORFOOT HILLS

With the Lammermuir Hills to the east, the Moorfoots form the northern rim of the Tweed basin. Hummocky and undramatic, the Moorfoots are often thought to be the least visually exciting of southern Scotland's hill ranges.

JOHN MUIR HOUSE
Dunbar, Lothian

High Street, Dunbar. Jun–Sept, daily except Wed and Sun 1000–1230, 1330–1630. Free (0368 63353).

The birthplace of John Muir (1838–1914), the naturalist and founder of the American national park system, is open to the public during the summer. The top floor has been restored to the 1838 period (the year of Muir's birth).

MUSSELBURGH
Lothian

On A1 5m E of Edinburgh.

Although a popular commuter town for Edinburgh, Musselburgh likes to keep its separate identity. Politically, it is distinct, as it is administered by East Lothian District Council and not by the City of Edinburgh. Once a bustling fishing harbour, the town's waters are devoted to pleasure boats. To the west of Musselburgh is Fisherrow, where the harbour lies. It was joined to Musselburgh in 1807 by a bridge built by John Rennie. The old bridge, which spans the River Esk, is now open only to pedestrians. Musselburgh has its own theatre and a coast-side racecourse (the oldest in Scotland) provides a further recreational option. Of historical interest is **Pinkie House**.

MUTHILL
Tayside

On A822 3m S of Crieff.

Muthill is an attractive 19th-century town of fine red sandstone buildings, made especially distinctive because the mortar between the stone has been picked out in white. The centrepiece of this sedate and contented settlement is a handsome church. Despite its own inherent charm, Muthill is best known for the ruins of **Muthill Church and Tower**.

MUTHILL CHURCH AND TOWER

At Muthill. All reasonable times. Free. HS (031–244 3101).

The ruins of this parish church consist of a tall 12th-century Romanesque tower, with all other parts dating from the 15th century. The church was used until 1818.

NEIDPATH CASTLE
near Peebles, Borders

On A72 1m W of Peebles. Thurs before Easter–end Sept, Mon–Sat 1100–1700, Sun 1300–1700 (087 57 201 or 0721 20333).

On the road above the dour stone castle, a sign at the roadside reads 'Please do not park here – it is dangerous'. A sheer drop to the **River Tweed** is the danger. The castle itself, a stern medieval keep with 12-foot-thick walls, is wedged into the hillside, looking out across the river. A rock-hewn well, a pit prison, vaults, a small museum and fine views from several floors are its internal features.

NEWARK CASTLE
near Selkirk, Borders

Off A708 4m W of Selkirk. Entry on application to Buccleuch Estates, Bowhill, Selkirk. Free (0750 20753).

This ruined five-storey oblong tower-house was a royal hunting seat for the Forest of Ettrick. Its courtyard was the scene of slaughter when, after the 1645 Battle of Philiphaugh, 100 prisoners were shot by the Covenanter General Leslie. Newark Castle is on the Buccleuch Estates, as is **Bowhill**.

NEWTONGRANGE
Lothian

On A7 8m SE of Edinburgh.

Once the largest coal-mining community in Scotland, serving the **Lady Victoria Colliery** which was closed in 1981, Newtongrange was designated a conservation area in an attempt to revive the economy of the village with new industries. A contribution to this revival was made when the Lady Victoria Colliery was reopened as a tourist attraction.

NEWTON ST BOSWELLS
Borders

On A68 7m N of Jedburgh.

A settlement which apparently evolved from its roots as a railway junction and a place where a livestock market was held, Newton St Boswells is what it sounds like – the new town of the lovely **St Boswells**.

NIDDRY CASTLE
near Edinburgh, Lothian

Off A89 10m W of Edinburgh. May–Sept, Sun 1000–1630. D (P) (0506 890 753).

Restoration works and an archaeological dig are being carried out at the site of this late 15th-century castle, the one-time refuge of **Mary Queen of Scots** as she fled from **Loch Leven Castle**.

NORTH BERWICK
Lothian

On A198 20m E of Edinburgh.

So special is North Berwick that Edinburgh people frequently holiday here, only a few miles from home. The beautiful unspoilt beaches of East Lothian are one

magnet, but the main appeal is
the town itself, which looks, with
its warm red sandstone glow, as
if the sun is for ever setting on it.
The harbourside fishing cottages
of deep red stone, the stately
Victorian beachside houses and
the pale mandarin sand make an
irresistible combination. The railway
station gives holidaymakers and
weekenders easy access to countless
guest houses and B and Bs. The
activities of golf, fishing and boating
are all available and sailings to the
Bass Rock depart from the harbour.
The only downside to North
Berwick can be the bitter North
Sea wind. Behind the town, on the
landward side, is North Berwick
Law, a rounded 613-foot hill of
volcanic origins which is topped
by an arch of whale jawbones and
the crumbs of a ruin. The dramatic
silhouette of **Tantallon Castle** lies
three miles east of North Berwick.

NORTH QUEENSFERRY
Fife

*Beneath Forth Road Bridge on N shore of
Firth of Forth.*

Partly sheltered by a small headland
which is sprinkled with gun
emplacements from World War I,
North Queensferry is dominated by
the **Forth Bridge** and, slightly further
west, by the **Forth Road Bridge**. A
hotch-potch of architectural styles
and mistakes – from large elegant
houses to bad conversions of old
cottages to modern bungalows –
the town none the less commands a
stunning view of the bridges. The
slipway, where the Forth ferry once
docked and off-loaded its cargo of
vehicles into the town centre, can
still be seen. The Fife coastal path
runs through the town.

OIL, see SHALE OIL AND JAMES 'PARAFFIN' YOUNG
panel p156.

ORMISTON
Lothian

Off A1 10m E of Edinburgh.

A pleasant tree-lined one-street village on the Tyne Water, Ormiston is best known for its 15th-century free-standing market cross, now in the care of Historic Scotland. It symbolized the right of Ormiston's inhabitants to hold a market. The village expanded greatly during the 19th century as a coal-mining town.

PASS OF KILLIECRANKIE, see KILLIECRANKIE.

PEEBLES
Borders

At junction of A703 and A72 18m S of Edinburgh.

Set amidst gently rolling hills beside the **River Tweed**, this likeable town has for its motto 'Peebles for pleasure'. Peebles remains a popular holiday destination and retirement town – it has within its parameters Peebles Hydro, the largest hotel in the Borders – and a popular touring base. **Kailzie Garden**, **Neidpath Castle** and **Traquair House** are all nearby. Peebles's main street is broad and assured, with a slightly superior

range of shops from delicatessens to silversmiths. A plaque outside the Tourist Information Office points visitors to the Old Town Wall, the **Cross Kirk** (the town's oldest site) and a clutch of parks and sports centres. In 1800 and 1802 respectively, Peebles was the birthplace of William and Robert Chambers, the Edinburgh publishers (to whose stable this book belongs). Novelist and Governor-General of Canada John Buchan grew up here. The town's **Common Riding** takes place in June.

PENCAITLAND
Lothian

On A6093 5m SW of Haddington.

A village in the heart of fertile East Lothian farmland, Pencaitland lies beside the Tyne Water, spanned here by a bridge which dates from the 16th century. Pencaitland's church has a 13th-century choir aisle. The village of East Saltoun, birthplace of Andrew Fletcher who opposed the 1707 Act of Union, lies just to the south-east of Pencaitland.

PENICUIK
Lothian

On A703 8m S of Edinburgh.

Penicuik (pronounced 'Pennicook') is the fourth largest town in Lothian Region and is a commuter town for Edinburgh. The settlement was moved from an earlier site to its current location south of the **Pentland Hills** in 1770 by Sir John Clerk. The paper-making industry was dominant in the town, although today other industries such as the

Shale oil and James 'Paraffin' Young

To the west of Edinburgh, the flattish Central Belt landscape is interrupted by huge flat-topped red mounds. These are shale bings, piles of residue left from the shale mining that once flourished in West Lothian. Rubbish tips, environmental pollutants and a scar on the landscape to some, the bings, which appear to glow as if the sun is continually setting upon them, are considered an important part of Scotland's industrial heritage by others. As such, many of them have been listed (and are therefore protected) as historical monuments – a lasting if unusual tribute to the work of Paraffin Young.

Glasgow-born James 'Paraffin' Young (1811–83) had begun research into a clear liquid by-product of coal-mining in the early 1840s. He needed a suitable source of coal and a mine at Boghead, between Armadale and **Bathgate**, emerged as the right contender. Young moved to the area, obtaining a site at Whiteside on the road to Whitburn. In 1848 he opened his oil refinery, where coal was heated and the resultant liquid drawn off. Faced with limited coal supplies, he subsequently started experiments on shale and discovered that it too was oil-bearing.

The years from 1853 to 1863 were a boom time for this new Scottish oil industry and for Young's Bathgate Chemical Works. Young had patented his discovery, thereby preventing any competition, and shale oil was shipped all over the world. Inventions such as Young's paraffin lamp, which enjoyed great success, followed. When Young's patent on the shale oil expired,

(continued)

James 'Paraffin' Young *(continued)*

the competition moved in. By 1871 there were over 50 oil refineries in West and Midlothian, all mining the area's shale seam.

Villages were taken over by oil fever – **Mid Calder**, East Calder, West Calder and **Broxburn** were dominated by shale mining. Finally, in the 1870s, sales of shale oil slumped in the face of cheaper, imported Texan crude oil. Young acted quickly again, expanding his line of products to include candles, fertilizer, rubber, paints and petroleum jelly. Then came steam heating, thermostats and refrigeration units.

Despite this, the shale oil industry gradually went into decline, until, by 1914, only seven refineries remained. These seven supplied the Royal Navy with fuel during World War I. After the war, they merged, becoming Scottish Oils. Dwindling returns and a poor rate of shale extraction led to a change of emphasis. Scottish Oils opened a crude oil refinery at Grangemouth and the shale industry concentrated on diesel production. A brief shale revival in World War II was followed by slump. By 1962, all refineries but one were shut down.

Even the heaps of residue, the shale bings, dwindled in numbers as a use was found for the red oxide in the 1960s. The surviving protected bings are now an important beacon of the area's once thriving industry, and are the very visible part of the shale tourist trail that criss-crosses West Lothian.

Edinburgh Crystal glassworks have replaced it.

PENTLAND HILLS
Lothian

Although the suburbs of **Edinburgh** have crept up to the base of the Pentland Hills, they are protected from further encroachment. The Pentlands run in a 16-mile strip to the south-west of Edinburgh, providing near and full-blooded hill-walking and a large recreational canvas for city-dwellers. The Edinburgh **Hillend ski centre**, visible at night from several points in the city, runs down the flank of one hill, but most of the range remains unspoilt. Views from the northern side of the Pentlands of Edinburgh and beyond are spectacular. The highest point of the hills is Scaldlaw at 1898 feet.

PERTH
Tayside

At N end of M90.

'So eminent for the beauty of its situation' said **Sir Walter Scott** of Perth, and its situation, straddling the broad **River Tay** with open parkland to the north and south, is indeed fine. In 1990, it was voted the place in Britain with the best quality of life for its citizens, a reflection of the city's facilities (theatre, shopping centres, leisure complexes), its environs (within easy reach of much that the Highlands have to offer) and the sedate attractiveness of its buildings. The city is often used for Scottish party political conferences. Perth was

the capital of Scotland from 848 for several centuries, and, even after the loss of its crown, the city continued to feature heavily in the momentous events of Scottish history. Here in 1437 James I was murdered; in St John's Church in 1559, **John Knox** delivered his famous, provocative sermon; in 1651, the city surrendered to Cromwell; in 1715 and again in 1745, Perth was occupied by Jacobite forces.

In recent times, the city has seen considerable growth, enabling the restoration of some of its most notable buildings and the tidying-up of its less desirable areas. In the city centre, medieval wynds and closes mix with Georgian neo-classicism and Victorian heaviness, while, in season, salmon fly rods whip the Tay's waters under the generous arches of the Old Tay Bridge. Combining its role as an important livestock market town with that of regional shopping centre, host of the whisky company **John Dewar & Sons**, the insurance company General Accident and location of numerous car showrooms, Perth seems to manage to accommodate and please residents and visitors alike. As well as the city centre attractions listed below, **Elcho Castle, Fairways Heavy Horse Centre, Huntingtower Castle, Megginch Castle Gardens** and **Scone Palace** are within easy reach.

PERTH, BALHOUSIE CASTLE (BLACK WATCH MUSEUM)

Facing North Inch Park, entrance from Hay Street. Mon–Fri 1000–1630, winter 1000–1530; Sun and public holidays (Easter–Sept) 1400–1630; closed 25 Dec–3 Jan. D (P). Free (0738 21281 ext 8530).

Balhousie Castle, built of the pale plum stone that recurs all over

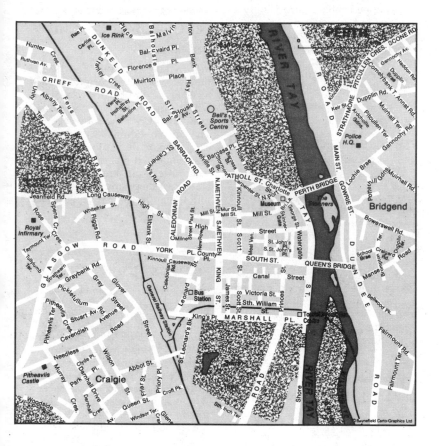

Town plan of Perth

Perth, was originally a 15th-century structure. It was subsequently completely rebuilt in the Scots baronial style, with turrets and crow-stepped gables. Surprisingly engulfed in Perth suburbia, the castle now houses the Black Watch Museum, and is the headquarters of the regiment. The museum describes the history of the regiment from 1740 to the present day.

PERTH, BRANKLYN GARDEN

Dundee Road. 1 Mar–31 Oct, daily 0930–sunset. D (P). NTS (0738 25535).

This garden, which covers two acres of a Perth hillside, is owned and run by the National Trust for Scotland. Begun in 1922, the garden and its notable collection of alpine plants were the work of John and Dorothy Renton. Condensed but impressive all year (snowdrops, rhododendrons, azaleas in spring, unusual hydrangeas in summer, red maples in autumn), it enjoys a considerable reputation.

PERTH, FAIR MAID'S HOUSE

North Port. All year. Mon–Sat 1000–1700. D. Free (0738 25976).

The Fair Maid's House has been, since 1968, a retail centre for Scottish crafts and a gallery. The house is built on a site which was first inhabited by a 13th-century monastery. Next on the site came the old Glovers' Hall, chosen by Sir Walter Scott for his novel as the house of Simon Glover, the father of Catherine Glover, Scott's *The Fair Maid of Perth*. Inside the building, visible as part of the

shop, is a portion of rough stone medieval wall.

PERTH, LOWER CITY MILLS

West Mill Street.

Restored between 1982 and 1988, the water-powered corn mill – with Scotland's largest working water wheel – produces flour and oatmeal, grinding for two days a week. The stone building also houses an exhibition on the Perth Mills, which have inhabited this site for over 900 years, a tearoom and a number of craft workshops and studios. The mill is signposted 'Working Water Mill' from the city centre.

PERTH, ST JOHN'S KIRK

St John Street. D (0738 26159/23358).

In 1559, in this fine cruciform church which dates from the 15th century, **John Knox** delivered his provocative sermon, calling for the 'purging of the churches from idolatry'. St John's was founded by David I in 1126. Restored in 1923–8 as a war memorial, its stern bare stone interior is softened by the colours of the stained-glass windows.

PINKIE HOUSE
Musselburgh, Lothian

At E end of Musselburgh. Mid Apr–mid July, mid Sept–mid Dec, Tues 1400–1700; appointment necessary. D (P). Free (031–665 2059).

This early 17th-century building, to which a considerable number of additions were made, is best known for its painted gallery and its plaster ceilings. It is now part of Loretto School.

PITLOCHRY
Tayside

On A9 25m N of Perth.

Because it lies on the Inverness railway line, and is therefore accessible to carless holidaymakers, Pitlochry is a busy summer holiday resort, full of hotels, B and Bs and guest houses. Amusements, wool shops and ice-cream counters cater for the seasonal visitors, while more high-brow hunting, shooting and fishing shops sell to Pitlochry's other clientele – the residents and weekenders from the surrounding area who participate in more expensive Highland pursuits. Day-trippers invariably come to the town to visit the famed **Pitlochry Power Station and Dam** for its so-called salmon ladder. Just above Pitlochry is the **Edradour Distillery** and at Loch Tummel is the **Queen's View**.

PITLOCHRY POWER STATION AND DAM
Pitlochry, Tayside

Pitlochry. Late Mar–late Oct, daily 0940–1730. D (A). Free (08824 251).

Visitors to the rather ugly concrete power station and dam have the considerable scenic compensation of the long, picturesque loop of Loch Faskally and a wide tract of wood and parkland. But scenery is not usually the visitor's intent: watching salmon leap up the purpose-built 'ladder' is. The ladder is in fact

stepped concrete chambers full of swirling dark water. They enable the salmon to move up from the River Tummel to spawn. The power station is a point on the 11-mile walk which goes beyond the loch to the pass of **Killiecrankie**.

PITTENWEEM
Fife

On A917 9m S of St Andrews.

Still a busy fishing harbour, Pittenweem has managed to sustain its industry where its neighbours have failed. At the eastern end of the harbour is a picturesque group of restored 16th-century houses called 'the Gyles'. An Edinburgh riot was started in Pittenweem in 1736 when two men robbed a customs collector. One of the offenders was subsequently hanged in Edinburgh. A mob then set upon and killed the guard commander, Captain Porteous. **St Fillan's Cave** lies by the harbour.

PORTOBELLO
Lothian

Just E of Edinburgh.

A seaside resort for Edinburgh citizens who come to paddle, stroll along the pink asphalt promenade or lick sticks of Portobello rock, Portobello is called 'Portie' by locals. It is somehow typical of a British seaside: multi-coloured benches on the seafront, fish and chip shops and amusement arcades. Much of Portobello High Street, which turns its back on the sea, is Georgian, built in sandstone. The sea air has taken its toll on peeling painted façades but Portobello, busy with shoppers and traffic, is not too worried.

PRESTONGRANGE, see SCOTTISH MINING MUSEUM.

PRESTON MILL AND PHANTASSIE DOOCOT
East Linton, Lothian

East Linton. 1 Apr–30 Sept, Mon–Sat 1100–1300, 1400–1700, Sun 1400–1700; 1–31 Oct, Sat 1100–1300, 1400–1630, Sun 1400–1600. Last tour 20 mins before closing. D (P). NTS (0620 860426).

The mill dates from the 16th century and is the oldest mechanically functioning, water-powered meal mill in Scotland. The mill buildings, resplendent in Dutch orange pantiles, are extremely picturesque. Uneven stone steps struggle upwards, a conical roof looks like a bent-over witch's hat and ducks and geese waddle around the site. The Phantassie Doocot, shaped like an elongated hummock, lies over the river and across a field from the mill.

PRESTONPANS
Lothian

On B1348 10m E of Edinburgh.

Once noted for salt-panning, oysters and coal, Prestonpans is now primarily remembered because of the 1745 battle which took its name. To the east of Prestonpans is the Prestonpans Battle Cairn which commemorates the victory of Charles Edward Stuart over General Cope. Just south of Prestonpans is the 17th-century Preston Market Cross, unusual because it is still in its original position. South-west of the town is Prestongrange and the **Scottish Mining Museum**.

PRIORWOOD GARDENS, MELROSE
Borders

In Melrose. Early Apr–24 Dec, Mon–Sat 1000–1730; Sun 1330–1730. D (A). NTS (089 682 2555).

Lying to one side of **Melrose Abbey**'s grounds are the National Trust for Scotland's small Priorwood Gardens, which specialize in dried flowers. Gravelled paths lead from growing beds towards the drying sheds while a shop sells the resultant produce. There is also a compact orchard.

QUEEN MARY'S HOUSE, see **MARY QUEEN OF SCOTS HOUSE.**

QUEEN'S VIEW
Loch Tummel, near Pitlochry, Tayside

On B8019 8m NW of Pitlochry. All times. Free (0796 3123).

A path leads from a car park to the viewing point, which gives a superb panorama of Loch Tummel and of **Schiehallion**, the 3547-foot Munro (a mountain over 3000 feet) beyond. The viewing point was visited by Queen Victoria in 1866 and is today a standard stopping place for coach parties in summer. The only slight hiccup for photographers is a caravan park down below.

RAVENSCRAIG CASTLE
near Kirkcaldy, Fife

Just E of Kirkcaldy. Apr–Sept, Mon–Sat 0930–1900, Sun 1400–1900; Oct–Mar, Mon–Sat 0930–1600, Sun 1400–1600. D (P). HS (031–244 3101).

Situated on a rocky promontory, the imposing ruin of Ravenscraig Castle is one of the earliest artillery forts in Scotland. It was begun in 1460 for James II and consists of two round towers, one of which was the home of James II's widow, joined by a range.

RED CASTLE
near Montrose, Tayside

Off A92 7m S of Montrose. All times. D (A). Free.

This ruined red sandstone tower, which probably dates from the 15th century, commands a good coastal defensive position on top of a steep mound in Lunan Bay.

RESTENNETH PRIORY
near Forfar, Tayside

Off B9113 1½m NE of Forfar. All reasonable times. Free. HS (031–244 3101).

A priory church of Augustinian canons, probably founded by David I, Restenneth is noted for its tall tower, the lower section of which is thought to be pre-Norman.

ROSEWELL
Lothian

On A6094 5m SW of Dalkeith.

A large section of this 19th-century company village, set up around a coal mine which closed in 1961, has been designated a conservation area. The village's housing clearly reveals a hierarchy of accommodation for the mine employees.

ROSSLYN CHAPEL
Roslin, Lothian

Off A703 7½m S of Edinburgh at Roslin. 1 Apr–31 Oct, Mon–Sat 1000–1700, Sun 1200–1645. D (031–440 2159).

This lovely 15th-century chapel, a miniature cathedral complete with small flying buttresses, is grafted on to what appears to be a much larger building. In fact the chapel is the choir of a church that was never built. The Prentice Pillar, ornate stone carvings, a ceiling studded with stone emblems, the small but perfect scale of the chapel and its location overlooking Roslin Glen add immensely to the chapel's charm. Just outside the chapel grounds are a row of cottages, once an inn which accommodated the Wordsworths, **Sir Walter Scott**, Dr Johnson and James Boswell and King Edward VII.

ROXBURGH CASTLE
near Kelso, Borders

Off A699 1m SW of Kelso.
All times. Free (0573 23333).

Only earthworks and fragments of stone remain of this castle, destroyed in the 15th century. Below the protective eye of the castle existed a town of the same name. It too was destroyed by the Scots, led by James II, after they had taken it from the English. The present village of Roxburgh lies a few miles south of the castle.

ST ABBS
Borders

On B6438 10m N of Berwick-upon-Tweed.

A small fishing village on the Berwickshire Coastal Route, St Abbs is comprised of red sandstone houses, which cover the colour spectrum from salami to deep pink. Mortar is picked out in white, adding to the distinctiveness of the settlement. To the village's left is the grass-topped headland, streaked with guano, which is part of the St Abb's Head Nature Reserve.

ST ABB'S HEAD NATURE RESERVE
St Abb's Head, Borders

1m N of St Abbs. Best season Apr–Jul. D (P). Free. NTS (08907 71443).

The 92-acre St Abb's headland, with 300-foot sheer cliffs, was made a national nature reserve in 1983. It is the most important location for cliff-nesting sea-birds in south-east Scotland, and there are colonies of razorbills, puffins, kittiwakes, herring gulls and guillemots. The waters off the headland are part of Scotland's first voluntary marine nature reserve.

ST ANDREWS
Fife

On A915 23m NE of Kirkcaldy.

The poet George Bruce captured something of St Andrews, the learned elder of Scottish towns and cities:

Old tales, old customs and old men's dreams
Obscure this town. Memories abound.
In the mild misted air, and in the sharp air
Toga and gown walk the pier.
The past sleeps in the stones.

Dominated by history, St Andrews in academic termtime is overwhelmingly a university campus town. Its shops and facilities have a student tilt (books, stationery) to them; its pubs show signs of student catering – solid meals at reasonable prices; and the air of the town itself hangs heavy with the weight of thinking and learning. In the summertime, this all gives way to levity and to holidaymakers who come for the sea and for lightweight recreation. Ink-pens are replaced by ice-creams and beach balls. Annual fixtures in St Andrews are, of course, the golfers, who tee off on blithe sunny days or on days when the foul, bone-piercing North Sea wind rages. Compact and attractive, St Andrews needs no marketing: it is assured of its own appeal, of the range of its purpose-built facilities and of its historical inheritance. As well as the attractions listed below, the Tentsmuir Point National Nature Reserve is within reach of St Andrews.

ST ANDREWS, BRITISH GOLF MUSEUM

Opposite Royal and Ancient Golf Club. May–Oct, daily 1000–1730; Nov–Feb, Tues–Sun 1000–1600; Mar–Apr, Tues–Sun 1000–1700. D (0334 78880).

A true golfing mecca, the museum is the new home of high-tech presentation equipment. Audio-visual displays and touch-activated

Town plan of St Andrews

screens bring **golf** to life, biographies of players are accompanied by videos and golfing knowledge can be self-tested on the touch-activated screens. The history of golf is also told in the museum's galleries.

ST ANDREWS, ST ANDREWS BOTANIC GARDEN

May–Sept, 1000–1900. Apr and Oct 1000–1600. D.

Established on its present site in 1960, the garden is best known for its Rock Garden and Peat Garden.

ST ANDREWS, ST ANDREWS CASTLE

At the shore. Apr–Sept, Mon–Sat 0930–1900, Sun 1400–1900; Oct–Mar, Mon–Sat 0930–1600, Sun 1400–1600. D (A/P). HS (031–244 3101).

From its dramatic setting, battered by the elements, the ruined castle looks out across the grey expanse of the North Sea. Founded in the 13th century, the building formed part of the stronghold of the archbishops of St Andrews. Many Protestant reformers were imprisoned here, and it was after the death of George Wishart, burnt at the stake by Cardinal Beaton in 1546, that a group entered the castle and murdered Beaton. They held the castle for a year. The castle buildings, many of which are later additions, were arranged around a courtyard. Today, visitors can cross the moat, circumnavigate parts of the castle and look down at the black rocks and seething sea below.

ST ANDREWS, ST ANDREWS CATHEDRAL

Town centre. Apr–Sept, Mon–Sat 0930–1900, Sun 1400–1900; Oct–Mar, Mon–Sat 0930–1600, Sun 1400–1600. D (A/P). HS (031–244 3101).

The beautiful ruins of the cathedral, once the largest in Scotland, to give some idea of the importance of this religious centre. Founded in 1160, the cathedral was not consecrated until 1318. The original size and shape of the complete building is marked out in granite chips, but only the east and west gables and a part of the south wall of the nave exist in any significant way now. The site also includes St Rule's Tower and the ruins of several monastic buildings.

ST ANDREWS, ST ANDREWS SEALIFE CENTRE

The Scores. Daily most of the year from 0900 (0334 74786).

Rock pools, 'touch' pools where children can have a hands-on experience of underwater life, tanks of fish and a seal pool merge education and entertainment in the Sealife Centre which opened in 1989.

ST ANDREWS, ST ANDREWS UNIVERSITY

Town centre. D (A) (0334 76161 ext 258/488).

The oldest university in Scotland was founded in 1411 and was originally tied to the cathedral and monastic community. St Salvator's

College and its chapel, St Leonard's Chapel and St Mary's College (the theological faculty of the university) were all early venues of 15th- and 16th-century learning.

ST ANDREWS, THE WEST PORT

W end of South Street. All times. D. Free. HS (031–244 3101).

One of only a few surviving Scottish city gates, West Port was rebuilt in 1589. Today it seems anomalous, for the town stretches far beyond it. The side arches are 19th-century additions.

ST BEANS CHURCH
near Crieff, Tayside

At Fowlis Wester off A85 5m NE of Crieff. D.

This 13th-century church, which was restored in 1927, contains an elaborately carved Pictish stone cross. Nearby is the Fowlis Wester Sculptured Stone, an eighth-century Pictish stone.

ST BOSWELLS
Borders

On A68 10m E of Selkirk.

Red sandstone dominates the picturesque houses of St Boswells, a town which retains its village green. The pretty village of Bowden, which lies just to the west of St Boswells, has a 12th-century church. To the west are **Mertoun Gardens**, the 20 acres of Mertoun House's grounds.

ST FILLAN'S CAVE
Pittenweem, Fife

Cove Wynd, Pittenweem. All year, 1000–1300, 1430–1730 (0333 311495).

The cave was the shrine of a group of ecclesiastical buildings which were constructed above it by 12th- century Augustinian monks. Prior to that, the seventh-century hermit saint is reputed to have lived in the cave, making use of its small well and perhaps its dramatic stone staircase. The cave was restored and rededicated in 1935 and is still occasionally used for worship.

ST JOHN'S KIRK, see PERTH.

ST MARY'S CHURCH
near Aberfeldy, Tayside

Off A827 3m NE of Aberfeldy at Pitcairn. All times. Free. HS (031–244 3101).

A low white-washed building adjoining a farm, St Mary's Church, which was endowed in 1533, has a sparse, dank interior. The surprise, when you turn on the timed light switch, is the delightful painted wooden ceiling. Part of 16th- or 17th-century modifications to the church, the ceiling is decorated with scriptural and heraldic panels, all painted in pale autumnal colours.

ST MARY'S COLLEGIATE CHURCH
Haddington, Lothian

Sidegate, Haddington. 1 Apr–30 Sept, Mon–Sat 1000–1600, Sun 1300–1600. D (062 082 5111).

The centrepiece of **Haddington** is St Mary's, a noble red sandstone medieval church. The choir and transepts lay ruined for 400 years, but have now been restored. The size of the church is enhanced by its riverside, grassy location.

ST MARY'S LOCH
near Selkirk, Borders

Off A708 14m SE of Selkirk. D. Free.

Noted for the loveliness of its situation amidst rolling green Borders hills, the three miles of St Mary's Loch are used for sailing and fishing. To the south of the loch is Tibbie Shiel's Inn, a meeting place for many 19th-century literati.

ST MARY'S PLEASANCE
Haddington, Lothian

Sidegate, Haddington. All reasonable times. D. Free (062 082 3738).

St Mary's Pleasance, which forms the grounds of Haddington House, has now been restored as a 17th-century garden. Rose, herb, cottage and sunken gardens have all been established.

ST MICHAEL'S PARISH CHURCH
Linlithgow, Lothian

Beside Linlithgow Palace on S shore of the loch, Linlithgow. Jun–Sept, daily 1000–1200, 1400–1600; Oct–May, Mon–Fri 1000–1200, 1400–1600; and by arrangement. D. Free (0506 842188).

Beside the bulk of **Linlithgow Palace** is St Michael's Parish Church, the cause of some parking congestion on Sunday mornings. The church sits at the top of Kirkgate, a street bordered by a wall which carries plaques listing royal successions from **Mary Queen of Scots** to Elizabeth II. The church, a fine example of a medieval parish church, is topped by a spiky modernist crown, the controversial work of Geoffrey Clarke in 1964, which replaced the medieval crown that collapsed in 1820.

ST MONAN'S CHURCH
St Monans (Monance), Fife

In St Monans on A917 12m S of St Andrews. All reasonable times. D (A). Free (033 37 258).

The squat turret and spire of St Monan's Church are the modest embellishments on a church which may have been founded around AD 400. It is reputed to have long been a place of healing: story has it that David I was cured of an arrow wound here. Alexander II and David II both repaired or made additions to it. It became a parish church in 1646.

SCHIEHALLION
Tayside

Off B846 10m W of Aberfeldy.

Its Gaelic name translates as the 'Fairy Mountain', and it certainly has a strange magnetism. From some angles, it has a long spine which struggles towards a slight peak. From others, it is a perfect cone. The mountain's unusual shape made it, between 1774 and 1776, the scene for experiments with a plumb line. In 1811, a Scottish mathematician, John Playfair, tried similar experiments, all related to gravity. At 3547 feet, Schiehallion appears on the Munro list of mountains over 3000 feet. Because of this, it is an over-popular climb, and the path that runs up the mountain's back can be quite badly eroded.

SCONE PALACE
Scone, Tayside

Off A93 2m NE of Perth. Easter–Oct, Mon–Sat 0930–1700, Sun 1330–1700; Jul and Aug, 1000–1700; other times by arrangement. D (A) (0738 52300).

The family home of the Earl and Countess of Mansfield, Scone Palace incorporates in its present castellated red sandstone form the 16th-century palace and earlier buildings. Here all the Scottish kings until James I were crowned. The last king to be crowned at Scone was Charles II in 1651. Contemporary Scone is a busy summer visitor attraction, with large grounds, collections of porcelain, furniture and photographs. There is also an adventure playground, a picnic park, gift shops and a coffee shop. The Moot Hill at Scone was the site of the famous Coronation Stone of Scone, brought to the hill in the ninth century and removed by the English in 1296 to Westminster Abbey.

SCOTSTARVIT TOWER
near Cupar, Fife

Off A916 3m S of Cupar. Apr–Sept, Mon–Sat 0930–1900, Sun 1400–1900;

Oct–Mar, Mon–Sat 0930–1600, Sun 1400–1600. Free. HS (031–244 3101).

Scotstarvit Tower is thought to have been built between 1550 and 1579. A handsome, solid, five-storey tower, its most famous owner was Sir John Scot (1585–1670) who wrote *Scot of Scotstarvit's Staggering State of the Scots Statesmen.*

SIR WALTER SCOTT, see panel p171.

SIR WALTER SCOTT'S COURTROOM
Selkirk, Borders

Market Place, Selkirk. Jul–Aug, Mon–Fri 1400–1600; other times by appointment. Free (0750 20096).

The bench and chair which were used by **Sir Walter Scott**, who was the Sheriff of Selkirk for 30 years, are on show here, along with a number of portraits of Scott, James Hogg, Mungo Park and Robert Burns.

SCOTT'S VIEW
near Galashiels, Borders

Off B6356 7m SE of Galashiels.

Reached via a twisty road, the summit of a 593-foot hill gives panoramic views of the surrounding countryside, including **Melrose** and the triple peaks of the **Eildon Hills** in the distance. The confident **River Tweed** curls around the base of the

Sir Walter Scott

A lthough Sir Walter Scott (1771–1832) was born and educated in **Edinburgh**, was published there and kept a house in Castle Street until 1826, he is primarily associated with the Borders where he lived from 1794 until his death in 1832. In the rebuilt and renamed **Abbotsford House** which he bought in 1811, Scott wrote his *Waverley* novels. Credited with reviving the fortunes of the novel, Scott was prolific – over 20 substantial novels, among them *Waverley* in 1814, *Old Mortality* in 1816, *Rob Roy* in 1818 and *Ivanhoe* in 1820, in 14 years – and incredibly popular. The reading public awaited each publication with considerable excitement. This anticipation was deliberately heightened by Scott's publishers who ran newspaper advertisements stating that shipments from Leith of the latest novel had been held up because of stormy weather. Such ploys became part of the extraordinary Scott phenomenon: a bestselling author who made novel-writing a lucrative profession. He was often carped at by critics, but was celebrated by the book-buying public at home and abroad.

Scott's legacy of romantic and historical fiction was matched by another, more politically pertinent one. He is often ascribed the role of champion of Scotland. He worked to restore valuable monuments, he initiated the search for the Scottish crown jewels, and he recreated Scotland in the minds of the British reading public. Mythologizing Scottish history, he imparted a heroism

(continued)

Sir Walter Scott *(continued)*

and bravura which boosted the flagging national ego. Outside his fiction, his romantic fancy had far-reaching consequences. For George IV's state visit to Edinburgh in 1822, Scott organized a parade of Highland chieftains, decked out in tartan and with all the paraphernalia that is now associated with the Highlands. Scott is, then, cursed in some quarters and celebrated in others for carving out a rather kitsch, romanticized Highland character which has been embraced by the world (and by some Scots) as the true image of Scotland.

Tourist bodies are happy to have a generalized Scottish image with which to work, just as they quickly latch on to the promotional possibilities thrown up by the innumerable real places and people that Scott recreated in his novels. Visitors to Scotland will find Scott mentioned almost everywhere from Perth (*The Fair Maid of Perth*) and Shetland (where his invented name of Jarlshof has been adopted for the islands' best-known archaeological site) to Edinburgh (*The Heart of Midlothian*). The Borders still has the strongest claim to him: the area around Abbotsford House has been dubbed 'Scott Country'. Within that tourist-built title are such imperatives as **Melrose Abbey, Dryburgh Abbey** (where Scott is buried), **Scott's View** and, of course, the intriguing Abbotsford House itself, where Scott died in 1832. Still owned by Scott's descendants, it has been a popular mecca for Scott enthusiasts since 1833.

hill, its banks perfectly parallel. No wonder then that **Sir Walter Scott,** while out walking, liked to pause here for the view. That view is now detailed on an etched plate which is screwed to a weathered stone plinth.

SCOTTISH DEER CENTRE
near Cupar, Fife

On A91 12m W of St Andrews. All year except Christmas and New Year; Apr–Oct, 1000–1700; later in summer weekends only; Nov–Mar special openings Christmas and Easter. D (P) (033781 391).

Describing itself as the 'total deer experience', this centre offers ranger-led tours to meet red, sika and fallow deer and reindeer. An exhibition tells the story of deer and explains their importance in Scotland. There are also viewing platforms, an aerial walkway, a nature trail and picnic areas.

SCOTTISH FISHERIES MUSEUM
Anstruther, Fife

At Anstruther harbour. Apr–Oct, Mon–Sat 1000–1730, Sun 1100–1700; Nov–Mar 1000–1700, Sun 1400–1700. D (P) (0333 310628).

Sea fishing through the ages, from sail to modern trawlers, and the life of a fishing community are the subjects of the Scottish Fisheries Museum. The museum includes two real fishing boats which are moored in the harbour, as well as indoor exhibits. Tableaux, information on ancillary trades to the fishing industry and a map of

fishing communities help illustrate the importance of the industry to this East Neuk coast. Many exhibits, the marine aquarium, the fishing and ship's tackle and the reference library are housed in a group of buildings known as St Ayles. They date from between the 16th and 19th centuries.

SCOTTISH MINING MUSEUM
Prestongrange, Lothian

On B1348 8m E of Edinburgh. All year. Tues–Fri 1000–1630, Sat–Sun 1200–1700. D (P). Free (031–663 7519).

A port of call on the Coal Heritage Trail, which includes **Lady Victoria Colliery**, the Scottish Mining Musuem has been established at the site of the former Prestongrange mine. Steam locomotives, an exhibition on mechanical coal extraction, a steam crane and a colliery winding engine are on show here.

SCOTTISH MUSEUM OF WOOLLEN TEXTILES
near Peebles, Borders

On A72 at Walkerburn 9m SE of Peebles. All year. Mon–Sat 1000–1730; Easter–Christmas, Sun 1200–1630. D. Free (089 687 619/281/283).

Fronted by a woollen-wear shop, this museum is composed of a handful of tableaux – a kitchen with wool socks hanging by the fire, stuffed sheep and a weaving shed – and displays on dyeing (dandelion for magenta, wild cress for violet) and spinning. There are also framed samples of traditional knitting designs. The emphasis is primarily on selling and a coffee shop caters for shoppers in need of refreshment.

SCOTTISH TARTANS MUSEUM
Comrie, Tayside

Drummond Street, Comrie. Apr–Oct, Mon–Sat 1000–1700, Sun 1100–1500; Nov–Mar, check times with office (0764 70779.)

This museum doubles as an important contemporary **tartan** centre, for it is here that the complete Register of all Publicly Known Tartans is kept. Commercialism is also rife – the historical element of the museum is rather subsumed by its other roles as a tartan shop, a tartan information centre and an issuing depot for the touristy gimmick of clan history certificates. There are, however, displays of Highland dress through the ages, a dye plant garden and a weaver's bothy. The museum is the headquarters of the Scottish Tartans Society.

SELKIRK
Borders

On A7 37m S of Edinburgh.

Composed of a hillside of houses and a valley floor with mill chimneys poking skywards, Selkirk has a pleasant, serious aspect. Its main street is top-and-tailed by two statues, both given a surprising coat of dove-grey gloss paint. One is of **Sir Walter Scott** and the other is of explorer Mungo Park (1771–1806). A number of traditional shops, among them the Selkirk Bannock

Shop, surround a small town square, which is in fact triangular. Also in the town is the Flodden Monument, a bronze statue of Fletcher, the man who returned from the Battle of Flodden with an English banner. This event is remembered in Selkirk's **Common Riding. Sir Walter Scott's Courtroom, Halliwell's House Museum** and the **Clapperton Photographic Studio** are all in Selkirk. **Selkirk Glass, Bowhill, Newark Castle** and **Yarrow Kirk** are close to the town.

SELKIRK GLASS
near Selkirk, Borders

Off A7 N of Selkirk. All year. Mon–Fri 0900–1700, Sat 1000–1630, Sun 1200–1600. Glass-making, Mon–Fri 0900–1630. D. Free (0750 20954).

Like the glass factories and paperweight-making centres near **Perth** and **Crieff**, Selkirk Glass provides local employment. Visitors can view craftsmen blowing glass and choosing coloured glass strands for the paperweight patterns.

SHALE OIL, see panel p156.

SILVERBURN
near Leven, Fife

Off A915 ½m E of Leven. Gardens open all times. Mini-farm open Apr–Sept, Mon–Fri 0830–1630; Oct–Mar, Mon–Fri 0830–1530; all year, Sat–Sun 1400–1600. D. Free (0333 27890 ext 214 or 0333 27568).

Silverburn Estate is criss-crossed with trails – a coastal trail, a tree trail and a nature trail – and has gardens, an old flax mill, a mini-farm for children and a children's play area.

THE SMA' GLEN
near Crieff, Tayside

On A822 just N of Crieff.

The dramatic scenery of the Sma' Glen is well worth a diversion from **Crieff**. A perfectly formed U-shaped valley, the Sma' Glen stretches from a stone bridge, spanning the River Almond, to the junction with the B8063. From the road, car passengers can see sheer schisty mountain sides, slicing down from their 2000-foot summits to the floor of the valley. There are picnic benches for those who like to eat amidst such grandeur.

ROBERT SMAIL'S PRINTING WORKS
Innerleithen, Borders

7/9 High Street, Innerleithen. Shop only: 1 May–mid summer daily except Tues and Sun; Restored printing works and shop: mid summer–31 Oct, Mon–Sat 1000–1300, 1400–1700, Sun 1400– 1700. D (P). NTS (0896 830206).

The National Trust for Scotland has restored this printing works and the various mechanisms and processing rooms. There is the Victorian office, stocked with historically appropriate items, a paper store with a reconstructed water wheel, and composing and press rooms. A resident printer shows visitors the ropes, and they are then given the opportunity to set type manually.

SMAILHOLM TOWER
near Kelso, Borders

Off B6404 6m NW of Kelso. Apr–Sept, Mon–Sat 0930–1900, Sun 1400–1900. HS (031–244 3101).

Smailholm, a fine example of a 16th-century rectangular Border peel tower, sits on a rocky knoll, commanding a wide view over the surrounding countryside and the **Eildon Hills**. Since 1983, the 57-foot tower has been the home of a collection of costumed dolls and tapestries taking the theme of **Sir Walter Scott**'s *Minstrelsy of the Scottish Borders*.

SOUTH QUEENSFERRY
Lothian

Beside Forth Bridge and Forth Road Bridge on S shore of Firth of Forth.

South Queensferry was a favoured port of call for sightseers in 1990, when the centenary of the Forth Bridge was celebrated, for it lies at the southern end of the massive cantilever structure. At the other side of the **Firth of Forth** is **North Queensferry**. South Queensferry has more intrinsic charm than its opposite number: its shoreside houses are picturesque and it retains something of the air of a holiday resort, with a yacht marina, watersports and a van selling shellfish.

STENTON
Lothian

On B6370 5m SW of Dunbar.

A conservation village, Stenton has the most attractive features of several East Lothian settlements – Dutch orange pantiles and red sandstone buildings. As an added bonus, it has a village green, upon which stands the Wool Stone, a weighing device used at the annual fair. Some cottages retain their outside stone staircases. Stenton was restored in 1970.

STEVENSON HOUSE
near Haddington, Lothian

Near Haddington, East Lothian. Jul–mid Aug, Thurs, Sat and Sun 1400–1730; other times by arrangement. D (A/P) (062 082 3376).

A guided tour leads visitors around the house, which dates mainly from the 16th century but was restructured and redecorated in the 18th century, to look at the collection of furniture, pictures and china.

STOBO
Lothian

Off A72 4m SW of Peebles.

Best known for Stobo Castle, the health spa, the small village of Stobo also has a restored Norman church which overlooks the **River Tweed**. Nearby is the place where the larch was reputedly introduced into Scotland in 1725.

STUART STRATHEARN
Crieff, Tayside

Muthill Road, Crieff. Jun–Sept, daily 0900–1900; Oct–May daily 0900–1700. D. Free (0764 4004).

Visitors can see the manufacturing processes involved in crystal-making, including the decoration of lead crystal which is available in the factory shop. There is also a video on glass-making.

THE STUDY
Culross, Fife

In Culross. All year by arrangement; Apr, Jun, Jul, Aug and Oct, Sat–Sun 1400–1600. D (P). NTS (0383 880359).

Up a cobbled street in the lovely restored village of **Culross** on the **Firth of Forth** is the Study, a tower and house which were built in 1633. White-washed harling is the building's exterior cladding (neighbouring houses are done out in pink or clotted cream harling), its roof is decked in orange pantiles and its windows are half-shuttered and half-leaded lights. There is a museum on the first floor. Views of the Forth can be had from the tower, which has a turnpike stair.

TANTALLON CASTLE
near North Berwick, Lothian

On A198 3m E of North Berwick.
Apr–Sept, Mon–Sat 0930–1900, Sun
1400–1900; Oct–Mar, Mon–Sat 0930–1600,
closed Wed and Thurs (am), Sun
1400–1600. D (P). HS (031–244 3101).

The magnificent outline of the red
sandstone Tantallon Castle, in its
lonely position on a promontory
above the crashing North Sea, can
be seen from some distance. The
massive 50-foot high 14th-century
curtain wall and circular towers
were strengthened in the 16th
century. A Douglas stronghold, the
castle's important strategic position
led to several attacks, and it was
finally ruined by General Monk
in 1651.

TARTANS, see panel p80.

RIVER TAY, see panel p178.

TEALING EARTH-HOUSE AND DOVECOT
near Dundee, Tayside

Off A929 5m N of Dundee, ½m
on unclassified road to Tealing and
Auchterhouse. All reasonable times. Free.
HS (031–244 3101).

This well-preserved Iron Age
earth-house consists of an uncovered
underground passage, an unusually
long curved gallery and small inner
chambers. The elegant, attractive
dovecot, which is nearby, was built
in 1595 to resemble a small house.

TENTSMUIR POINT NATIONAL NATURE RESERVE
near St Andrews, Fife

S and E of Tayport between estuaries of
Rivers Tay and Eden, on B945 from St
Andrews or Tayport (0334 54038).

This nature reserve, which lies at
the north-east corner of Tentsmuir
Forest, includes foreshore (Abertay
Sands), an area of dunes and some
marsh. It is an important breeding
ground and nesting area for
migrating birds.

THIRLESTANE CASTLE
Lauder, Borders

Lauder. Easter week, May, June and Sept,
Wed, Thurs and Sun only; July and Aug,
Sun–Fri 1200–1800 (grounds), 1400–1700
(castle). Last admission 1630. D (P)
(05782 430).

The seat of the Maitland family, the
oldest part of Thirlestane dates from
the late 16th century. Additions
were made until the 19th century. A
large collection of toys, lavish state
rooms and fine 17th-century ceilings
are Thirlestane's particular merits.
The grounds contain a woodland
walk and the Border Country Life
Museum. The latter traces the
history of rural life in the area from
prehistoric to modern times.

The River Tay

F rom its source 3000 feet up the side of Ben Laoigh, the the Tay river system wends its way from the west to the east towards **Dundee** and the North Sea, nearly splicing Scotland in half. A primary artery in Tayside and, at 120 miles, the longest river in Scotland, the Tay means many things to many people.

To fishermen, it is one of the great rivers, full of the promise of salmon and trout. To the dwindling numbers of licensed pearl fishers, the river's freshwater pearls are a livelihood. To canoeists, its falls and currents present considerable challenges. To those paddling their weary way in the annual raft race from **Kenmore** to **Aberfeldy**, the Tay is a back-breaker. To even the most casual observer, the Tay is temperamental, changing from moody, tar-coloured depths to violent angry surge and to wide, blithe sweep, all in the space of a mile.

Much of Scotland's history resides on and around the river's banks: at Aberfeldy, the Tay, once an obstruction in the path of **General Wade** and the English army, now pushes under one of General Wade's finest remaining bridges. At **Dunkeld**, it passes **Dunkeld Cathedral**, the one-time spiritual centre of Scotland. On the opposite shore lies **Birnam**, linked to Dunkeld by a Thomas Telford bridge.

At **Perth**, the Tay is perhaps at its most magnificent. It is said that a legionary in Agricola's army caught sight of the Tay here, and, marvelling at its size, said 'Ecce Tiberis' ('Behold the Tiber'). Scornful of the comparison, **Sir Walter Scott** replied in verse:

> Behold the Tiber, the vain Roman cried,
> Viewing the ample Tay from Bailgie's side;
> But where's the Scot that would this vaunt repay
> And hail the puny Tiber for the Tay?

Like **Edinburgh**, Dundee has a toll road bridge and a rail bridge, both of which cross the river. Here, within 20 yards of the present rail bridge, the Tay's worst tragedy took place. During a storm in 1879, the rail bridge collapsed, killing an estimated 100 people whose train plunged into the river.

Beyond Dundee and **Broughty Ferry**, the Tay spills into the North Sea and, discharging more cubic feet of water into the sea than any other British river, adds another superlative to its reputation.

TORNESS POWER STATION
near Dunbar, Lothian

Off A1 6m SE of Dunbar. May–Sept,
guided tours Mon–Sat 1000–1600. Free
(0368 63500 ext 3871/2).

Painted an innocent baby-blue
which sometimes melds with the
sky, the rectangular bulk of Torness
Nuclear Power Station is visible
from the A1. Like other nuclear
power stations working to win the
confidence of the public, Torness has
introduced guided tours. (Torness
'produces a quarter of all the
electricity consumed in Scotland').

TORPHICHEN PRECEPTORY
near Linlithgow, Lothian

On B792 5m SW of Linlithgow.
Apr–Sept, Mon–Sat 0930–1900, Sun
1400–1900. HS (031–244 3101).

The remains of the Preceptory
(community) consist of the tower
and transepts of a church which
was built in the 13th century by the
Knights Hospitaller of the Order
of St John of Jerusalem. This was
planned as the Scottish centre of
the Knights. An exhibition tells the
history of the founding of the Order
and of the Knights in Scotland and
abroad.

TORWOODLEE HOUSE
near Galashiels, Borders

Off A72 2m NW of Galashiels.
1 Jun–31Aug, by appointment (0896 2151).

Constructed on the site which has
been the home of the Pringle family
since 1501, Torwoodlee House is
a small Georgian mansion with
Victorian additions. It was built in
1783 by the 9th Laird, James Pringle.

TOWN HOUSE
Culross, Fife

Sandhaven, Culross. Easter weekend,
1 May–30 Sept, Mon–Fri 1100–1300,
1400–1700, Sat–Sun 1400–1700; or by
arrangement. NTS (0383 880 359).

One of several buildings restored by
the National Trust for Scotland in
the picturesque **Firth of Forth** village
of **Culross**, the 1526 Town House
has, unlike its harled neighbours,
been left as bare stone. It has served
as a prison and a meeting place for
the town council. Its external double
stair (now concrete) and its clock
tower give the building something
of a toytown flavour.

TRANENT
Lothian

Off A1 10m E of Edinburgh.

A former mining and industrial
town, Tranent takes its place
in Scottish history books as the
place from which the Highlanders
advanced to win the Battle of
Prestonpans. Tranent was also the
location of one of the first two
railway stations in Scotland. The
railway was built in 1722 to carry
coal to ships at **Cockenzie**. The
ruins of the old parish church date
from medieval times. There is a
16th-century dovecot in the town.

TRAPRAIN LAW
near Dunbar, Lothian

Off A1 5m W of Dunbar. All times. Free.

To 'trapan' someone means to remove part of their skull, and it has been suggested that the long flattened, summitless Traprain Law, rising strangely from the otherwise flat landscape, may draw its name from the unattractive verb. The 734-foot hill has upon it an Iron Age fortified site. The site was probably used as an easily defended settlement until the 11th century. Fourth-century Christian and pagan silver was discovered on Traprain Law in 1919. It is now kept in the Royal Museum of Scotland.

TRAQUAIR HOUSE
near Peebles, Borders

On B709 8m SE of Peebles. Easter week 1330–1730; May, Sun and Mon 1330–1730; 26 May–30 Sept, 1330–1730, July and Aug, 1030–1730. Last admission 1700. D (P) (0896 830323).

The white-washed Traquair House, which dates from the 12th century, is said to be the oldest continuously inhabited house in Scotland. **Mary Queen of Scots**, Edward I and Edward II are only three of the 27 English and Scottish monarchs who have visited it. Perhaps the most famous aspect of the house is its Bear Gates, shut after the 1745 Jacobite uprising, and not to be reopened until the Stuarts regain the throne. Rooms open to visitors include halls, the drawing room, dining room, museum room, library, a wash-house and the chapel. The reception and shop are located in outbuildings. Traquair also boasts its own 18th-century brewhouse which produces 210 barrels of ale each year. The house and grounds are situated beside the **River Tweed**, which was once much closer to the buildings but was diverted to avoid flooding. Events such as the Traquair Fair are annual fixtures.

TULLIBARDINE CHAPEL
near Crieff, Tayside

Off A823 6m SE of Crieff. All reasonable times. Apply adjacent farmhouse. Free. HS (031–244 3101).

Situated in Strath Earn, the delightful Tullibardine Chapel, founded in 1446, is one of the few medieval rural churches in Scotland that was completed and remains unaltered today. Its open timber roof is particularly notable.

TUMMEL FOREST CENTRE
near Pitlochry, Tayside

On B8019 6m NW of Pitlochry. Mon before Easter–last Fri in Oct, daily 1000–1730. D (A/P). Free (03502 284).

A Forestry Commission centre, it offers an audio-visual slide show and displays on aspects of local history and industries. Tummel Forest has forest walks, a reconstructed Highland clachan and a partly excavated ring fort.

RIVER TWEED, see panel p181.

The River Tweed

In his travelogue *Scottish Journey*, Edwin Muir writes of 'the toy landscape of the Tweed Valley'. He is right: the Tweed valley is somehow a model river valley, too ideal to be true with its rich agricultural land, rounded hills, tidy towns and villages, lush vegetation and, of course, the river system.

During the river's 97-mile journey from its Tweedsmuir Hills source in the west to the North Sea at Berwick-upon-Tweed, the Tweed and its tributaries (Jed Water, Yarrow, Ettrick, Gala Water, Borthwick, Teviot) pass through the principal Border towns – **Peebles, Selkirk, Galashiels, Hawick, Kelso** and **Jedburgh.**

The mighty river system has been the lifeblood of the Borders' **wool industry** in these towns, but its best face is its rural one. The Tweed twists easily around the low, rounded Borders hills, sliding blithely through woodland or moving in generous curves through open farmed valleys. The Tweed basin, edged by the **Lammermuir** and **Moorfoot Hills** to the north and north-west and by the Tweedsmuir Hills to the west, is overwhelmingly fertile.

Vantage points like **Scott's View**, where the Tweed is strangely self-assured, give a proper perspective. The view is of a patchwork of fields and warm red sandstone earth, of abundant deciduous trees, and of the lumpy **Eildon Hills** in the distance.

The Tweed's strategic importance as a defensive boundary is reflected by the number of towers and castles along its

(continued)

181

The River Tweed *(continued)*

banks. Among them are some of the Borders' best-known visitor attractions. **Neidpath Castle** near Peebles sits on a hill above the river; **Traquair House** by **Innerleithen** lies within a stone's throw of it – the house orginally sat beside the river but one of the owners had it diverted because of persistent flooding.

Further downstream is **Sir Walter Scott's Abbotsford House** and **Dryburgh Abbey** in its beautiful riverside setting. To the east, where the Teviot joins the Tweed, **Floors Castle**, on the outskirts of Kelso, looks across fields down to the river.

Just beyond Kelso, the Tweed becomes the England–Scotland border, flowing between **Coldstream** on the Scottish side and Cornhill on the English bank. A little further on, the only substantial English Tweed tributary, the Till, joins the river as it heads for Berwick-upon-Tweed, the subject of many England versus Scotland ownership battles. The town now lies within the realm of England's Northumberland, although Scottish nationalist voices can be heard sporadically calling for its return to Scotland.

At Berwick, the wide Tweed estuary is spanned by the 15-arch Old Bridge, now superseded by an uglier, newer road bridge, and by the Royal Border Bridge which carries the main east coast railway line. Beyond, the Tweed, mecca for salmon fishermen and symbol for all things Borders flows into the sea.

UNION CANAL, see panel p184.

UNION SUSPENSION BRIDGE
near Paxton, Borders

On unclassified road across 2m S of Paxton, across River Tweed (0835 2230).

Built by Samuel Brown in 1820, this was the first bridge of its type designed for road traffic in Britain. It joins England and Scotland.

VANE FARM NATURE RESERVE
Loch Leven, Tayside

On B9097 on S shore of Loch Leven. Apr–Oct, daily 1000–1700; Nov–Mar, daily 1000–1600, except Christmas/New Year. D (P) (0577 62355).

A converted farm building contains displays which interpret the surrounding countryside and the loch. From the end of September to April, large numbers of geese and wild ducks feed and rest on the loch. There is an observation hide (binoculars are provided) and a nature trail.

Union Canal

Within earshot of the roar of traffic on the M8, the water of the Union Canal slides between its wooded, leafy banks at a sedate, untroubled pace. Although built, like its many Victorian contemporaries, for trade and transportation with a sideline in leisure, the Union Canal's modern purpose is purely recreational. The waterside towpaths have been cleared for nature ramblers; the silted waterway has been dredged and passenger-carrying barge boats can again meander along part of its length. Canoeists and boat club members ply the canal waters, joined by ducks and moorhens. However, only sections of the original 31½ miles, which joined **Edinburgh** to the Forth and Clyde Canal via 11 locks at Falkirk, are now navigable. Some stretches have been diverted irreversibly into culverts; others are yet to be reclaimed from the overgrowth and from silt.

Under the eye of engineer Hugh Baird, building work began on the canal in 1818. Three ports were dug at the Edinburgh end: Hopetoun, Hamilton and Lochrin Basin, all of which are now filled in. Thomas Telford came to inspect the plans of the aqueducts, of which three – Almond, Slateford and Avon – were modelled on his own designs. The Almond aqueduct, which carries the canal 75 feet above the River Almond, has attracted sightseers since 1834. From that time, people have come to see the opening of the sluice gate which allows canal water to cascade to the river below. It was also from this aqueduct that a 75-foot-long icicle, known as the Broxburn Icicle, formed in February 1895.

Countless navvies – from Ireland and from the Scottish Highlands – were employed on the building project and many of the colourful anecdotes about the canal's construction concern them, their rowdy behaviour and the stupendous amounts of whisky, bought from canalside distilleries, that they consumed. Two of their number were the notorious body-snatchers **William Burke and William Hare** who met while working on the canal.

The first Union Canal passenger boat sailed in 1822, and managed the journey from Edinburgh to Falkirk in four and a half hours, travelling at around nine miles per hour. Although built primarily to carry coal, sandstone, slate and granite cobbles to Edinburgh, the canal's days as a busy trade highway were limited. By 1910, such traffic had almost ceased. In 1965 the canal was officially closed to navigation. Its subsequent renaissance as a recreational area has been gradual and work is ongoing.

GENERAL WADE, see panel p186.

WATER OF LEITH, see **EDINBURGH.**

WATERLOO MONUMENT
near Jedburgh, Borders

Off B6400 5m N of Jedburgh.
All times. D. Free (08353 306).

The monument rests on top of 741-foot Peniel Heugh Hill. It was built in 1815 by the Marquess of Lothian and his tenants to mark the Battle of Waterloo victory. A walk from the **Woodland Visitor Centre** leads up to it.

WEAVER'S HOUSE AND HIGHLAND TRYST MUSEUM
Crieff, Tayside

64 Burrell Street, Crieff. Summer, daily 0900–1830; winter, Mon–Sat 1000–1630. D (P) (0764 5202).

An unusual and popular 'hands-on' museum where children are encouraged to dig into the dressing-up chest and to play Victorian games. In a row of 18th- and 19th-century weavers' houses, visitors can watch craftspeople at work, weaving tartan on hand looms and spinning yarn. There is also a coffee shop and an archive with records of 2000 tartans.

WEST CALDER, see **MID CALDER.**

WEST LINTON
Borders

On A702 15m SW of Edinburgh.

Now partly a commuter village for Edinburgh, West Linton lies on the Lyne Water below the south-east slopes of the **Pentland Hills**. It was once the rough and ready gathering place of drovers and their herds as they went on their way through the Pentlands pass of Cauld Stane Slap. The village was renowned for its stone-masons, who were responsible for the 1666 carving on Lady Gifford's Well.

JOHN WOOD COLLECTION
Coldingham, Borders

Fishers Brae, Coldingham. 1 Apr–31 Oct, Mon–Sat 0900–1800. Free (08907 71259).

Photographs of Border life in the early 1900s have been printed up from the original glass plates which were found in a potting shed, to form this exhibition.

WOODLAND VISITOR CENTRE
near Jedburgh, Borders

At Monteviot, 3m N of Jedburgh at junction of A68 and B6400. Easter–end Oct, daily 1030–1730 or by prior arrangement for parties. D (P) (08353 306).

Primarily an interpretation centre and educational centre on the theme of woodlands and timber. Exhibitions, woodland walks, games and puzzles and an adventure play area also subscribe to the theme. The home farm which houses the centre

General Wade and Wade's Roads

I n July 1724 General George Wade (1673–1748) was sent to Scotland on a military mission for George I. In the continuing uncertainty after the 1689 and 1715 Jacobite Risings, he was to 'inspect the present situation of the Highlanders' and to 'make strict inquiry into the last law for disarming the Highlanders'. Wade's subsequent report calculated that the majority of Highland men able to bear arms were ready to do so against the crown. George I immediately appointed Wade Commander-in-Chief, North Britain and Wade began to organize crown garrisons in the Highlands.

The general planned to mobilize his soldiers throughout the Highlands, quelling, disarming and forming allegiances with clans as he went. By summer 1725 the first military road was being built. The military objective was quickly achieved and several of the clans gave up their arms.

Between 1728 and 1730, Wade's men built the road from **Dunkeld** to Inverness, connecting **Perth** and Inverness. By July 1728 Wade was able to write in a letter that he had 300 men working on the road, that 15 miles of it were finished and that he hoped to have 40 miles completed by October.

In 1730 the road from **Crieff** to Dalnacardoch was constructed, connecting Stirling with Inverness. Passing from Crieff through the **Sma' Glen**, through **Aberfeldy** and on up to Loch Tummel, its line remains largely the same today. Even though the road was finished, Wade had yet to bridge the **River Tay** at Aberfeldy. Construction, to a design by William **Adam**, began in 1733. Although it was completed in well under a year, Wade wrote: 'The Bridge of Tay ... was a work of great difficulty and also much more expensive than was calculated.' At a cost of over £4000, the bridge became the most expensive item on his road-building programme.

By 1739 Wade's Highland Companies had become the Black Watch, a regular regiment which is commemorated by a memorial beside Wade's fine Tay Bridge. The Black Watch's regimental museum is in **Perth's Balhousie Castle**.

Promotion finally ended Wade's work in Scotland. He left in 1740, handing on the road-building reins to Major William Caulfeild. His name is not remembered to anything like the same extent: Wade was the entrepreneur who forged into the Highlands, much to the regret of the Scottish independence movement but doubtless to the relief of the road-travelling public.

has been restored using different timbers.

WOOL INDUSTRY, see panel p188.

YARROW KIRK
near Selkirk, Borders

On A708 W from Selkirk.

In the lovely Yarrow valley, justly celebrated by **Sir Walter Scott** and James Hogg (who grew up near Yarrow), and in the village of the same name is Yarrow Kirk which dates from 1640. Scott's great-great-grandfather was minister at the church.

YESTER PARISH CHURCH
Gifford, Lothian.

On B6355 4m S of Haddington.
Apr–Oct at all reasonable times. D
(P). Free.

Gifford's Dutch-looking Yester Parish Church dates from 1708. It has a late medieval bell and a 17th-century pulpit. A plaque inside the church commemorates the Reverend John Witherspoon (1723–94) who was born in Gifford and who was the only cleric to sign the American Declaration of Independence.

JAMES 'PARAFFIN' YOUNG,
see panel p156.

The wool industry

Commercial knitting on frames began in Scotland in 1771 when Baillie Hardie of **Hawick** introduced four hand-worked frames for the manufacture of stockings. Although Hardie began with the intention of supplying to order for individual customers, he was able to expand his business to the extent that it produced 2500 pairs of stockings annually. The industry spread to Denholm, **Kelso**, Langholm, **Melrose** and **Selkirk**. In 1780 Hardie sold out to a Nottingham man, John Nixon. By 1791, 4000 pairs of hose, mostly now in lamb's wool as opposed to linen or worsted, were manufactured each year. Despite its relatively slow beginnings, in the 19th century the industry took off. In 1816 there were 1500 knitting frames in Scotland, over 500 of which were in the Hawick area. By 1838, over a million pairs of stockings was the Borders' annual tally.

From 1850 onwards, there was a change in emphasis. Production of woollen underwear and clothing increased. In 1858 the first steam-powered frame was brought to Hawick. Ten years later, very few had been installed, and the preference was still for hand looms. In the early 20th century, the Borders knitwear industry turned to outer clothing more and more. This was given added impetus with the high demand for jerseys and cardigans for the armed forces during World War I. After World War II, underwear production decreased further. In 1951, only just over £1 million worth of underwear was manufactured, as opposed to £16 million worth of outerwear.

Today, Scottish Borders knitwear concentrates on quality clothes. Mills are still thriving and the industry, as well as being attractive to visiting shoppers, has become more involved in tourism. The Borders Woollen Trail encourages car-borne visitors to stop at towns, wool mills and wool museums where tweeds, tartans and woollen products from mittens to shawls can be seen.

LOCAL COLLECTION